FAITH
AND
Heresy

FAITH
AND
Heresy

BY
REUVEN AGUSHEWITZ

TRANSLATED
BY
MARK STEINER

THE MICHAEL SCHARF PUBLICATION TRUST
of the YESHIVA UNIVERSITY PRESS
NEW YORK

Library of Congress Cataloging-in-Publication Data

Agushevits, Re'uven.
  [Emuneh un apiòkorses. English]
  Faith and heresy / by Reuven Agushewitz ; [translated by Mark Steiner].
     p. cm.
  Includes index.
  ISBN 0-88125-910-1
  1. Faith (Judaism) 2. Materialism. 3. Philosophy, Jewish. I. Title.
BM729.F3A4813 2005
296.3'9--dc22
                                        2005026522

Manufactured in the United States of America

Distributed by
KTAV Publishing House
930 Newark Avenue
Jersey City, NJ 07306
Email: orders@ktav.com
www.ktav.com

Table of Contents

Translator's Introduction[1]

I

The Importance of the Work

We have before us a fascinating document, an original philosophical work written in the Yiddish language by Rabbi Reuven Agushewitz (1897-1950) . By the word "original" I mean that this book contains philosophical arguments and ideas that may never have appeared in print before. I mean that the book is not just an account of other philosophers' thought (of that genre there are many books and articles in Yiddish), but is meant as a contribution by the author. It is also a polemical work, a sustained attack on philosophical materialism, ancient and modern, as well as an attempt to show that religion in general, and Judaism in particular, are in complete harmony with the scientific world view (when both science and Judaism are properly understood). And it was written by an ordained rabbi with no degrees in philosophy, in fact who may never have studied even a day in any university (cf. below).

The interest in this book is, therefore, threefold: we have here (a) a work containing original philosophical material; (b) written in Yiddish; (c) by an autodidact rabbi who emigrated from Lithuania to the U. S.

All in all, we have before us a unique work; there is, to my knowledge, nothing like it. Of course, there were Eastern European Jews who became philosophers (Solomon Maimon, Morris Raphael Cohen), but they abandoned Orthodox Judaism. There were Eastern European Jews who studied philosophy without abandoning Judaism, such as, of course, Rabbi J. B. Soloveitchik, who knew Agushewitz well and wrote an approbation for his Talmudic novellae on *Bava Kamma*. As it

---

[1]In this translation, Yiddish words written in English letters are given in YIVO orthography. The dialect assumed is what is called "Standard Yiddish" which is in any case close to our author's Lithuanian dialect.

happens, I have also worked on translating Rabbi Soloveitchik's essays from Hebrew into English, and a comparison is very instructive.

Classical Western philosophy, from Plato to Kant inclusive, mainly involved an attempt to prove, or at least give good reasons for believing, philosophical theses, by rigorous logical reasoning from acceptable premises. (I will not attempt to define here "philosophical thesis.") Another form of classical philosophy was the attempt to refute philosophical theses, or at least to show that no valid reason had been given for holding them. Much contemporary philosophy, particularly in the English speaking countries, could be called "classical" in this sense, but much contemporary philosophy cannot be so called, even in the English speaking world. I myself was trained by what you certainly could call "classical" philosophers and attempt to write in that vein, even when I take on "large" subjects such as the place of the human species in the entire cosmos.

R. Soloveitchik, I would claim, was not a "classical" philosopher despite his extensive knowledge of classical (and non-classical) philosophy. The value of his work (and it is certainly an important contribution to modern Jewish thought, particularly to Orthodox Jewish thought) rests in other relations to philosophy than that he was able to confirm or refute philosophical theses and proofs in new ways. Rather, I would say that R. Soloveitchik has the following three relations to philosophical discourse:

(a) R. Soloveitchik's essays provide material for classical philosophical thought. That is, they have philosophical value even for the classical philosopher, without being themselves classical philosophy. My favorite example is Halakhic Man, where he puts forward the idea that halakhic Judaism involves intrinsically an alternative description of the world than that of natural science. I think this idea itself—that of redescription—could be developed in classical philosophical style.

(b) R. Soloveitchik utilizes the concepts treated in philosophy, including classical philosophy, to provide attractive descriptions of the outer and inner life of the halakhic Jew. This is sometimes called "phenomenology." What I mean by this is that by reading the works of R. Soloveitchik, one gets an intuitive insight into the meaning of concepts like "freedom" as applied to halakhic man. These insights defeat the detractors of religion, or Judaism in particular (e.g., Kant or Spinoza who claim that Judaism is enslaving), in ways different from (and often better than) merely refuting their arguments. In some cases, they didn't even *have* arguments, but provided loaded descriptions of religion in general, or Judaism in particular, whose tendency was to weaken the hold of Judaism on its practitioners. For example, Voltaire provided no new arguments against theism, but rather used the old material to make theistic religion look ridiculous. The satirical and polemical essays and poems by the 19th century maskilim in Judaism had a similar effect. R. Soloveitchik's essays redescribe his brand of Judaism to make the criticisms simply beside the point. Philosophical categories serve him in this endeavor.

(c) R. Soloveitchik's essays attempt to "tame" philosophy by outflanking it. One of his strategies, which he employs in "Uvikashtem Misham," is to describe philosophy itself (even nonreligious philosophies) as a manifestation of the relationship between Man and God.

I would not underestimate or belittle the value of R. Soloveitchik's success in undermining the paralyzing psychological effect of the intellectual attacks on Judaism, which was more devastating than the intellectual challenge of the arguments themselves. By describing Judaism in philosophical terms (b), and describing philosophy itself in religious terms (c), R. Soloveitchik made Judaism, including the intensive study of Talmud, intellectually respectable to an entire generation (as his disciples in Boston told me when I went there for a sabbatical recently). And I think that the redescriptions themselves have philosophical value in themselves (a).

It should be not assumed, however, that R. Soloveitchik's (re)descriptions of Judaism had only a defensive purpose. In the case of Liberal religion, R. Soloveitchik used his philosophical descriptions of ideal types to discredit, to distance halakhic Judaism from, its alternatives. He has nothing but disgust for the idea that religion is a palliative, or a means to "peace of mind," and makes no effort to show that his prototype of Halakhic Man, R. Haym Brisker, was at peace.

Having said all this, it remains that R. Soloveitchik, by sidestepping, for the most part, the actual arguments of classical secular philosophy against religion, leaves an objective lacuna in contemporary Jewish thought. It is this lacuna which R. Agushewitz tried to fill, consciously or unconsciously, and thus purported to be a classical, if theistic, philosopher. His work comes to grips with the actual "proofs" ("bavayzn") of classical philosophers such as Spinoza or Kant. He does intend to construct original philosophical arguments and to confront directly (by refuting them) the arguments of others, particularly the materialist atheists. And to an amazing extent, especially for a writer who had no degrees in philosophy, he actually succeeds in doing so.

Surely a book like this (and I don't know whether there are any more like this) should be redeemed from oblivion.

II

The Author

Who was Reuven Agushewitz? Let's begin by translating the Hebrew biography written by his late nephew, a well known Borough Park physician. The biography appeared as an introduction to R. Agushewitz' Talmudic novellae, *Bi'ur Reuven* to *Bava Kamma*:

The Life of the Rav, the Author
by his nephew, Dr. Haym Shmuel Agus

The author did not have the opportunity (*lo zakhah*) to see his work of Talmudic logic in print, for he passed away suddenly in Eretz Yisrael on erev Rosh Hashana, 5710 (1950), only fifty-three years of age.

The Gaon, Rabbi Reuven ben Eliyahu, of blessed memory, was born in the town of Svislotz, Grodno district, to a noted rabbinic family. As a child, he amazed those who knew him by his powerful memory and sharp mind. At the beginning of World War I, he was forced to end his yeshivah studies. In those days of ferment, he devoted all his powers to agitation for Zionism and social justice. With great energy and youthful fire, he went from town to town as an orator on behalf of the new Messiahs of the generation. But his father, an outstanding Torah scholar, before his death, prevailed upon his son to give up this adolescent behavior and to cleave to Torah and wisdom. He returned to the Mir and Slobodka yeshivot, earned his reputation as a brilliant and indefatigable scholar, and received ordination with highest honors [rabbat hitpa`alut]. Afterwards, he journeyed to Western Europe, where he acquired secular wisdom at the Sorbonne [It is hard to reconcile this statement with that of Agushewitz' brother's memoir, quoted below, that R. Reuven Agushewitz could not afford to study at the Sorbonne; I rely on Chaim Shmuel's testimony—M.S.]. His friend, Rabbi Amiel, who would later become Chief Rabbi of Tel-Aviv, appointed him as Rosh Yeshiva of Antwerp, where he served for five years.

His literary work began to flourish in the United States, of which he became a citizen in 5689 (1929). He adopted the following regimen: to content himself with the bare necessities of life, while pursuing a literary career. From then on, he lived the life of an ascetic, taught a few disciples, and occupied a niche in the [New York Public] Library. He had great powers of abstract reasoning, which led him to the study of philosophy. But his common sense, prodigious learning, and clear, straightforward elucidation, strengthened his ties to his disciples and to the Talmud. Henceforth, he had a twofold soul: the soul of a pious Jew, trembling at the word of God, and the soul of the scientist, the scholar, who seeks philosophical truth. Beginning with 5695 (1935), he published three books in Yiddish (besides many newspaper articles): *Ancient Greek Philosophy*--a sharp criticism of the major trends in Greek philosophy; *Principles*--a theoretical essay on the nature of existence according to the latest philosophers as well as Talmudic aphorisms; and *Faith and*

Heresy--a sublime work reconciling religion and science, which became widely known in the Jewish world, and which is being published in Hebrew in Jerusalem [It was published in 1951 by Mossad Harav Kook as *Emunah u-Kefirah*—M. S.] He wrote his commentaries to the Talmud in the margins. He left elucidations and emendations on Nezikin, Nashim, and Mo'ed of which the present work [*Bi'ur Reuven* to *Bava Kamma*] is one example. One of his disciples, well known philanthropist Harry Fischel, founder of the Institute which bears his name in Jerusalem, encouraged him to prepare his commentaries for publication. For this purpose he moved to Israel--but fortune was not kind to him. As the Talmud says of the purely righteous, his work was now finished by others.

Learned, brilliant, straightforward exegete [*pashtan*], clear expositor--few were like him in Israel, but his good heart was paramount. He was unique in his humility, his goodheartedness, in his willingness to say a good word for every man, in his feeling the pain of every despondent soul, in his generosity and in his frugality. He did not leave a wife or children. But his three brothers and their descendants, his hundreds of disciples and friends, and his thousands of readers, will memorialize his name with a feeling of holiness and admiration.

We learn from this short obituary that R. Agushewitz was an active Socialist, if not a Communist, for a period of his life, but then "returned" to traditional Judaism and Torah scholarship (he left a commentary on three quarters of the Talmud, most of which has never been published). This conclusion is confirmed also by an article about him in a reference work published by YIVO. Here we have an explanation for Agushewitz' preoccupation with materialism, and his conviction that materialism is the essence of atheism.

We learn, further, that, in philosophy, R. Agushewitz was mainly self-taught. As a rule, autodidacts do not do very impressive work. Yet Agushewitz, unencumbered by the constraints of family, was able to sit uninterruptedly in the New York Public Library at 42nd Street for years. The product is remarkable; *Emune un Apikorses* (*Faith and Heresy*) displays both encyclopedic knowledge of the history of philosophy, and the analytical skills necessary to be a player in that very history.

At the same time, R. Agushewitz was, and remained a Talmudic *illuy* (genius). His published novellae on Tractate Bava Kamma, referred to above, appear with approbatory letters from none other than R. Joseph B. Soloveitchik and R. Aharon Kotler. These Talmudic giants differed sharply on their attitude toward the study of philosophy, but they concurred wholeheartedly on the scholarship of R. Agushewitz.

III

The Work

Emune un Apikorses is an ambitious work. It contains discussions of an astonishing range of topics and authors. Among the thinkers discussed in the book are (in no special order) Democritus, Lucretius, Zeno, Hobbes, Spinoza, Descartes, (Ludwig) Buechner (the once influential, now forgotten, 19th century materialist), Bergson, Russell, and even the mathematician Georg Cantor. It is noteworthy that the chapter on Spinoza has already been found worthy of being published (in excerpted form) in an international Spinoza journal (*Studia Spinozana*, vol. 13, 134-140), and is an excellent introduction to Spinoza's metaphysics, as it shows how Spinoza's ideas about a Perfect Being grow out of those of Descartes. Not contenting himself with historical analysis, Agushewitz analyzes and criticizes Spinoza's actual reasoning, pointing out various logical fallacies in his proofs. The ultimate goal of the Spinoza chapter is to prove that Spinoza was actually an anti-materialist, and that the materialists cannot claim Spinoza as one of their own—i.e. that the common interpretation of Spinoza's "monism" as a materialism is totally misguided. (This thesis of Agushewitz, and, more generally, the positive attitude of many Religious-Zionist thinkers toward Spinoza, is discussed in some detail by Dov Schwartz — who read Agushewitz in the 1951 Hebrew translation—in Chapter Three of his recent book, *Faith at the Crossroads : a Theological Profile of*

Translator's Introduction

Religious Zionism; translated from the Hebrew by Batya Stein [Leiden: Brill, 2002].)

Among the topics covered in the work (and there is no point in listing everything) are the nature of matter and energy; of force; the concept of infinity; Zeno's paradoxes of motion and their solution; the nature of religion, as distinct from idolatry; the nature of Greek mythology; the question of free will; the nature of scientific (inductive) reasoning; the meaning of Jewish history; and, of course, the relation of humanity to the rest of the Universe. Taking the offensive against materialism, old and new, he argues, inter alia, that materialism, far from representing a progressive form of thought, is nothing but a new form of idolatry; modern science, rather than representing the triumph of materialism, has transformed the very concepts of physics into mathematical abstractions, thus making the thesis of materialism pointless. The argument that since everything else in the Universe is material, so must be Man, Agushewitz dismisses scornfully as question-begging, with the analogy: suppose you notice that all the passengers on the ship are American—does that mean that everything on the ship is American, even the furniture? The chapter on free will, a clear and well informed essay on a difficult topic, has already been found worthy of publication and has appeared separately (*Torah U-Madda Journal*, vol. 11, 1-34; I have borrowed here freely from the Introduction I wrote for *Torah U-Madda*)—expert readers have voiced their opinion that it could serve as a useful introduction to the subject.

Agushewitz intrepidly takes on even the mathematician Georg Cantor and his enthusiast, Bertrand Russell. Russell had touted Cantor's "arithmetic of infinity" as providing the final and only answer to Zeno's paradoxes of motion. Agushewitz, on the other hand, held that Cantor did no such thing, and, in any case, that Cantor had not treated of the historical and ordinary language concept of infinity, but of an invented concept. Here, I believe, he was over his head—his mathematical knowledge was not up to this task, though to his credit, he did show *Emune un Apikorses* to a mathematician, Professor Yekutiel Ginsberg of Yeshiva University. He makes a number of mathematical blunders, which I point out in my notes to the texts. At the same time, it must be said that on the main point, whether Cantor's theory of the infinite solves Zeno's Paradoxes, I believe that Agushewitz has the better of the argument.

Agushewitz even has some original things to say about the paradoxes themselves, though one would have thought that there is no longer anything to say about them. For example, taking his lead from Einstein, Agushewitz investigates Zeno's paradoxes from the point of view of a moving reference frame and, in an argument which I had not seen in earlier literature (see below), demonstrates that the paradoxes survive Aristotle's attempt to solve them by rejecting the mathematical concept of a dimensionless point in favor of "quanta" of minimum length.

IV

Philosophizing in Yiddish

Jews used to say: all other languages are spoken, but Yiddish "redt zikh aleyn" (lit., speaks by itself). Of course, this is a joke based, like many Yiddish jokes, on a philosophical fallacy. (Recall the beggar's boast "If I were Rothschild, I'd be richer than Rothschild, because I would still be a *shnorrer* on the side.") It is similar to the story that Ludwig Wittgenstein used to tell about the Frenchman who argued that French was the perfect language, because only in French do the order of the words follow the order of thought. But there is no question that Yiddish has a flexibility which can, on the one hand, afford great philosophical expressiveness, and on the other hand, make translating it a daunting task.

For example, during the twenty-three years I have been teaching philosophy in Hebrew, I have been looking for a Hebrew equivalent to the English expression "explaining away," which was used by my late, and much lamented mentor, Professor Sidney Morgenbesser, himself a native Yiddish speaker who liked to use Yiddish expressions to make clear subtle philosophical concepts. He distinguished between explaining a phenomenon and explaining it away, the latter being an explanation only of why

Translator's Introduction

people erroneously thought there was a phenomenon in the first place. There actually is no way to convey this in Hebrew, so when I started translating Chapter Three of "Emune un Apkorses," on Greek materialism, I was bowled over when I read that Democritus' atomic theory amounts to "oyspshetln bedoykhek" human action and desire in terms of mere atomic motion and collision. This has a flavor and an irony which is hard to convey in terms of the "pareve" (if literal) expression "to explain away with difficulty." (Incidentally, "pareve" is one of the many Yiddish words that express halakhic concepts, or Jewish practice, for which there is no translation into Rabbinic Hebrew. The Talmud, as well as some Jewish communities, uses "fish" as a prototypical "pareve" dish. Another is "yohrtsayt.") To really appreciate what Agushewitz accomplished with the term "oyspshetln bedoykhek," one needs to appreciate the Jewish study hall (besmedresh), where one studies "pshat," the plain meaning, avoids the pseudo-pshat or "pshetl," (the contemptuous diminutive of "pshat" in Yiddish), avoids "doykhek" (forced or strained interpretations), hence "oyspshetln" or "explaining away."

In what other language, I ask you, could the antinomy between unity and diversity be referred to as an "eybiker vayisroytsetsu," (cf. Gen. 25:22); and the opposites themselves, unity and diversity, be referred to as "tsvilling fun hipukhim" [antagonistic twins, Jacob and Esau] which are compelled "nebekh" to live together in one bed ["tzuzammenvoynen in eyn nare"]? Could Kant have written such a sentence? What European philosopher would phrase the mind-body problem as the question: how does a physical representation creep kit and caboodle (that's the best I can do with "arayngegrokhn hak un pak") into our mind? What historian of philosophy ever characterized Spinoza's metaphysics as covering Descartes' idea of a perfect being "un nokh mit a smitshik" [lit., and a bit more]? Or "advised" atheists to dissociate themselves from Spinoza, remarking that his rationalism coheres to materialist philosophy "vie arbes tzum vant" (the best I can do here is "like oil with water"; the literal meaning is "like peas to the wall").

And what other language but Yiddish could generate--in the standard dictionary (Weinreich, p. 758)--the following three successive entries: (1) *ay* (but then, precedes an objection) (2) *ay ay* (terrible) (3) *ay ay ay* (wonderful)?)

   But Agushewitz is not only a Yiddish writer. Unlike most of them, he is a *talmid hakham*, a talmudic prodigy. This produces special problems of translation. In dismissing the arguments of the nineteenth century atheist materialist, Ludwig Buechner, as an equivocation, Agushewitz complains, as the Talmud does in *Bava Kamma* 27a: "Er heybt on mit a fessl, un er endikt mit a krigl" [lit., he begins with a barrel and ends with a pitcher]. Agushewitz goes on to chide Spinoza for forgetting the gemore-logic he learned as a youth, otherwise he would have never have committed a "tartey-desasrey" [inconsistency].

   On the other hand, Agushewitz's talmudic training often makes it easier to translate his work. He is a masterful teacher and "balmasbir" [expositor], who remains in the "besmedresh" even when writing in his nook in the 42nd Street Library. For example, his chapter on Spinoza's metaphysics is an extremely lucid introduction to a very difficult subject, from which I learned a great deal. His prose is pellucid and, as a great teacher, he has the patience even to repeat phrases for pedagogical purposes. (For example, he never says that A is X and B is not, but always: A is X and B is not X.) All his pronouns have clearly defined, unmistakable antecedents.

   Agushewitz' Lithuanian Yiddish is naturally closer to German than is Polish Yiddish. But the subject matter, too, has its own influence. Agushewitz naturally uses German words when discussing Kant and other German writers, but not only there. The need to extend the Yiddish language to encompass the various fields he is discussing (even Cantor's set theory) lead him to make use of German vocabulary even where Weinreich's dictionary has Yiddish equivalents. Thus I found myself using German dictionaries as much as Yiddish ones.

V

Some Personal Reflections

When I was a boy, I used to visit my grandparents on Friday night. My grandfather used to spread out the Morgen Journal and I would read the Yiddish texts aloud. Little did I know that fifty years later, I would be involved in Yiddish translation. And not on the level of Leo Rosten's *The Joys of Yiddish*, nor that of borscht belt comedy, but a serious philosophical work (though, as we have seen, Yiddish, with its hatred of pomposity, tends to lend a humorous vein even to "serious" discourse).

Some time ago, Rabbi Aaron Feder, a retired businessman and *talmid hakham* in his own right (see his talmudic novellae, *Shalom Behelekh*, published with the approbation of R. Zelik Epstein, the respected *rosh yeshivah* of Sha`ar Hatorah in Kew Gardens, Queens), asked me to consider translating the philosophical works of his rebbe, R. Agushewitz, from Yiddish into English. Feder, one of Agushewitz' disciples, had studied Talmud with Agushewitz privately on a daily basis while attending private school in Manhattan. He had previously helped publish R. Reuven's Talmudic writings, and now wished — as a labor of love — to memorialize his rebbe by publishing translations of his philosophical works, to ensure that they too would be widely acknowledged. I was unsure that my Yiddish was up to the task, so I leafed through "Emune un Apikorses." I was amazed to see an informed discussion of Zeno's paradoxes, for example, "Achilles un der tsheripakher." I saw right away that I didn't have to look up "tsheripakher" and that I was capable of doing the job. (A note to the philosophically uninitiated or linguistically challenged: the word means "tortoise.") Reading further, I was astonished to see an improvement of Zeno's arguments to take account of an objection by Aristotle ("Avade iz Aristotle gerekht, uber..."), an improvement I had never seen in the "goyishe" literature. The closest thing to it was an article I had read by Professor Max Black of Cornell University, published well after "Emune un Apikorses" appeared, and not anywhere near as deep. I reported back to

Feder, and a few months later, I started to work on the book, which I now present to the public. The reactions I have received from the already published excerpts from this book, including reactions from members of the philosophical community, have persuaded me that an important mitzvah has been done in producing this translation.

Agushewitz wrote an Introduction to *Emune un Apikorses*, which, for some reason, was not included in the Hebrew edition. In the Introduction, which contains no philosophy at all, he depicts his home town (shtetl), Sislovitch, which had been destroyed by the Nazis, as a memorial. He describes the almost unbelievable devotion to scholarship in the town, the outstanding geniuses that lived there, as well as the outstanding works of charity performed by the citizens of Sislovitch—all of this wiped out by the Nazi bestiality. By publishing this translation, we are thus not only rescuing R. Reuven from oblivion, but also his entire cultural milieu, as a fulfillment of his last will and testament. We cannot bring the six million back, but at least we can thwart the final goal of the Nazis: to obliterate the memory of the six million, and the memory of their crimes against humanity.

Rabbi Soloveitchik, in his approbation to R. Reuven's hiddushim (novellae) to Tractate *Bava Kamma*, wrote: "I believe that the Torah community neither knew him nor appreciated him properly." Rabbi Feder explained R. Reuven's invisibility as a result of his modesty, his shrinking from publicity. Still, it is astonishing, indeed, that a man whom R. Aharon Kotler described (in his letter) as a "gadol batorah uvahokhma" (great in Torah and wisdom), could have suffered such neglect in the Torah world.

It wasn't only the Torah world, however, that neglected our author—and Rabbi Soloveitchik was not the only one who bemoaned Rabbi Agushewitz' obscurity. Shortly before I wrote this Introduction, a member of Agushewitz' family, Dr. Saul Agus (a grandson of R. Reuven's brother), showed me an obituary in the Morgen Journal written soon after Agushewitz' sudden death in Ramat Gan, Israel, in 1950. The author bemoans the fact that Agushewitz, a quiet modest man, never enjoyed the fame he deserved for his outstanding scholarship. A great scholar, he was never properly eulogized (a serious transgression in Jewish law);

on the contrary, few knew who he was, and died unappreciated, even by the Yiddish literary world, who should particularly have mourned his passing. "What this quiet thinker accomplished," mused the author, will perhaps be appreciated in less disheveled (tseshoyberte) times... And though I can't honestly say that we today live in "less disheveled" times, I humbly offer this translation in the hope that it will provide a measure of redress. May it serve as the eulogy he never received; may it make clear, finally, to all, what a loss the Jewish world suffered when Rabbi Reuven Agushewitz left this world suddenly at age 53.

VI

Appendix: A Tale of Two Brothers

Well after writing this Introduction, I found out that R. Reuven's brother, Chaim Shmuel (see Agushewitz' own Introduction for details of his life), who had adopted the name Rubin to avoid the Czarist draft, had written an autobiography, and that Professor Shaul Stampfer of Hebrew University had a copy. I thus came upon a totally unexpected source of biographical information about our author. I reproduce below verbatim, Chaim Shmuel's account of his meeting with R. Reuven in Antwerp, 1928. Chaim Shmuel was returning to Eretz Israel after a stay in the United States, where he had completed a degree in chemistry. (This work was translated into English by Dr. Haim Agus, R. Reuven's nephew; I made a few stylistic corrections.)

We docked at last in Antwerp. I was hoping to see my brother waiting for me on the pier, but then I realized that it was Saturday. I would not dare take a cab since he probably lived with ultra-orthodox people, for which Antwerp was famous. So I dragged myself on foot, more than one Sabbath distance, till I reached my destination. I passed many bearded Jews with streimels. I knocked on the door, introduced myself as the brother of Reuven and was received with sincere joy. The house exuded the spirit of Sabbath. But my brother was out of town. He had received my letter, but could not meet me at the pier on

Saturday. The landlord, a rich diamond merchant, expressed respect and veneration of my brother. At first I thought that there had to be a family tie between my brother and this family, but it became clear that it was pure love and adoration. I waited impatiently for Reuven's arrival. When he appeared, our encounter was very emotional, with flowing tears of joy. He did not want to tire me and was concerned about quarters for me for the night.

He took me to my lodging. My host belonged to a fanatically religious sect. He was against Zionism and opposed to free thinkers migrating to the Holy Land. Naturally, it was useless to have any discussions with him. I preferred to learn from him about my brother's living conditions. He spoke of him with great respect. He told me that Reuven exists on the income of several private lessons and of holding a Talmud class for adults under the auspices of the chief rabbi, Amiel. The latter admired Reuven's genius and befriended him. From his earnings Reuven supported a young man who was indigent.

Let me give now a thumb-nail biography of this remarkable, modest man, my brother. After graduating from cheder, he elected to continue his studies in the yeshivah of Slobodka, known as Knesset Israel (named after the great Rabbi Israel Salanter). This school was renowned for its emphasis on Ethics and Morality, known as Mussar. Reuven had absorbed the teachings to the full and adopted that system as a way of life. He shied away from ordination as rabbi as being an expression of flaunting pride. Father was greatly distressed that such a talent should not be properly crowned. Being a determined young man with righteous conviction, my brother resisted all arguments. It was only after my father took seriously ill, that he went to Grodno and was ordained enthusiastically by one of the great rabbis, at the remarkable age of seventeen. At the end of World War 1, after the October Revolution, he became a social activist and made the rounds, preaching justice and social equality based on religious tenets and principles. It was his belief that religion was the foundation of morality and ethics. The new Polish government, virulently anti-communist, branded him as a dangerous radical and issued an order for his arrest. Luckily, he got wind of it in time and managed to escape to Germany. From there he went to Belgium. Rabbi Amiel (later, chief Rabbi of Tel Aviv) became his patron and mentor. From his letters I learned that he planned to get a doctorate in France. Indeed, he traveled to Paris and prepared to enroll in Sorbonne University. But his economic poverty was unbearable. His physical appearance, short and thin, did not help either in finding a job. He was hungry and ill-clad and was sure that he headed for tuberculosis. Completely frustrated, he decided to go back to Antwerp. There he embarked on a study of philosophy in depth. He researched late in the night and wrote a critique on Immanuel Kant, which is still in manuscript. Years later he published, in Yiddish, three books on philosophy–on Old Grecian, Middle Ages and Modern Theories finding fault with such giants as Aristotle, Spinoza and Descartes–which received favorable reviews. His last book, *Faith and Apostasy*, was translated into Hebrew by Prof. Chaim Lipschitz and published by Rabbi Kook's Institute. His ethical stature was towering and unforgettable. I took a long stroll with him and was amazed at his tremendous erudition and profundity of thought. He had a positive attitude towards Eretz Israel and Aliyah. I asked him to explain to me the reasons for his excessive religious observance. He said that once he became convinced that Judaism was the true religion and that the practice thereof is an essential principle, he followed the commands of the Shulchan Aruch to the letter. He took me around to visit many homes. Wherever he went he elicited respect and was welcomed at all times. When he stopped at a chess game, play would become serious and when he smiled at a certain move, it would arouse increased attention. I conveyed to him that Juda Leib would like him to come to New York, and offered to help him to settle there. He said that he got a letter from him to that effect and that he was debating whether he could adjust to the materialistic spirit of that country. Nevertheless, he decided to answer in the positive, mainly because of the wonderful libraries of New York. Too bad I could not stay longer than two days. At the railroad station, on the way to Paris, we parted tearfully. A young man came over later and asked me: "That fellow, the one who gave you such an emotional good-bye, what is he to you?" I said: "That's my brother, why?" He said: "If there is any truth to the legend of the Thirty Six just men, then he is one of them. That's the reputation he has in the diamond industry. "

In the two hour train ride from Antwerp to Paris by way of Brussels, I felt very depressed about the eternal fate of righteous people, as exemplified by my brother. At home he suffered more than any other child, because he was headstrong, because of his extraordinary brainpower that could not be confined to the world of the Talmud, and because of his demands for justice for all. He missed motherly love -- he hardly knew her. Father was always full of resentment about his own hard life and the orphans grew up in sadness. As Reuven matured, his great soul was buffeted by the new storms in society that promised justice and equality and strongly challenged the traditions. Father considered these vacillations as deviations from the straight path. His [i.e., Reuven's] foreshortened life thus passed without a spark of pleasure. His only satisfaction was the philosophical speculations that he incorporated in his three published books and the several articles in the Jewish press. Very few books, however, are destined for eternity and in the course of time, as Solomon says, it is all forgotten.

***

In preparing this work for publication, I have done my best to insure that R. Reuven Agushewitz is not forgotten.

June 15, 2005

A Word to the Reader

Religious belief can be accepted even by someone who is not entirely convinced. After all, most things are accepted — and must be accepted — only on faith. For example, we accept on faith that lands and cities exist which we have never visited, or that wars we did not see took place, etc. We go so far in this, that on the basis only of faith in a doctor, we endure the worst suffering, and undergo the most perilous operations.

It is, however, different when the issue is [handlt zikh] rejecting an old faith. If someone should tell you that the city of Tel-Aviv has never existed, you would not take his word for it unless you had made a thorough inquiry and had become convinced that it is true. This is certainly valid when at issue is a religion which is fortified by a tradition thousands of years old. And, in particular, when one rejects religion one rejects the best gift that humanity has received: in religion there is hope for the downhearted and the crippled; in religion the lonely and the persecuted find comfort; religion gives the elderly the feeling that they are not yet dispensable [iberik], that they can still make progress by increasing their "stock" of good deeds [mitsves].

It is, therefore, incomprehensible folly [umbagrayflikhe laykhtzinigkeit] to reject religion without a thorough inquiry. And to aid such an inquiry, the author offers this book.

I would like to take the opportunity to thank Dr. Yekutiel Ginzburg [a mathematician at Yeshiva University] for the deep interest he took in this book and for his learned comments in the chapters concerning the infinite.

———••❖••———

Foreword

A.

This book is dedicated to the memory of our six million martyrs [kedoyshim], among them my two sisters with their families, whom the Nazi criminals [reshoim] murdered [umgebrakht] together with all the other Jews of Sislevitz, Grodno district. Some of them were shot to death in a nearby forest, on 22 Heshvan 5703 [20 October 1942], and some were murdered a little later, in the Nazi gas chambers. May their souls be bound up in the bond of life.

The Jewish communities [kehilles] of the Yiddish-speaking cities and shtetls were torn up from the roots. All that was left of them is their memory, i.e., their history; and just as children hold dear, and seek out everything related to, the memory of their mother [a mamen], so should we, children of these communities, investigate their history. However, I am not a historian and all my efforts to plumb the source from which Jewish Sislevitz flowed were to no avail. The farthest I got [alts tsu vos ikh hob zikh dershlogn] is a date from the year 5570 (1809 or 1810), when the volume *Mar'ot ha-Tzov'ot* by the Gaon, R. Moshe Ze'ev b. R. Eliezer, was published, with the approbation [haskome] of the Gaon R. Yehezkel "Katznalenpogen," chief rabbinic authority of Svislotsh.[1]

---

1 Svislotsh is the Russian name of Sislevitz. It should also be noted that R. Yehezkel *z"l* [Hebrew: of blessed memory] was the third son of the famed Rabbi of Brisk [Brest-Litovsk], R. Avrohom Katzenelenbogen *z"l*, who had seven sons (Cf. *Da'at Kedoshim*, by Eisenstadt and Wiener, p. 17), and was already married in the year 5487 [1726 or 1727], because this year is given in all the sources as the date in which R. Avrohom came to visit his father-in-law in Vilna, and he was there so charmed by the seven year old genius [illuy], who was later known as the Gaon of Vilna *z"l*, that he took him with him to Kaydan. It thus appears [kumt oys] that R. Yehezkel was already an old man in the year 5487. We see this also from the fact that the same volume, *Mar'ot ha-Tzov'ot*, contains an approbation of the Rav of Brisk, R. Aryeh Leyb *z"l*, who is a son and successor of R. Yehezkel's brother, R. Yosef *z"l*. And since R. Yehezkel was rabbi in no other place than Sislevitz — no other rabbinic position is given for him in *Da'at Kedoshim* — it is plausible [shikt

Forty seven years later, in the year 5617 [1856 or 1857], Sislevitz already has as rabbi the famous Gaon of the generation, R. Meir Yonah Shatz *z"l*, who authored the commentaries *Sha`ar he-Hadash* and *Petah ha-Dvir* to the *Ittur*; *Har ha-Moriah* to Maimonides' *Code* (Laws of the Temple Service); *Mei ha-Shiloah*, to the *aggadot* of Tractate *Berakhot*; and *Pesah Leyl Shimurim* to the Passover Haggadah. Aside from these works [seforim], which he had succeeded in publishing, there remained the manuscripts "prepared for publication . . . a short commentary on the entire Jerusalem Talmud"; a voluminous commentary on the *Halakhot Gedolot* [a Geonic work] which he authored during his tenure as Chief Rabbi of Brisk; *Mei ha-Shiloah*, a commentary on the *aggadot* of the Talmud, *Seder Mo`ed*; halakhic novellae on the entire Talmud; responsa; and marginal glosses to the Talmud, to the Alfasi, to the Rosh, to the Ran, to the *Zohar*, to the *Tikkunei Zohar*, and to the *Mahzor Kol Bo*.[2] R. Meir Yonah died in the year 5651 or 5652 [1891 or 1892].[3] And from 5617 until his death he occupied the rabbinate of Sislevitz — except for a certain period in between, when he was Chief Rabbi of Brisk-Lithuania. This shows how surpassingly [vayt] important the Sislevitz community had already become in that time; and this we see also from the "marriage" [shiddekh] between Sislevitz and Brisk-

zikh] that he had already been rabbi in Sislevitz for a long time, because one usually occupied one's first rabbinical position as a young man.

We see also, that R. Yehezkel was then considered important [khoshev] and famous among the learned [bney toyre]: although R. Moshe Ze'ev was himself so great in Torah that he was the chief rabbinic authority in Bialistok, he nevertheless sought the approbation of R. Yehezkel even after he had that of the celebrated Rabbi of Brisk. This shows, therefore, that even then Sislevitz possessed a very important community.

2 Cf. the eulogy [hesped mar] for R. Shmuel Moliver, written by R. Meir Yonah's son, R. Mordechai, who was also rabbi in Sislevitz.

3 In the above mentioned eulogy, R. Mordechai writes [in Hebrew], "These are the seven famed great and purely righteous *Geonim* who passed away during the last seven years . . . the first was our Master, R. Meir Yonah." R. Shmuel Moliver, whom he reckons as last of the seven, passed away on the 11th of Sivan in the year 5658 [1898]. R. Meir Yonah, therefore, passed away about seven years previously. In the year 5650 [1889 or 1890] R. Meir Yonah was just able to publish his *Har ha-Moriyah*.

Lithuania, because the Brisk rabbinate was then the most important in the region. This very thing is what R. Meir Yonah writes himself concerning Sislevitz in his introduction to *Petah ha-Dvir*, published in 5634 [1873 or 1874; I translate from the Hebrew]: "It is customary to honor one's host [dorshin be-khvod akhsanya], namely the holy community of Svislotsh [Russian name of Sislevitz, see fn. 1 above], among whom I have been dwelling since 5617, and they supply all that I need. And they are an illustrious congregation [eda nikhbada] and among them are outstanding Torah scholars [muflagei torah] and God-fearing people, supporters of Torah. And in their House of Study there is a library full of new and old volumes."

The "outstanding scholars" of the year 5634, I probably missed knowing. I did, however, hear many stories about the Torah scholarship [lomdus] of my late grandfather, R. Chaim Shmuel (the father of my late mother, Rochel) about whose greatness elderly Jews used to tell tales, and who merited the honor that in the Old Study Hall [besmedresh] where R. Meir Yonah prayed, the congregation waited for my grandfather to finish his prayers before going on [khazoras hashatz].[4] I later heard also about R. Borukh Ayin who lived ultimately in Amdur. That R. Borukh was among the Sislevitzer "outstanding scholars" of R. Meir Yonah's times is confirmed by his volume with the title *Dvar Mitzvah*, Concerning the 613 Commandments, Exegesis of the words of the Rambam [Maimonides] in his Book of the Commandments, and the Fourteen

---

4 This was reported to me by R. Dovid Bershkovsky, one of the elderly Sislevitz Jews, who is a sexton [shames] in the Beth Israel synagogue on West 93rd Street, New York. One can rely on R. Dovid's testimony, because he was already not a young man, and it is not yet sixty years since my grandfather's passing: "Up to sixty years, a man remembers" (*Ketubot* 20b). I am in any case [bikhlal] happy to have known R. Dovid closely because the Sislevitz piety which R. Meir Yonah had mentioned is reflected in him. It appears that R. Dovid believes strongly in the Talmudic adage, "Night was created only for the study of Torah" (*Eruvin* 65b); he sits every night until around 2 a.m. over the Mishnah, but on the other hand does not see himself as a scholar [talmidkhokhem], who should not engage in fasting (*Ta`anit* 11): he fasts the *Behab, Erev Rosh Hodesh*, and in general at every opportunity. He used to fast every Monday and Thursday, but his second wife objected to this and he stopped doing so.

Principles [for classifying the Commandments] that he [Maimonides] there laid down, by Borukh, son of Eliyohu Ayin of Svislotsh, [published in] Warsaw, 5634. In order to assess R. Borukh's genius, it will be enough to mention the following fact: when Sislevitz burned down, in the summer of 5670 [1910], and the Old Study Hall burned with the "library full of new and old volumes," R. Borukh came to help with a gift of over five hundred different valuable volumes. My older brother, R. Yehuda-Leyb, was then the librarian [gabbai sforim] in the Old Study Hall and he had to catalogue them. But my brother was also a great scholar [lamdn] (he is today the rabbi of the Talmud Study Society [khevre shas] in the Shomrei Emunah synagogue of Boro Park) and he enjoyed perusing Talmudic books [sforim]. He was astonished to find R. Borukh's books full of R. Borukh's own brilliant glosses. Of course, this evoked the enthusiasm of the scholars of Sislevitz — and don't forget, these were only some of his volumes.

R. Moshe-Zalmen Rubinstein, of blessed memory, whom I was still privileged to know, should have also, according to his age, been one of the "outstanding scholars" of 5634. Concerning R. Moshe-Zalmen's scholarship and piety legends circulated [arum gegangn], which I found not to be true — yet this very fact [i.e., that false stories of his brilliance were circulated –Tr.] shows how great he was [because people make up stories like that only of people who are already known to be brilliant –Tr.].[5] R. Moshe-Zalmen in his old age sat and studied day and night in the Study House of Amstivev. There my rebbe, R. Moshe Dovid, of blessed memory, also studied and attended prayers; he was the greatest melamed [teacher] of the shtetl, and was extremely versed [shtark bahavent] in the Talmudic commentaries, early and late [rishoynim un akhroynim].

---

5 A granddaughter of his lives in New York; she is married to Avrohom Ayin, secretary of the "Help for Sislevitz Landsleit." Avrohom Ayin is also a relative of R. Borukh Ayin, and to the same family also belonged the great Boro Park scholar [talmidkhokhem] and intellectual, the late R. Ze'ev Ayin, who passed away three and a half years ago in Boro Park. His older brother, R. Moshe Ayin, whom I found studying Talmud, gave me important information concerning the family tree of his relative, R. Borukh Ayin.

In the New Study Hall, a number of rabbis attended prayers [hobn gedavent]: R. Dovid Meisel — a man with a brilliant mind [ofene kop] — and Shmuel Melscheinker's two sons-in-law, R. Meir Leibush and R. Avrohom Alkanitzky.[6] Also attending services there was R. Shlomo Belkin, father of Dr. Samuel Belkin, President of Yeshiva University. R. Shlomo was known chiefly as knowledgeable [kenner] in the Hebrew language [loshnkoydesh], and teaching [lereray] was, in fact [takeh], his profession; but when he reached his middle age, R. Shlomo traveled to Slonim where he received rabbinic ordination [smikhe].

Yet the greater number of scholars [lomdim] of the shtetl could be found in the Old Study Hall. Attending services there were R.

---

6 R. Shmuel Melscheinker himself represented a type which must be mentioned. A Jew who was perfect in all virtues, he dedicated all these perfections to the New Study Hall, which was therefore called, in fact, Shmuel's Study Hall: he served there as Torah Reader, Cantor for the High Holidays, he taught public classes in Mishnah, and saw to it that boys away from home should sit and study there. When the Study Hall burned down, he harnessed himself to dirty work [shvartse arbet] (he was a strong man [a yid a gever]) and carried stones, bricks and clay. Of course he carried on his shoulders many other public works [kolshe arbetn], and he did nothing for personal gain [oylomhaze]. It should be added, also, that R. Shmuel was by no means an exception in our circle [bay uns] in this point, R. Yosef Katzenelenbogen (Yoshke Grodzenkes, a descendent of the abovementioned Brisker Rabbi, R. Avrohom Katzenelenbogen) also dedicated his long life to the Talmud Torah, Zionism, etc.; he was in fact also a delegate to one of the first Zionist Congresses. My late father, who worked very hard to make a living [parnose], was imposed upon to do important public work: warden [gabai] of the Old Study Hall, help for the needy before Passover [moes khitim], the Great Charity Fund [tsdoke gedoyle] (my late father was a very quiet and unassuming [basheydener] man and affluent [a gvir] he certainly wasn't — from the five or six rubles a week that he made, he used, like the saintly Hillel of yore, to give around a half for Torah tuition [skhar limud] — I actually don't know how it come about that they imposed such important trusteeships [gaboesn] to him). One of my father's disciples in public work was R. Feivl Lev (Feivl the Goralnik), he subsequently took upon himself all the public work [tsorkhe tsibur]. R. Meylekh of Valk should also be mentioned, a saintly man [tsadik], who did, so to speak, the dirty [shvartse] altruistic labor: he used to visit the sick (even during epidemics, when doing so was very dangerous) and the heavy-hearted, who needed to be consoled; upon seeing somebody working around the house, he himself set to work, so as to fulfill "Thou shalt surely release it with him" [Ex. 23:5].

Mordechai Slutsky (nicknamed "Motye Esther-Rochel's" [son]), "a wise man and a scribe," who himself was an author who also edited the works of others,[7] and R. Yisroel Zeltzer, the sexton [shames] of the Study Hall. The Old Study Hall also boasted [farmogt] the most diligent scholar [masmid] among the shtetl's laity [balebatim], R. Leybe Chaikes; also attending services there was R. Yoshe Drettschiner, for whom all had great respect [derekherets]; even the rabbi of the shtetl, the Gaon Rabbi Yosef Rosin, who is today Chief Rabbi of Passaic [New Jersey], paid attention to his every word. The greatest scholar of the Study Hall, however, was considered to be R. Yerachmiel, who sat up front [mizrekh sheni] on the same bench as my late father.

Concerning my father I will allow myself to relate the following fact. On a visit once to Bialistok, I entered a study hall [besmedresh] in order to show off my power of Talmudic disputation [mefalpl zayn], which I had brought along fresh from the Yeshiva of Mir. Upon learning that I was from Sislevitz, one of the older laymen [balebatim] asked me, "Whose son are you?" "The son of Elia of Horodne [=Grodne]," I said. "Would that [halvay] you know ten years from now what your father knew."

B.

This is not the place to describe our shtetl, particularly since my friend Avrohom Ayin did it already.[8] I will only relate my earliest

---

7 R. Mordechai's book [sefer] is catalogued in the library of the Jewish Theological Seminary under the title [I translate from the Hebrew here]: "*Azharot Poems* [Azharot are liturgical poems for the Shavuot festival in which the 613 Commandments of the Torah are enumerated –Tr.] for the Shavuot Festival, by R. Eliyahu the Elder, with the commentary *Hiddur Zaken* [Hebrew: Honor to the elder, an allusion to Lev. 19:32], by Mordechai Slutzky of Sislevitz. Warsaw, 5640."
8 Cf. Avrohom Ayin's "The Shtetl Sislevitz," in YIVO Bletter of Sep./Oct. 1944, as well as (Yiddish) "The Economic Life of Sislevitz," May/June 1945. I brought to

reminiscence, a game in which my father took part and therefore made quite an impression upon me — what kind of game?

As you know, when it comes time for [es halt baym] individuals to repeat the Talmud lesson [gemore], the best [student] goes first. However, there were two "best" in my father's primary school [kheder], my older brother Chaim Shmuel and "Arke" [diminutive of Aharon] the rabbi's son [dem rov's] (a son of the rabbi of Sislevitz, the Gaon R. Shneur Zalmen Piness, of blessed memory), and there was no other solution [eytse] but to cast lots [varfn goyrl] who of the two should have the privilege [zkhiye] of going first.

These two friends took up different paths in life. My brother Chaim Shmuel divided his powers between Torah and secular knowledge [haskole]: he received rabbinic ordination from the yeshiva in Lida, and a diploma from a [teacher's] seminary in *Eretz*

Avrohom Ayin's attention a number of omissions, which he himself would like me to correct. For example, in describing the Sislevitz wedding, he failed to mention "The Poor Man's Supper" [di oreme vetshere] about which it wouldn't hurt American Jews to know; the night before a wedding there was a custom to make a dinner for the poor — a dinner which was certainly no worse, and sometimes even better, than the wedding dinner for the families and their guests. Don't forget that with this dinner the idea was not to make an impression on [oystsufaynen] anybody, but to succeed with [oystsunemen bay] the Master of the Universe, upon Whose will the entire happiness of the young couple depends. Aside from this dinner, generous donations were set aside for the poor. At the dinner, poor people from the surrounding shtetls convened, among whom one could find usually also comic talents, merry beggars [freylikhe kabtsonim], who wanted to show their stuff and thus regaled the entire crowd [oylem]. I myself was present at a Poor Man's Supper at my brother's wedding — it was the best meal I have ever had, even better than the dinner of the Hospitality Committee [khevre line, society which arranges free accommodation for travelers] to which my father used to take me.

He also forgot to mention many of the charities of Sislevitz, the *Maot Hittim* [help to the poor before Passover], the *Tzedakah Gedolah* [the "great" charity fund], and *Hakhnasat Orhim* [hospitality for wayfarers]. I actually happened to see these charities first hand: as stated above, my later father was the trustee for *Maot Hittim*, and *Tzedakah Gedolah*, and my rebbe, R. Zelig ("the schoolmaster from Alivud"), was the trustee of *Hakhnasat Orhim* — so I saw the fine manner in which benefactors gave and also the poor were served. I saw how, without any "appeals," the Sislevitz laity brought their contributions to *Maot Hittim* (usually the same as the previous year) and I saw what honor my father bestowed upon the noble [eydele] strangers, "guests," who were the recipients of the *Tzedakah Gedolah*.

Yisrael; studied chemistry in Pittsburgh; and returned to the field of education. During Word War II he was the principal of the high school [gymnasium] in Petach Tikva. On the other hand, "Arke" the rabbi's son took up the way of Torah only, where he had great success. In [the yeshiva of] Slabodke he was already known as the prodigy [illuy] from Sislevitz, about whom anecdotes were narrated even in other *yeshivot*. Today he is considered the greatest yeshiva head — the Gaon of the generation, R. Aharon Kotler.

Another friend of my brother, the Gaon R. Feivl Ruin, of blessed memory, also became famous in the yeshivot of Lida and Ponevez as a genius [illuy] and a Torah great. Circumstances however led him to stay in his grandfather's tannery, where he was destined [bashert] to remain "a vial of perfume in a dirty place" (*Sanhedrin* 108).

Another friend of mine who had great success [shtark matsliekh] in Torah and became an eminent yeshiva head was the Gaon R. Shimon Langbard, head of the Volozhin yeshiva, which today is relocated in Israel. R. Shimon (as a boy known as "Shimon-Aryeh's" [son], grandson of my rebbe, R. Gedalya Sender) was always better than I in the *kheyders* and *yeshivot* where we studied together. Also better than I in many respects were my friends Yitzchok Antzevitz, Moshe Slutzky, Shimon Vatnik and the late Yehuda Belkin.

The last of these was an older brother of Rabbi Dr. Samuel Belkin [president of Yeshiva University]. Dr. Belkin himself belonged to a younger group, which included my brother's children: Dr. Avrohom Yitzchok [Irving] Agus, author of the award-winning book, *Rabbi Meir of Rothenburg*; Rabbi Dr. Yaakov Dov Agus, author of the profound works *Banner of Jerusalem* and *Modern Philosophy of Judaism*; and the well-known Boro Park physician and intellectual [maskil] Dr. Chaim Shmuel Agus. In the same group one must also include my former disciple, the physicist and intellectual [maskil], Dr. Feivl Panter.

This is only a small part of the intellectual fruit that grew on the tree with the name Sislevitz — fruit which grew right around me and to which I was an eyewitness. I must however add that what "grew around me" was rather meager, because I was very rarely in the shtetl and knew very few;[9] I did not even know all the friends of my younger brother Yitzchok Dov, who was all of three years removed [opgerukt] from me (he lives now with his wife in the Borochov neighborhood). And taking into account that Sislevitz occupied only a small point on the map of Jewish cities and shtetls where the Nazi monster rampaged, we can already get an idea [hasoge] of the kind of intellectual garden this wild animal had rummaged in.

Finally, I would also like to mention my untimely deceased brother, Shammai, and his wife Esther, who had a stake in this publication.

--------◦⟨◆⟩◦--------

---

9 As example I will give here only Dovid Lewis (Lasch), a well-known lawyer and the National Secretary of the Canadian Socialist Organization, of whom I can speak only from second hand [eyd mipi eyd], though according to the time we left Sislevitz, after World War I, I could have known him personally.

Introduction

A.

People customarily take stock at the end of a period: they probe their deeds, they scrutinize the events of the period, and attempt to draw conclusions for the future. Every good businessman does this; at the year's end he examines the books. We Jews now stand at the end of a very important period in the life of our people, and therefore we must look over our books.

Obviously, we will not review here everything we have done or everything that has happened to us during our long Exile, but we would like to take note of a great miracle that befell us: the miracle that we were able to persist among so many hostile nations, without being debilitated, physically or spiritually, by the persecution which we had to contend with. This very miracle is certainly the greatest in the history of humanity; nothing like it has been observed in the case of any other nation.

In reviewing our chronicles, we see that this particular miracle continually recurred; what happened to us was not a single miracle, but many similar miracles. How often were we deprived of life? How many mortal blows and catastrophes did we have to suffer: the destruction of the first and second Holy Temples; religious persecution at the hands of the Syrians, the Romans, the Moslems, and the Christian nations in Western and Eastern Europe. Yet these deadly afflictions, wonderfully, healed, and often the cure had been prepared before the onset of the malady.

Thus, the Jewish center in Babylonia had been made ready before the fall of the one in Israel. Similarly, the Jewish torch had been carried marvelously to North Africa and Western Europe even before it was entirely extinguished in Babylonia. In the same manner did Jewry in Eastern Europe begin to show its strength even before Jewry in Western Europe had been altogether enfeebled. And so is it with the destruction of Eastern European Jewry, which took place before, and which we have seen with, our very eyes — even here has the remedy been prepared before the affliction.

The Holocaust in Eastern Europe is still fresh in our minds and it would seem a desecration of the honor of our near ones, to attempt to find even the slightest consolation in this catastrophe. Yet on the other hand we must not close our eyes entirely to the glow of Divine Providence over us, which reveals itself in this very darkness. We must ask ourselves the question: what would have happened if the Holocaust had, God forbid, occurred a few decades earlier, i.e., before we managed to gain a foothold in the Land of Israel and on the American continent?

The glow of Providence is much wider and much clearer when we take into account that such horrible suffering was prophesied in the Torah; it is emphasized in the *Tokhehot* [Moses' Warnings] of Leviticus 26 and Deuteronomy 28, as well as the Song of Moses (Deut. 32). In fact, our prophets have prophesied concerning a time when there would remain "one out of an entire city" (Jer. 3:14). And our Talmud is also full of tragic descriptions of the "birth pangs of the Messiah": "Let the Messiah come, but let me not see him," is the well-known expression of some of our sages.

B.

In the same manner, the second part of the prophecy is being fulfilled before our eyes, the prophecy of the final Redemption, which accompanies almost every prophecy concerning our suffering in the Exile — the Promise that our suffering will eventually turn out to be the birth pangs of the Messiah. And it should be added that our Redemption, like the Exile, does not just "happen"; that here, too, we see manifest miracles before our eyes.

We are not yet in the last act of the Drama of Redemption, and it is a little too early to sum up events. Nevertheless, it is already possible to say that if we were to pile up all the obstacles we have encountered on our way they would together be a mountain which we could not conquer with our feeble powers. Recall the many horrors we have endured in the last year alone [1948], the many times during the year when many of us looked with despair and cries of despondency on the entire affair.

During the last year horror and despair befell us when we learned of the deceptions of the Palestine Mandatory regime; how they did everything in the world to make the Jewish restoration impossible; how they disarmed the Haganah and gave the guns to the Arabs; how they disbanded the Jordan border patrol and allowed the Arab policemen to take their arms with them; how they brought in the British-Arab Legion from Transjordan and groomed them to inherit the Land; how they opened the Syrian border to a well-armed band of 7,500 men, among them German Nazis, Polish antisemites, Yugoslavian collaborators, and English fascists; in other words, all those who thirsted for Jewish blood.

During the last year horror and despair befell us when we learned that the U.N. resolution of 29 November, upon which we had pinned our hopes so much, is no more than a piece of paper; we learned that the United Nations could do nothing — or, in some cases, would do nothing — in support of their own resolution. We learned of England's continual violations: according to the resolution, she should have cleared a port for unrestricted Jewish immigration; instead she did the opposite, guarding all the routes, so that not a single Jewish immigrant could enter even by stealth; according to the resolution, England should have worked together with the representatives of the U.N. to prevent chaos after the surrender of the Mandate; in fact, she did everything to foster as much chaos as possible in the Land. The final blow was when our own America suddenly had a change of heart concerning this very resolution, which she had helped bring to pass, and began working with all her might to repeal it.

During the last year we had to bear the great horror when, on the first day when Israel had declared its independence, enemy armies began marching toward it from all sides; armies dispatched by nations compared to which Israel was like a drop in the bucket [botl beshishim]; armies equipped, more or less, with modern armaments: tanks, airplanes, and heavy artillery — instruments of war, which our underground fighters could not possibly hide from the eyes of the British (and thus could not obtain).

And during the last year we endured the many horrors caused by the multifarious manipulations of the British, inside and outside the Security Council. Certainly we recall our mood of despondency on the Saturday night when the radio reported the news, that England had succeeded once again in preventing the application of sanctions against the attacking Arab nations; and certainly we remember still how terrified we were over the British-inspired Bernadotte plan, which robbed us of our ability to build, and therefore also to exist; and certainly we have not yet forgotten the British air force's reconnaissance flights over our positions.

The English maneuvers are a wonderful chapter by itself. They present a strange spectacle: England, the master spider, virtuoso of entangling others in her web, here confounded herself again and again by her own strategems; she maneuvered herself out of a point to which she tried with all her might to return. Not for nothing do we say in the Psalms "Then will our mouth be filled with laughter" [126:2].

This is not the place to expand on this subject. It is enough to point out that the appeal to the United Nations, the demand to send a commission, and the so-called British "neutrality" during the negotiations concerning the partition plan — things which turned out to be very useful to us — were certainly not meant for our good. Similarly, it wasn't meant for our good when the Arabs were advised to evacuate any land on which our Haganah set foot. Even the first cease-fire, a product of British initiatives, and which was clearly meant to give the Arabs time to catch their breath and start a new march (the Syrian delegate, Alkoory, said this explicitly), ended not at all badly for us. Similarly, the latest British maneuver, sending spy planes over our positions, did us no harm.

Finally, it will perhaps not be out of place to mention, that the fact that we relied entirely on an agreement, which was given to us only on paper, recalls the tradition of a paper bridge, which we will have to cross in the end of days and which will prove stronger than the iron bridge of our enemies. Forget not as well, that the agreement itself was miraculous, because some of the nations immediately thereafter regretted their vote, as though they had cast it in an ominous time, against their will — and at every opportunity thereafter voted the contrary.

C.

There are those who do not believe in miracles, and attempt to account for everything superficially [`al pi pshuto]. They obviously cannot deny that our survival in Exile is extraordinary and our Redemption marvelous; but, they say, there are simple explanations for our extraordinary survival in Exile and for the marvel of our Redemption. What are the explanations of our extraordinary survival in Exile?

One explanation, they say, is this very thing: the promise that our troubles will end with a wonderful Redemption. This gave us the stoic courage to bear the worst troubles — this had the effect, that during each tribulation we hung our hopes on the Redemption; we believed that these are nothing but the birth pangs of the Messiah. And this supplied the weapons through which we were able to endure in every war — for who would surrender when he believes that he is on the threshold of victory?

A second explanation for our survival is that since the destruction of the first Holy Temple we were never concentrated all in one land: "God dealt with us charitably, when he dispersed us among the nations" (*Pesahim* 87). In this way the number of Jewish centers increased, and for that reason Judaism was never defeated, for when Esau came upon one camp and smote it, the remaining camps escaped [Cf. Gen. 32:9].

A third explanation for our survival may be that we have been outstanding in philanthropy; members of no other nation help one another in time of trouble as do we Jews. This is why the Jewish people could endure a time of trouble better than other nations; for though people of other nations were often lost in captivity and slavery; captive Jews were usually redeemed and remained among fellow Jews; and while in the case of other nations the uprooted mostly perished, in the case of Jews they found a brotherly hand, helping them take root somewhere.

A fourth explanation of our survival in Exile may be we that were outstanding in the study of Torah; already nineteen hundred years ago the high priest Yehoshua ben Gamla instituted universal education among us; and this institution succeeded to the extent that there was literally no example of Jewish children who did not study Torah. And the study of Torah certainly had the effect of strengthening the bonds of the Jew with his people, with his faith and with everything Jewish; for, learning Jewish history, the Jew necessarily acquired a stronger national feeling; learning Jewish religion and Jewish ethics, the Jew was obliged to regard as good or evil only what was good and evil from the Jewish standpoint.

A fifth explanation for our survival may lie in the habits and emotions which the 613 Commandments of the Torah instilled in us — habits and emotions which erected a barrier between our world and the Gentile world, a psychic barrier which we could not transgress. For example, the prohibition of eating pork engendered in us a feeling of disgust both toward the pig and also toward anyone who eats or raises pigs. This barrier was only strengthened by the inhuman behavior which the Gentiles displayed towards us, since through this behavior they debased themselves in our eyes.

So much concerning our survival in Exile. As for the wonders of our Redemption, further, they attempt to account for them by one thing — "no alternative": we are fighting with our back to the wall; we know that on this battle depends our last chance for survival as a free people. And we know also, that if we lose *this* battle, our lives are worthless, we will forever be in danger of being cast to the mad dogs, or else remaining like dirt under the feet of wild pigs — so we had to undertake this impossible battle, and had, therefore, to fight relentlessly, exhibiting marvelous bravery.

Yet it has to be added that the reliance on "my power and the strength of my hand" (Deut. 8:14) cannot here explain all: it does not explain the consent of the United Nations, it does not explain the flight of the Arabs, etc. It has to be added, as well, that a feeling of "no alternative" does not always lead to courage and strength: one Nazi could lead hundreds of us to the slaughter, and most of the time we did not even try to storm and disarm him, even though we knew that we had nothing to lose by making the attempt.

The same can be said concerning the previous explanations for our survival in Exile — they explain, but not everything; in any case they do not explain the fact that our prophets and sages successfully predicted both our horrible troubles and our wondrous Redemption. If someone were to predict, and the prediction were completely fulfilled, that you would have to traverse a dangerous path, with a thousand destroyers lurking in ambush, but that you would be saved from all of them, then surely you would not cease from wondering over this thing, even if you could identify the explanation for each individual deliverance.

D.

When you consider the above explanations for our survival, you see that they all depend on faith: our great suffering was always bound up with hope for Redemption, because we always believed in the words of our prophets and of our sages. Being dispersed over many lands actually helped us to survive; because everywhere, under the most difficult circumstances, we held on to our Jewishness (dispersion means, after all, a fragmenting of power, which usually causes destruction); we remained prodigious benefactors [groise ba'aley-tsdoke], we learned much Torah, and we distinguished ourselves generally with our 613 Commandments, because we heeded that which our faith demanded of us.

In other words, faith is the cause behind all the other causes of our survival. Nay, it goes *before* them all. Our parents showed the greatest heroism precisely when what was at stake was the highest principle of the faith, namely Sanctification of the Divine Name [martyrdom], and bore all the expulsions and exiles, in order only to find a little place to practice Judaism. Faith was thus, directly, the greatest factor — and, indirectly, the only factor — in our survival, i.e., the manifest cause for our having outlived all the other nations in a similar situation was, that we were ardently religious — more religious than the other peoples.

One must add, however, that recently the wheel has turned, we have become less religious than most other peoples, the proportion of atheists among us is greater than among them — all polls show this. Why is this so? If you ask a "secular" Jew, he will naturally applaud this [darshn leshvakh]. He will say that it follows from the fact that Jews are a progressive nation, a "wise and understanding people" (Deut. 4:6), and they therefore accept progressive ideas more quickly, ideas better supported by science.

It is not possible to assess how far the contemporary Jew's understanding goes; but on the other hand we can say with certainty that the average Jew has no ability to analyze [funanderklaybn] the question of faith or atheism, a question which requires much more knowledge than the average Jew possesses. To judge the question of faith or atheism it is necessary to know the philosophy of both; otherwise, one does not know even what faith is and what atheism is.

The problem with the contemporary Jew is that he thinks he knows it all, having gone to Hebrew school [kheyder] he thinks he knows what faith is; and being a little familiar with popular science, he knows what atheism is.

What is the result of this? It is that our "understanding" is a fault, rather than a virtue. Because of our self-styled understanding, we draw conclusions from the little we know, and we become, therefore, so to speak, half philosophers or quarter philosophers. This is in fact the main cause of our atheism — compare the well known philosophical saying, which Hegel cites in his *Philosophy of Right* (here quoted in English translation): "It is a celebrated saying that a half philosophy leads away from God, while a true philosophy leads to God."

In the following chapters, we will see what a "half philosophy" means; and also why a half philosophy leads away from, while a true philosophy leads to, God. We will see what faith means and what atheism means — and we will see that atheist ideas are far from being as progressive as they pretend to be, and that their pretension to be based on science is also false.

————•◦◆◦•————

Chapter One

Religion and Atheism

A.

Atheism was not born today [nisht ersht geborn gevorn]; atheism is by now at least as old as Democritus' atomism, that is, close to 2,500 years [fuftzig yoyveln] — so whence the assumption that atheism is based on progressive ideas? Upon what grounds can the atheists pretend that atheism is the last word in thought?

This pretension rests upon the ground that atheism is, allegedly [kloymersht], supported by the findings of science, which is the last word in thought. We see, therefore, that every atheist administers [git] his little bit of atheism sandwiched [eingesendvitsht] among scientific findings, as though his atheism actually followed from those findings.

This at once [shoyn] gives the atheist, as a matter of course, an opportunity to dress up in borrowed glory [zikh tsu putsn mit fremde federn], that of the scientists, and makes it possible for him to write bulging tomes [beikhiger bikher] on popular science which successfully draw many readers, lured by the genre, into his web. We see that the scientific pretensions of the atheist serve him doubly.

On the other hand, what ground is there to link atheism with the findings of science? Well, some things and occurrences, which traditionally used to be ascribed to a Divine power, are today through science linked to a natural principle. This could easily lead to the conclusion that tradition is quite unreliable and that the assumption of a Divine power is completely superfluous and misleading.

Many scientists have come to such a conclusion, especially those for whom a successful discovery has turned their heads [fardreyt dem kop]. Similarly for the socialist theoreticians, who regarded themselves as awesome scientific innovators [gevaltike mekhadshim]. In this way also, atheism automatically became popular among the working masses, who followed the socialist theoreticians blindly.

These scientists and socialist theoreticians, however, err grossly; they see not the forest for the trees; they see not that it is atheism which rests au fond [in zayn toykh] upon unscientific grounds, while religion, or at least the Jewish faith, rests, on the contrary, on scientific grounds.

The scientific method demands that one should not come to a conclusion without adequate evidence, and when such evidence is lacking, the conclusion must be left suspended; the matter, moot. But the atheist will not hear of it, he draws a conclusion concerning something which is and must remain doubtful. In this he follows in the footsteps of the idolaters, with whom he finds himself, of necessity [mimeyle], in a primitive stage of human thought. To prove this, let us proceed immediately to the chief distinction between atheism and religion.

B.

Religion consists of two elements: (a) belief in G-d,[1] and (2) belief in prophecy, which purports to account for the relationship between G-d and the world. The atheist does not believe in G-d and perforce for him prophecy is already ruled out. The chief conflict between religion and atheism, therefore, is over the belief in G-d.

Now in what does the belief in G-d consist, i.e., what does 'G-d' mean according to the pure religious standpoint? It means an unknown Power which is posited in connection with various operations which we discern in nature, just as we say in the Song of Unity, "We have not found Him, nor have we known Him, but through His deeds do we recognize him."

In connection with what operations is the unknown Power posited? Much has been written already about this in all literatures, and in Yiddish as well — cf. the present author's book, *Principles*, wherein these various operations are more fully depicted and

---

1 [The author also uses the dash in Yiddish. –Tr.]

classified. Here we will give in outline only some of the main classifications from that book, namely, "unity," "diversity," and "progress."

Concerning unity, it is enough to mention the operations of "bonding": physical bonding, which is manifested through cohesion and gravity; biological bonding, manifested through the cooperation among the parts of a living organism; epistemological bonding, manifested in sensory contact, or cognition; and intellectual bonding, i.e., the bonding between cognitions, which is manifested in general concepts, logical systems, conscious and unconscious memory, etc.

Regarding diversity it is enough to mention the operations of "separation": physical separation, expressed in the intervals of space within matter, and also in the separation of matter itself into various elements and physical forms; biological separation, thanks to which organisms continually procreate and change; and epistemological and intellectual separation, thanks to which our feelings and opinions do not remain fixed, and are different in different individuals: "As their visages are not alike one to the other, so are their opinions not alike one to the other" (*Midrash Tanhuma*, Pinhas, 10).

Briefly put, regarding progress we will mention only the fact of progressive activities among persons. Here we see so clearly how much power is invested [avekgelegt] in the striving to outdo others, just as in the effort to "outdo" oneself, to be in the future something more than in the past. We see also clearly how in this striving we are continually driven by something, because when we just try to stop for a moment, we feel as though our entire lives have become empty, without purpose.

As stated, I have already written concerning all these elsewhere. I add, however, that by these operations, the existence of an Active Power is actually exhibited, not inferred. In other words: the Active Power is discerned directly, through these directly observable operations, which in fact are, essentially, nothing other than Active Power itself.

C.

Are we in a position to recognize also something concerning the essence of this Active Power? Can we say what He is, how He is? About this, too, there has been no end of writing and speculating, and from this mountain a few attributes can be selected which our cognition entitles us to ascribe to this Power.

Thus we are entitled to ascribe to Him the attribute of rapidity, which manifests itself to us quite adequately through the speed of light rays, a speed of 186,000 miles per second. Thus we are entitled to ascribe to Him the attribute of might, which was manifested quite adequately over Hiroshima and Nagasaki. We are entitled to ascribe to Him the attribute of greatness (in quantity), because however far we can reach with the biggest telescope the domain of this Power is manifested.

The cognition of these attributes entitles us to add, that the essence of Active Power is beyond our comprehension; none of us can comprehend the speed of a light ray, how it is possible that something could traverse such an immense space in so small a time, or how it is possible that in such a small time something could have managed [zikh bavayzn] to be in all the locations of such an immense space. Similarly, none of us can comprehend the extent of the energy [gvure] in the matter of the cosmos, in comparison to which the puny atomic bomb [bombele] is certainly not more than a drop in the sea. Nor can any of us fathom the quantity of this power, best illustrated by taking it in the small.

We all know today, in fact, how small an atom is: that an ounce of the heaviest element, uranium, contains approximately one hundred billion billion atoms; that an ounce of the lightest element, hydrogen, contains approximately twenty million billion billion atoms. And these very atoms contain interstitial spaces, i.e., even in such an inconceivably small quantity the Active Power must be admitted, expressing itself, as everywhere, through binding and separation.

D.

If the Active Power we discern is unknown by us in its essence, we can perforce know utterly nothing concerning its origin; we cannot know if this Power exists of itself or whether there is over it some other power which designed it. That is, we know utterly nothing concerning the highest source of the Active Power; we know only, that it must exist (because even if the Active Power exists of itself, it is nevertheless itself its own highest source).

This is actually the standpoint of the Jewish faith. Indeed, we all know that in the Torah, G-d is designated by the following two names: "Existence" and "Power." We know, as well, that which the Torah declares in the Ten Commandments: "You shall not make any image of G-d" [Ex. 20:4]. And in Deuteronomy this declaration is even stronger: "Be careful with your souls, because you did not see any image on the day when G-d spoke to you . . . " [4:15].[2]

We find this also in the Talmud. For example, it is enough to mention here what Rabban Gamliel replied to the atheists, who "argued" in jest that they know what goes on in Heaven: "What is here on earth, you know not; but you know what goes on in Heaven? . . . What is in your own mouth you do not know, but you know what goes on in Heaven?" (*Sanhedrin* 39). Note that the logic of this argument is exactly that which was elucidated above: if that which we discern is unknown to us, we can certainly not know what is higher than it.

It is certainly true as well, that both in the Talmud and in the Prophets there are very often depictions of G-d, even depictions which are largely anthropomorphic. But we immediately see that these depictions are a matter of style, metaphoric [Hebrew: le-shabber et ha-ozen]: in the Talmud the [Hebrew] word "*kebayakhol*" [in a manner of speaking, lit., if it were possible] is usually added immediately, which shows explicitly that a personification is involved. Concerning the prophets, again, their entire style is

---

2 [I have translated the Yiddish translation of these verses, not the verses themselves. –Tr.]

personification and metaphor. Yet, on the other hand, sometimes it happens, that the prophet takes fright from his own style, and when he is on the verge of a personification he cries out: "Woe is me, for I have personified G-d[3] . . ." (Isa. 6:5).

E.

Some philosophers have also come to the conclusion, that above the known must be something unknown. Yet in the course of their philosophizing they turn the wagon shaft, turn around, and go precisely in the opposite direction; they talk as though the unknown were known, in one way or another.

Take, for example, Herbert Spencer. He concludes in favor of an unknown, which ought to be the highest cause of the known. But at the same time, he philosophizes concerning Nature as though the unknown stands entirely on the side, as though He had no connection with the progressive course of Nature. But from whence does he know this? How does he know that the unknown is so "Deistic," that although He is the ultimate cause of nature and must therefore be able to determine her direction, He nevertheless intervenes no longer in her course?

Or take the famous Immanuel Kant. He also comes to the conclusion that behind what appears to us there must be something that does not appear — behind the phenomenon there must be a "noumenon." But although the noumenon is unknowable, Kant nevertheless knows that it is outside space, outside time, and perforce also outside causality, which is, just as the other "categories," tied to time — but how does he know that?

Or let us go back even earlier, to Spinoza. Spinoza knows, as well, that something is unknown; nevertheless, he goes on immediately to describe it as though he was standing nearby: it is an infinite substance, which manifests itself through an infinite number of attributes, of which we know only two, Space and Idea; of the others we cannot have any conception. But here the question arises,

---

3 [Hebrew *nidmeiti*, "I am undone"; the author gives a very nonstandard Yiddish rendition. The source would seem to be Albo, *Sefer ha-Ikkarim* 3:17. –Tr.]

how is it possible to describe that of which we cannot have any conception?

Nevertheless, in this matter these particular philosophers sin less than those who rule out the unknown altogether, like, for example, the materialists, who suppose that everything that exists must be just as our senses represent them to us. In the next chapter, we will see that this very thought concerning knowability was, in fact, the chief principle of idolatry, against which our faith came to do battle.

———••❖••———

Chapter Two

Idolatry

A.

Idolaters were of various kinds. They worshiped terrestrial objects: inanimate objects, plants, animals, and people (even in our time, the Mikados were the official gods of the Japanese). They worshiped heavenly bodies: the sun, the moon, and the stars. They worshiped natural phenomena, such as the gale wind, thunder, and even the seasons (the Tammuz). They worshiped also spiritual objects: the souls of the dead, good and evil spirits, etc. What do all the various sorts of idolatry have in common, and what sets them apart from the pure Jewish religion [emune]?

The common wisdom concerning the distinction between monotheism and polytheism is: the idolater believed in the existence of many gods, while the achievement of the Jewish religion was belief in the existence of only one G-d; for idolaters, the functions of nature are divided up into many hands, while Jews introduced the idea of one dominion over all of nature.

It is doubtful, however, whether this distinction is applicable to every idolatry. Some of them were not even genuinely [azoy] polytheistic. For example, in the Greek and Roman pantheons, a kind of "monoidolatry," rather, dominated: one idol was there elevated to a position of full dominion over the others, so that the others were not more than his officials, charged with performing certain functions. Their place, therefore, in the pantheon was rather that of servants, or angel-gods, rather than as gods.

True, these angel-gods had, indeed, full autonomy, they could do as they pleased, they could act even against the will of their lord. But this autonomy was not derived from restrictions on the dominion of the all powerful god, but from the anthropomorphism of the idolater himself — from the human-like free will with which the idolater invested his gods. In accordance with his free will, a god had to have the ability to violate even an explicit command of his powerful master. But just as a insubordinate human servant is direly punished, just so fares the god in the legend who dares to reveal the secret of fire to man.

However this may be, this is certainly not the entire distinction between the pure Jewish religion and idolatry. It is not even the main distinction, because monoidolatry is as much against the pure Jewish religion as is polyidolatry; were men to set aside all their gods in favor of one idol — for example, the Baal — would they be any less "worshipers of strange gods" [oyvdei avoydezore] than if they worshiped many gods; they would in any case transgress the explicit commandment: "Thou shalt not make unto thee any graven image or any likeness" [Ex. 20:4].

The main distinction between the Jewish religion and idolatry lies not in quantity but in quality; we Jews believe that G-d is of an entirely different nature from the object of the idolaters' belief. What, therefore, are the qualitative distinctions and which among them is the chief distinction?

B.

The qualitative distinctions are of three kinds: (1) differences over the very essence of G-d; (2) differences over His characteristics [mides]; and (3) differences over how to serve Him.

The very essence of G-d is, according to the Jewish religion, unknown, as was shown in the preceding chapter. In contrast, the idolaters not only depicted how their gods looked, but described their exact nature and even their biographies.

The virtues of G-d are, according to the Jewish religion, ideal, incommensurably higher than ours. In contrast, the idolaters usually ascribed the same characteristics to their gods as they themselves exhibited [praktitsiert].

Concerning the proper manner of serving G-d, the Jewish religion, on one hand, abolished all of the evils of idolatry — human sacrifice, burning children, blatant depravity, etc. — and on the other hand, introduced the "mitzvot ma`siyot," statutes and laws, which install [makhn] each individual in the active service both of G-d and of society.

Now of these three distinctions, wherein lies the chief difference — the element of which we can say with certainty, that it pertains to the pure Jewish religion only, or conversely, to idolatry only?

The differences in the manner of serving G-d are certainly very important, so important that our Sages put the emphasis [trop] on them, and devoted themselves much more to them than to the other differences; after all, idolatry is described by our Sages by the name `avodah zarah — a "strange" manner of worship, different from that of the Jewish religion; and to this "strange worship" an entire tractate of the Talmud is devoted. But this importance is only from the practical standpoint, because of the way a man's character is influenced by the way he worships G-d. From the theoretical standpoint, in contrast, our Sages certainly did not find here the chief difference between the Jewish religion and idolatry, because worshiping the gods in the same manner as the Jewish religion prescribes for worshiping G-d is, according to the Talmud, even more idolatrous than worshiping the gods in other manners.[4]

The same goes for the differences in virtues. Certainly these differences are also very important from the practical standpoint, because certainly the virtues of G-d have a great influence on the character of men. Thus, Jews always attempted to improve their virtues by aspiring to align [oysglaykhn] them as much as possible with those of the Master of the Universe: "As He is merciful, so shall you be merciful . . . as He clothes the naked . . . so shall you clothe the naked" (Cf. *Shabbat* 133b, *Sotah* 14a). Nevertheless, no one would say that herein lies the main distinction between the Jewish religion and idolatry, that a god to which is ascribed ideal virtues, would by this alone cease to be an idol, that the Mythrians, for

---

4 Cf. *Sanhedrin* 60b, where it is said that worshiping an idol in the manner practiced in the Holy Temple is called idolatry [Avoyde-Zore] even if the devotees of the idol themselves do not worship it that way; while worshiping an idol in some other way is called idolatry only when the devotees of the idol worship it in that way.

example, are not idolaters because they ascribed exceptional virtues to their god.

What remain, therefore, are only the differences in the very essence of G-d, among which the chief difference must be sought. There is no doubt that here must it be found — if only because a difference in the very essence of things must be found whenever the things exist, and perforce must be included in all the forms under which they appear: now, the proscription "Thou shalt not make unto thee any graven image or any likeness" [Ex. 20:4] must be found always in the Jewish religion, and where there is such a proscription there is an element of the Jewish religion.[5] Conversely, every form of idolatry includes an element of "graven image" and "likeness," and whenever we are confronted with such an element, we are confronted with an element of idolatry.

C.

In light of the above master distinction, the source from which the greatest part of the theory and practice of idolatry issues is bared before our eyes. We see clearly that the chief characteristics of all forms of idolatry stem from the idolater's attempting to picture to himself [oysmoln zikh] an image [bild] of the unknown. At first this led to animism or (what is better called) pan-anthropomorphism, to the belief, that every object possesses a humanlike soul. Second, this led to the cult of the dead, to the belief that the dead have the same needs as, and are gifted with more powers than, the living. And finally this attempt led to polytheism and to the various later forms of idolatry. How so?

First, everyone understands that an image which we picture to ourselves must come from something which is known to us, because what we know not, we know not how to depict. True, we can imagine a monster which we have never seen, or a man with horns, but even in that case we do not really imagine something we have

---

5 "Whoever denies idolatry is called a Jew" (*Megillah* 13).

never seen, but rather combine together what we have seen separately.

So how can the idolater picture to himself an image of that which is unknown to him? He can do this only by clothing the unknown with a garment made of something he does know. The image is therefore not of the unknown, but of something different: the known.

And because everyone knows himself best, it further emerges that when the idolater attempts to picture to himself an image of the unknown in each thing, he must fill out each thing with characteristic features taken from his own person: for him, the inanimate, the plants, and the animals, appear like his own self, like men; the dead must be for him not much different from the living — the difference being nothing more than this, that we see them not, that they are invisible; the Active Power which manifests itself in nature must be imagined as that of a powerful man, a man who has in his power to rule and activate the whole of nature — from whence, the entire paraphernalia of idolaters originates.

Filling out the image of a man, he must eat, drink, and procreate; he must possess a desire for these needs, just as for everything he does; he must be happy, or unhappy, when things are done, or not done, in accordance with his desire; he must possess lust and anger, love and hate — in a word, all the weaknesses and all the virtues of a flesh and blood human being.[6]

Procreation brings about children, which must be of the same species. In this way, an entire family of gods must be imagined, a polytheism. Filling out the image with an analogy to a royal family, ruling over many lands (for he who rules over all nature has, in fact, every land in his dominion), these prince-gods must have settled in many lands, each of which being the "*ba`al*" or lord of his place. Procreation of the *ba`al* of the land brings with it, furthermore, the idea that some of the men of the place, the kings and heroes, are descended from him.

---

6 The only weakness which the idolaters did not ascribe to their gods is mortality, because death is not accepted as an essential property of life, but as a visitation coming from the hand of the gods and which, therefore, a god itself need not suffer.

The conception that the gods must have a desire for the deeds they do can further point to the manner which each god can be worshiped: the one that causes light must be worshiped through fire, the one that produces wine must be worshiped through drunkenness, and so on. From here the various modes of worshiping the idols originate. Here, too, is the basis for the exceedingly shameful manner in which some of the gods are worshiped, for in nature, in fact, these kinds of activities, among others, go on.

D.

It follows from what we said, that the general and chief character of idolatry is a baseless gnosticism, a delusion [aynredenish] that we know the unknown. And it is this very delusion, with all its ugly associated consequences, with which the Jewish religion was to do battle.

This agrees, actually, with the theory of the renowned scholar, Max Miller, that the evolutionary path in religion goes from the perceivable to the unperceivable. In accordance with Miller's theory, the culmination of this evolution brings about something which is altogether unperceivable, completely unknown; and this means, further, that the standpoint of the Jewish religion represents the most progressive ideas in this field.

Later we will see that the whole achievement of atheism is to drag human thought back to the standpoint of the idol worshiper and therefore atheism itself must be lowered many rungs downward on the ladder of progress.

————◦§◆§◦————

Chapter Three

Ancient Materialism

A.

Atheism and materialism are not, of course, synonyms. The two are not even strongly associated; atheism need not be a kind of materialism. Take, for example, the outspoken atheist, Arthur Schopenhauer; he was actually a Kantian, i.e., he held that space, time, and therefore matter are nothing but appearances, presentations, which come only from, and do not at all exist outside, our consciousness. This is the opposite of materialism, in which space, time, and matter are the Prime Movers; their existence is certain, eternal, infinite, and necessary.

But even if not equivalent, there is, nevertheless, an essential association between them — a one-sided association, which entails that every materialist should be an atheist. This results from the following: the core of atheism is the denial of the unknowable of religion, and thus it intersects with the core of materialism, which is the theory that that which our senses take in (matter and its properties) is the highest source of all nature, and it follows that there is no unknowable.

This relationship with atheism makes materialism very much like idolatry; just as idolatry, so must materialism invest the unknowable with apparel taken from the known. The difference between the two lies only in the place from which the apparel is taken and thus also in the quality of the garments: the idolaters take their apparel from human nature; and the materialists, from the matter of everything known. The former were attracted to a garment rich in color, and therefore forgo quantity; while the latter were attracted to a broader garment and therefore had to forgo quality, and satisfy themselves with the colorless word "property."

Because of this relationship between materialism and atheism, the former became the prophet of the latter — materialism led to atheism. Materialism, furthermore, remains the chief bastion of atheism:

whenever the former is strong, the latter sits fast in the saddle as well, and when the first is weakened, the latter loses its grip. The history of atheism is, therefore, mainly a history of materialism.

B.

Materialism led to atheism in two ways: (1) by denying outright the existence of an Active Power, or (2) by denying the separate existence of such a Power, by interpreting it as a property of matter. The first way was taken by the ancient materialists, and the second by the modern materialists.

The history of materialism begins, of course, with the theories of the Ionic school — Thales, Anaximander, and Anaximenes. It must be added, however, that these philosophers did not yet explicitly deny the existence of an Active Power. According to Aristotle's testimony, they did, on the contrary, believe in such a Power, or powers: "All things are full of gods and the magnet lives because it has the power to move iron" — these very words Aristotle ascribes to the father of the Ionic school, Thales the Miletian. If so, it is more probable that these philosophers were animists; they believed that even "inanimate" matter lives, although in another manner than the animals.

Atheism manifests itself, however, in its fullest expression in the heir of the Ionians, Democritus of Abdera, who already denied explicitly the existence of any Active Power whatever. According to him it turns out that everything that happens follows from a passive activity, a spontaneous [mimeyledike] descent. How so?

The substance of all things consists of atoms: suchlike invisible and indivisible bits [pitzelekh] of matter, which continually fall from above to below in a bottomless space. These atoms are controlled by no power, internal or external. They therefore have no qualities, because every quality is an internal power, which makes a thing behave in a particular way. Now being without qualities, they cannot be distinguished from one another by different qualities — so how are objects which manifest different qualities constructed from them? Where do all the differences between things and events come from?

They come from differences in the externality of the atoms, from differences in their form, their size and therefore in their weight (I say "therefore," because difference in weight was linked by Democritus to difference in size, that which is larger and has in it more matter must *therefore* be heavier). He made everything depend on the differences in weight. How so?

Differences in weight have the effect, that in descending, the atoms fall on one another, the heavier upon the lighter. This causes collisions. The collisions have the effect, one the one hand, that the atoms cohere and build larger or smaller bodies; and on the other hand, that the bodies break apart once again. This brings about the birth and the death of all the large and small bodies we see.

The collisions have the effect also that the atoms and the bodies collide in different directions. From this come the different movements and different wishes we experience. Each desire is an impulse in a certain direction, an impulse which follows from a collision. And in this matter all activities and all differences can be explained away [oysgepshetl't] with difficulty [bedoykhak].

C.

This is, in brief, the Democritean metaphysics, which is considered by philosophical authorities as quite sound [oysgehaltn] from the materialist standpoint — from the standpoint "that only matter is real."[1] It is in fact true, that in several of its premises Democritus' theory is as materialistically sound [oysgehaltn] as those of his modern colleagues, but on the other hand, it is not hard to find premises which are unsound even from the materialist standpoint. This we can see by examining the premises presented above.

---

1 These are the words of Bertrand Russell in his introduction to the English translation of Albert Lange's *History of Materialism*: "The two dogmas which make up the essence of materialism are: first, that matter alone is real; second, the rule of law." It is clear that these two dogmas come from the belief of materialists that there is no unobservable, and if the laws that we observe today were not eternal, we could not predict the future and therefore something would be unobservable.

First, concerning those premises which are materialistically sound. The Democritean premise, that the atoms are not permitted to have any qualities, is certainly materialistically sound, because every quality, even if tightly bound to matter, must be taken for an immaterial existence. This is, actually, the difference between quantity and quality: quantity has to do with the essential stuff of a thing, its matter, while quality comprises everything the thing expresses except for its essential matter.

Materialistically sound, likewise, is the Democritean premise that the "falling" of the atoms is not brought about through any power — whether internal or external to the atoms — but occurs spontaneously. This very premise follows from the first premise, because even a power *in*, can be taken only for a quality *of*, the atoms, and therefore as an immaterial existence.

On the other hand, there is an explicit contradiction between the premises that the atoms are differentiated by their size, and that they are, nevertheless, indivisible. Difference in size of atoms means necessarily that the matter of the larger atoms takes up a larger space than the matter of the smaller atoms, so why cannot a piece of matter be cut off from the former, so far as to equalize their volume with that of the latter?

This can be reconciled only through the idea that the matter in the atoms is so cohesive, that it cannot by any means be taken apart. But if so, what holds the matter together? Is there not need for a power — something excluded according to Democritean materialism?

From the same standpoint the premise that the atoms are distinguishable by their weight is similarly inconsistent. Every rational person understands that if the atoms are indistinguishable in their qualities, they must also be indistinguishable in their kinds of motion, and therefore in the velocity of their descent from up to down.

The resolution [teretz] that the difference in atomic weight is derived from the difference in their size, is nonsensical blather [umzinige ployderay], and one can scarcely believe that it came out of Democritus' mouth. One need not be a great mathematician to calculate that if matter has no powers, then more matter has no more power than less matter, and the former can, therefore, move no faster than the latter.

D.

The last premise was, therefore, rejected even by Democritus' close followers. Epicurus and Lucretius already held that the atoms are not distinguishable in weight. Left alone, the atoms would continually fall in a straight line, never coming to a collision. What then? Some atoms must at some time have received an impulse from somewhere else — an impulse which perturbed their path and which caused all of the succeeding collisions and everything that follows from them, all according to the teaching of Democritus.

It is superfluous to say how far this concession deviates from the Democritean line, how far the impulsive factor breaks through the wall of the exclusively materialist existence and how far the impulsive activity fills up the void of absolute spontaneity. Yet a deviation by itself does no harm; a deviation can mean improvement and progress. But on the other hand, we need to know: from whence comes this impulse?

Well, concerning all this Epicurus is silent [makht a shvayg]. This agrees even with his practical philosophy, to make inquiry only concerning what is practical, that is, only what allows of inquiry. As a practical maxim, this is not bad. But one must remember, concerning this, that that which does not allow of inquiry can occupy a place in the generality [sakh hakl] of what allows of inquiry, and when we omit the former, we cannot achieve a full — i.e., a correct — account of the latter. This is what Epicurus did not know, or did not want to know.

Lucretius, on the other hand, did, in fact [shoyn], attempt to give an answer to this question. But listen to his novelties [hert khiddushim]: he holds that such an impulse could have come from a kind of initiative of the will, which we observe in men and other higher living beings. In other words: Lucretius believes that these living beings possess in their wills a power of initiating, a power to begin a new activity — a power we call free will — and this very power could have initiated another kind of movement.

E.

Some will undoubtedly say that the existence of a power to initiate a new activity [tetigkayt] not only conflicts with the Democritean postulate, that immaterial powers and qualities do not exist, but fails also to agree with Democritus' first principle, "From nothing, nothing comes" — a principle which was taken over by all materialists and for which Lucretius himself moves heaven and earth [legt ayn veltn].

And this claim is certainly correct, unless we postulate that Lucretius construed the principle as referring to the "coming" of substance or form, but not as referring to the "coming" of a small amount of activity, even though that very activity causes the coming of new forms.

But let us make a new attempt to understand the full meaning of the postulate itself, that the first impulse which led to the collisions between atoms, could have been derived from free will. This, obviously, cannot mean free will of humans or of other living beings, which are themselves products of the collisions between the atoms and could, after all, not have existed at the time of the first impulse, which led to these collisions. But if not from the free will of humans or other living beings, from where else could this "free will" be derived?

This question leaves Lucretius with two alternatives:

(1) To accept that the atoms themselves have "free will" and that they are living beings themselves. Or

(2) To accept that even during the first impulse something outside the atoms already existed, having the power to impel the atoms in the way of creation.

The first alternative is the way of animism, which Lucretius rejects. In his poem, Lucretius ridicules openly the thought that the individual atoms should possess vital properties. What remains is then the second alternative, i.e., that even the materialist Lucretius cannot do without the existence of an active, vital Origin, which is the putative cause [zoll zayn di urzakh] of the world's creation.[2]

Thus we see how the ancient materialists failed utterly in the matter of atheism. We will see, in what follows, whether their counterparts [khaverim], the modern materialists, have had more success in this respect.

————•◦◦◄◆►◦◦•————

---

2 It is possible that even Epicurus tacitly [beynoy leveyn atsmoy] accepted this postulate, and that this was actually the reason he construed the local gods as living eternally, and as perfect beings. He argued only that as such they would have to be indifferent to all that goes on in the world.

Chapter Four

The New Materialism

A.

In the second half of the seventeenth century, Newton published his famous calculations, which established the law of gravity. Of course, there could then be no more talk of the spontaneous, continuous fall of atoms. Everyone had to admit then that the fall of objects is caused by a force and that the same force could suspend it occasionally as well.

Similarly, everyone then knew that the cohesion of the atoms does not stem from an external pressure, caused by a collision, but from an internal force, or, as it is called today, an internal energy. Naturally one could not then assess the extent of this force, as it manifests itself in atomic power. But little by little this also has begun to be gauged, and in the period before atomic power was discovered, scientists had already begun to anticipate [nehen a baytl, lit., sew a money pouch] what can be accomplished by success in releasing this hidden energy.

Once the existence of energy was established, there was no longer any ground for attempting to distort the facts, for refraining from calling every source of activity by its proper name, that is force or energy. All at once, one became energy conscious; every kind of activity was now designated as a kind of energy: chemical energy, electrical energy, nervous energy, thermal energy, optical energy, etc. This went so far that some believe today that the only thing that exists is energy, and that matter is itself a kind of energy.

This, naturally, gave the death blow to the Democritean version of materialism; this compelled the modern materialists to change their color and modify their language. Today's materialists no longer, therefore, say that only matter exists; rather, what exists is "matter and energy."

B.

So what does materialism look like after this metamorphosis — namely, allowing the existence of something other than matter — can it remain so "materialistic" and so atheistic as before, under Democritus, or must it yield a little concerning these principles?

In order to answer this question, we need only mention the correct postulate of the materialists of the past, that a power or quality in matter is not the same as matter itself, and that the existence of such a power must therefore be construed as the existence of something that is immaterial, as the existence of an immaterial essence.

So much concerning materialism. But atheism undergoes the same setback. When the modern materialists pack into the word "force" [kraft] all kinds of energy, they perforce invest the immaterial essence with all sorts of powers; and when they account for "force" as the cause of everything that originates and everything that happens, they concede, ipso facto, that all events arise from the immaterial essence.

This is not yet all. The materialist philosophers usually hold also a practical philosophy, a materialist ethical teaching, in which they demonstrate, with signs and wonders [oysesumoyfsim], that our moral feelings are nothing but correct calculations of what is expedient: it pays to go in good paths and avoid the bad ones, because good ways lead naturally to human happiness and bad ways lead naturally to human unhappiness.

This was the philosophy of Epicurus and Lucretius in the past and this is also the philosophy of the modern materialists: "What we call 'moral feelings' are derived from the social instincts or habits, which every human (or animal) society develops, and must develop, to avoid being destroyed by its own incompetence." These are the words of L. Buechner in his *Force and Matter*, the materialist bible of the second half of the nineteenth century.

Rewarding good deeds with good, and evil deeds with evil, is nothing other than the old system of reward and punishment, which occupies such an important place in every religion — except that, while in every religion reward and punishment are meted out by a

Power, according to materialism they follow naturally. But "following naturally" must for the modern materialist mean, following from the nature of matter, i.e., from its qualities, and thus, once again, from its immaterial essence. The immaterial essence that goes under the name "force" must therefore also possess the power and the virtue of meting out rewards and punishment, so how does it differ from the immaterial essence in which the religious believe?

C.

The addition of "force" to matter dictated, therefore, that the modern materialists should renounce both the narrow materialism and the atheism of their former friends. They are, however, not ready to sacrifice so much, and they attempt, therefore, to save themselves by the postulate that force and matter represent the same thing: "Matter and force are separable only in thought; in reality they are one."[1] In reality, only matter exists; and force exists eo ipso, because it is one with matter. It is clear that with this premise, the modern materialists seek to jump once again upon the well-trodden path of the ancient materialists — matter possesses force intrinsically, or moves itself, just as for the ancient materialists the atoms fall spontaneously from above to below.

There is, however, a great difference between "falling" and "force," and if "falling" could formerly be admitted as a spontaneous occurrence, this can no longer be done with force: falling is usually taken for a negative occurrence — which follows from the absence of any power — a thing having no power to hold itself up, falls; falling thus can well be described [oyfnemen] as spontaneous. It is otherwise with force. The activities though which force manifests itself are taken for positive occurrences; when we see that a thing attracts or repels, we must admit a power which performs [tut] these actions — so how can we say that force is intrinsic, and does not imply a separate existence?

---

1 A quote from A. Meier, cited by Buechner in the beginning of his *Force and Matter*.

Besides, it is in any case difficult [stam shver] to understand how one can undertake to determine what force "really" is. After all, force is never perceived by our external senses; every materialist will surely admit that he has never seen, heard, or felt force. Everything we know about it is through reason [gedank], which adduces it as the cause of observed activities — so what right do we have to contradict our reason, to declare that reality differs from what reason represents to us?

True, we know that our reason is fallible, that a thing can be different in reality from what our reason takes it to be. We therefore always have the right to doubt what reason tells us about something — even when reason alone acquaints us with that thing, we may think that perhaps the thing is in reality different from what reaon takes it to be. But how do we know for sure, in such a case, that the thing is, in fact, different from what reason takes it to be? Nay more, how do we know *in what respect* it is different, that is, *how* the thing is in reality?

D.

The materialists themselves, realizing that they have no effective weapons against thought, attempt to plead for an acknowledgment by reason itself of the unity of force and matter. Buechner argues that force and matter must be the same thing, because separately they cannot exist, cannot be imagined, nor even thought:

"There is no force without matter — no matter without force. By itself, neither is more possible or imaginable than the other. If we try to think of electricity, magnetism, weight, or heat . . . without the substances in which we have observed the manifestation of these forces . . . what is left over is nothing but an empty idea, a word-token, which we can use only with the end of designating and classifying a certain class or group of material phenomena."[2]

But the above passage can serve as an sample of Buechner's frivolity in making assumptions and bringing proofs. First of all, he

---

2 *Force and Matter*, first chapter.

"begins with a barrel, and ends with a pitcher" [i.e., he equivocates; cf. *Bava Kamma* 27a] — the examples in the passage show, chiefly, that force without matter cannot be imagined or thought, not that it cannot exist. In any case, the argument is valid at most for force without matter — but not matter without force.

Let us at least see how matters stand concerning the unimaginability or the unthinkability of force without matter, which happens to be true. But we cannot imagine force *with* matter, either — because we cannot imagine force at all! Why not? Because our imagination can only reproduce or reflect what we cognize with our senses, and since force is not cognized by the senses, we cannot imagine it.

And since we cannot imagine force, we must imagine all matter as though it lacked force. We learn about force quite independently, though its effects, such as motion, attraction, repulsion, etc.[3] The truth is, therefore, diametrically opposed to Buechner's view: not only can we, but we *must* imagine matter without force.

For the same reason, we must also cognize force separately from matter, because cognition takes over matter from the imagination, and cognizes it, therefore, just as it takes it over from the imagination. This fact is, actually, conceded by the materialists themselves, when they say, that force and matter are separable in thought; this has to mean, that we think the two as separated — force separate from matter and matter separate from force.

But if so, what about the examples of force that Buechner cites — do they not manifestly show that force without matter cannot be thought?

The answer is, that these examples do not represent pure force, but rather force mixed with matter. Electricity, for example, is the action of force on the material particles we call electrons. Clearly,

---

3 This does not mean that we first learn about force only by observing these effects. By analogy, we can very well reckon in advance the possibility of those effects. For example, when we observe a pigeon flying we assume that another pigeon would possess also the same ability; so for force: by induction, everyone knows from his personal powers what force might be.

electricity, as such, cannot be thought without matter, which takes part in it, because without matter there is in fact no electricity. On the other hand, the cause of electricity — what drives the electrons to come together or fly apart — that is the pure force which is thought separately.

E.

Let us even suppose, however, that force and matter cannot exist separately. This would not mean, after all, that force and matter are actually one thing, so far as to say that the existence of matter *implies* that of force. For this we need a Spinozistic unity, through which force and matter are taken to be two separate manifestations of the same thing, so that force should be essentially matter and matter essentially force.

So in order to preserve their darling, namely atheism, the modern materialists are prepared to go equally far with the unity of force and matter. We find such an attitude in Buechner's writing: "Separated from one another, each one becomes an empty abstraction or idea, which are used to show two sides or manifestations of the same existence, the nature of which in itself is unknown to us. Force and matter are fundamentally the same thing thought from different standpoints."[4]

It will be observed immediately, however, that this is not authentic Spinozism — if only for the fact that for Spinoza, force and matter are not different manifestations, but rather different modes of the same manifestation, namely space.[5] On the contrary, again, thought, which is for Spinoza a separate manifestation, is for the

---

4 Taken from the first chapter of the fifth edition of *Force and Matter*.

5 A manifestation, or an attribute, is something that possesses an infinite existence, that is, for example, there is no boundary of spatial existence, neither in location nor in time. On the other hand, the modes are bounded both in place and in time; we can very well imagine a body which exists in one place but not in another, in one time but not in another.

materialists only a mode of force: "Thought," says Moleschott, "is a movement of matter."[6]

We have here, then, only an imitation of Spinozism. We will see presently whether Spinozism allows itself to be imitated in this way.

————••❖••————

6 *Force and Matter*, in the chapter with the name "Thought."

Chapter Five

Spinoza's Metaphysics

A.

S pinoza is known as a Rationalist, whose philosophy excels in its accordance with reason, more than that of any other philosopher.

And surely he earned the title honestly [kosher]: more than any other philosopher, he endeavored to give his philosophy a strongly logical appearance; his famous *Ethics* is an anomaly among all other philosophical works in that it has the format of a geometry textbook, in which the propositions are linked in a continuous logical chain, the later ones following logically from the earlier.

To accuse Spinoza of illogic should therefore be impossible, unbelievable. And yet there are those who cast against him this very accusation. There are those who find nonsense or logical errors in most of the propositions of the metaphysical part of the *Ethics*.

Of course, this is not the place to set forth Spinoza's metaphysics or the criticism thereof — criticism which itself, of course, is strongly disputable. Here we will dwell upon only a few propositions, which are the most important ones of his metaphysics and which appear more awkward than his other metaphysical propositions.

One of these propositions we have mentioned in the last chapter, that space and thought represent two manifestations of the same being (essence). This proposition seems quite meaningless: space is taken for something that is; thought is taken for something that is performed. Space and thought are therefore taken as different as a substantive is from a verb, as different as the earth is from our traveling upon it — so how can the two be taken as the same being?

The second such proposition is the one upon which rests virtually the entire Spinozistic metaphysics — the proposition, that there must exist a perfect being, a being that is infinite or unlimited in every respect. In this proposition lie the flaws in the proofs, which are full of logical errors. Here we will, indeed [shoyn], pause and consider the demonstrations which are to be found in the *Ethics*, Proposition XI.

B.

Spinoza adduces no less than [gantse] four demonstrations for this proposition. Here these demonstrations will be communicated in popular form. Whoever would like to see them verbatim can find them in Nathanson's (Yiddish) translation of the *Ethics*.

First comes the proof from "*causa sui*," from the rule that a perfect being must be the cause of its own existence. The proof goes as follows: such a being cannot have the cause of its existence outside itself, because being infinite in every respect, there can be nothing outside it. It must, therefore, have the cause of its being within itself. And since the rule of causality requires, that that which has a cause of existence must exist, and since, having the cause of its existence in itself, the perfect being always has cause to exist; the perfect being must, therefore, always exist.

This demonstration, however, contains the following glaring logical fallacy: from the premise that a perfect being cannot have the cause of its existence outside itself, it does not yet follow, that it must contain the cause of its existence in itself. It is possible that there should be nowhere such a cause — not in itself or outside itself. And having no cause for its existence, it should, in fact, according to the requirement of the rule of causality, not exist at all.

The second proof for the existence of a perfect being Spinoza adduces from the premise that there cannot be any cause of the *nonexistence* of such a being: everything that exists must have, either inside or outside itself, a cause for its existence, just as everything that does not exist must have within itself or outside itself a cause for its nonexistence. For example, an existing man has the cause of his existence outside himself, in his parents. By contrast, a four-sided circle has the cause of its nonexistence within itself: it does not exist because it contains within itself a contradiction, because its existence is logical nonsense, and therefore impossible.

Now, the infinite being cannot have outside itself a cause for nonexistence, because being infinite, nothing outside it can exist. Nor can it have such a cause within itself, because then it would never exist, and what does not exist cannot cause anything. Since, then, it has neither within itself, nor without itself, any cause for nonexistence, the infinite being must exist.

This demonstration is even more absurd than the previous one. Had Spinoza recalled the logic of the Talmud [gemore] which he had studied in his youth, he would have immediately at the beginning of this proof discovered a contradiction: if it is said, that in order to exist, a thing must have a cause, it is thereby presupposed, that without a cause the thing will not exist, i.e., that nonexistence needs no cause. The same in reverse. If it is said that nonexistence requires a cause, it must thereby be presupposed, that without a cause there will be existence, i.e., that existence requires no cause.

C.

The third demonstration is what is called by Kant the "cosmological argument." It begins with Descartes' "*Cogito ergo sum*": I think, therefore I am. From this it follows that something must exist. Even if we suppose, that all our cognition and all our ideas are not more than dreams and empty fantasies, the dreams and the fantasies themselves must exist, i.e., the mind that dreams and fantasizes.

What should be, however, the essence of that which exists? There are three possible alternatives: (1) that only imperfect beings exist; (2) that only perfect beings exist; (3) that both sorts of beings exist. The first alternative is excluded, because that which exists is more powerful than what does not exist, then if only imperfect beings exist, the result is that imperfect beings have more power than perfect beings — which is absurd. What remains, therefore, only the last two alternatives, according to which it results that perfect beings must in any case exist.

The fourth demonstration goes the same way, except it leaves out the a posteriori element, the part which is supported by our experience that something exists. It starts, therefore, immediately from the premise that existence means power; and since a perfect being can certainly not lack any power, it cannot lack existence either. This proof is known in philosophy as the "ontological argument," which traces its pedigree [yikhes] from the ancient Scholastics.

The last two demonstrations are both based on the premise, that existence means power — which implies that anything in which we understand [derhern] power must exist, and the more the power, the more the existence. But if so, one should have been able to argue in the same vein, that the lion should have existed when the amoeba began to exist, inasmuch as the lion possess more power and thereby must exist more or longer than the amoeba.

Spinoza himself senses that something is awkward [nit glatik] with the premise upon which the last two proofs are based, and he attempts to smooth [fargleten] it over with the claim, that a finite being, which exists in virtue of [durkh] something else, is in this respect unlike an infinite being, which exists in virtue of itself. He must mean by this, that a being that exists in virtue of something else, must depend for its existence not on its own power, but upon something else, and therefore the extent of its existence cannot be deduced from the extent of its own power.

Yet even so, the same objection remains: if existence means power, it should follow [oyskumen] that the stronger species which received from an external source more power, received, thereby, more existence — then why has the amoeba existed longer than many other, far stronger, species, which began to exist far later, and of which there is today no trace?

Perhaps it will be said, that existence is a special sort of power, a power to exist, and that the amoeba was able to acquire more of that particular sort of power than the other species did — although the other species acquired more of what we usually understand by the word "power." But if these are two kinds of power, and we cannot deduce one sort from the other, we cannot deduce it either in the case of the infinite being.

The one thing we can perhaps say is, that in the case of the infinite being, there can be no difference between one kind of power and the other, since, being perfect, the infinite being must include the power to exist as it includes all other kinds of power. But if the idea of perfection should include the power to exist, as it includes all other kinds of power, then existence would have to be entailed directly by this idea, just as all other sorts of power, such as strength, wisdom, etc., are entailed by it — so why is existence not entailed directly by the idea of perfection? Why must it here be smuggled in under the apron [fartukh] of "power"?

This shows that something here is not so smooth [glat], that existence is different from power and cannot be dragged along [mitgeshlept] with it. This difference was later exposed by Immanuel Kant — and Kant's distinction between power and existence consists in this: power is a quality of a thing, of which it is a part, and in the idea of the entire thing, in which all its parts must be included, its power must also be included. By contrast, existence is not a quality of a thing, but rather a assertion concerning it — when I say that this or that thing exists, I assert that this or that thing, which I have in my mind, exists outside my mind — and such an assertion is not a part of the essence of the thing, and is, therefore, not included in the concept of the thing; I can very well have in my mind an idea of perfection, which may not exist outside my mind.

D.

So what's the matter with Spinoza, who cannot, after all, be dismissed with a wave of the hand [avekmakhn mit de hand]? In many ways Spinoza shows himself to be a master of logic — so how is it possible that the master should sometimes be a master bungler [portazh shebeportazhes]. Isn't there some catch, a resolution of these difficulties? Actually, it is not hard to find a resolution if we investigate the background of Spinoza's metaphysics — a background which lies in the philosophical speculations of Spinoza's predecessor, the French philosopher René Descartes.

Descartes (a star of the Renaissance period) occupied himself with finding fixed axioms, truths to which everybody would have to agree — just as everyone agrees that two times two equals four.[1]

But where will such truths be found? As for the conclusions of the philosophers — that's out of the question [upgeredt]; they have no conclusions to which everyone must agree. Even the sciences upon which these conclusions are based, even the elementary knowledge which we receive from the senses, is not always reliable, because even the senses sometimes do deceive us. They deceive by illusions as, for example, that huge stars appear to us to be minuscule points. And we get false knowledge all the time in our dreams — and how do we know that even when we are awake we are not dreaming, that the demon who deceives us by night, is not deceiving us by day? From whence do we know, that our waking time itself is not a deception — do we not in a dream also think that we are awake?

All our knowledge thus lies under a pall of doubt — all, except the knowledge that my thought exists. Even to deceive me I must be thinking; and dream, illusion, and doubt, are also thoughts. Thus have I already found a certain truth — my thought (mind?) certainly exists.

I examine my own mind, and find therein ideas and images [forstellungen]. I can have no doubt, that at this moment there exist in my mind such ideas and such images. The only question is, whether I can rely on what these ideas and images represent [viln hobn], that what they represent actually exists outside the mind.

I examine further my ideas and images, I find among them one idea concerning which I cannot doubt, that what it represents exists outside the mind. That is the idea of a perfect being, which must really exist — for the following reason:

Every idea must come from a mind. An idea of perfection must come from a mind, which has in it perfection, because perfection cannot come from imperfection. There must, therefore, exist a mind, which has perfection in it — a perfect mind. This cannot be my own mind, because from the very fact that I doubt and can be deceived, I

---

1 The following philosophical speculations are found in Descartes' *Meditations*.

see indeed, that I know not everything, and that my mind is not perfect. External to my mind there must, therefore, exist a perfect mind, a perfect being.

Of course, a perfect, or infinite, being cannot be limited by something else, which exists outside it. Everything that exists must therefore stem from it. My mind, or my power to cognize existing things, must therefore also stem from it. And no falsehood can come from a perfect being (since falsehood means the opposite from that which exists; means the lack of existence, which a perfect being cannot suffer), my power to think and to cognize cannot be false either. With this the entire pall of doubt, which was cast upon our knowledge, disappears at once.

But at this point the question poses itself: if so, from whence originate our false thoughts and cognition? The response is, they originate from two sources that are found outside our mind: (1) from our free will; and (2) from bodily disorders.

Our false thoughts are false calculations which we make because of the rashness [behole] of free will, which the perfect being has endowed us with in order to give us the power of choice, so that we should not act mechanically.

In other words — when the mind bides its time with the sum total until it has counted everything there is to count, then it will never make a mistake. It happens very often, however, that while the mind is in the middle of its calculation, the will dashes out and drags down the sum total; making a decision, when the calculation is very far from being finished. Thus it seems, that on the basis of inferences of little acceptability, which we happen to have in mind at the time, our will decides to indulge a harmful lust; or, on the basis of insufficient cognition of things seen from afar, we judge of four-sided things, that they are round, or of large things that they are small.

Further, bodily disorders comprise the source of errors in perceptual matters — sense impressions and feelings. The mind never receives perceptual material directly, but transmitted by the nerves, which bring this material from all parts of the body to the brain, the seat of thought. And how does the mind know from whence this material comes? How does it know, for example, that the feeling of pain is an SOS sent from the finger and not from another part of the body?

The mind must surmise it from the way that the perceptual matter is transmitted — the pain which is transmitted in such and such a way, is a pain in this or that finger. This is fine as long as the body is working in good order. Every now and then, however, there is a disorder in the body, the nerves in the brain do not work properly, and then the feelings and sense impressions perform differently from usual, and thus, too, the mind's interpretation of them is different from the usual. The error is not in the mind's assertions, but in the material, which the nerves or the brain present to the mind.

And this sort of disorder in the nerves or brain usually dominates a person when he sleeps, or when he is drunk, or delirious, or, in general, when people are disposed to having illusions.

E.

The main points of Descartes' theory can be found also in Spinoza's metaphysics; Spinoza, as well, took as his starting point the idea that something must exist; and he, too, ended up with the ideas: that there exists a perfect being, that everything that comes from the mind is true, while falsity lies in what does not come from the mind. However, Spinoza carries out the work with more dexterity, and consequently his theory has much more logical continuity on this point than Descartes'.

Let us take first the idea that something must exist. Spinoza begins with his famous division of existence into three sorts: substance, attributes, and modes.

Take, for example, some water. It has liquidity, cohesiveness, weight, etc. These qualities are not taken as existing in and of themselves; there is no liquidity or cohesiveness without something which is liquid or cohesive. They must therefore be taken as existing in something else — something which stands under them, their substance. They merely indicate the form of existence of the substance and therefore they are called *modes* — forms.

What is the *substance* of water? It will be undoubtedly said, the atoms arranged in the order H_2O. But these atoms, too, already possess qualities, which exist in something else, namely space. Only space exists in nothing else. That is, space must be taken to be the absolute substance of the atoms and of anything which consists of atoms. Yet even space cannot be taken to be absolute substance, and here is why:

There is a difference between absolute substance and the modes as to the cause of their existence: the modes follow from the nature of their substance — the rigidity of iron stems from the nature of iron — while the absolute substance cannot follow from something else, because in that case it would depend upon something else and would therefore not be absolute. Absolute substance must, therefore, have within itself the cause of its own existence; it exists because it possesses of itself the property of existence.

Possessing the property of existence means *being* existence, just as possessing the property of red means being red.[2] Absolute substance, being existence, excludes any form of nonexistence, including the limitation of existence — which includes in itself nonexistence. Absolute substance must therefore be unlimited in its existence, and nothing outside it can exist, for the existence of something else outside it would limit it. For this reason, space cannot be considered as absolute substance, since there is, in fact, existence outside space: ideas do not take up space, and thus exist outside space.

On the other hand, space is not a mode either, because a mode must exist in something else, while space does not exist in anything else, but in itself. Even if we were to imagine that space existed in something else, this something else would have also to be space. In this way, it emerges that space is neither an absolute substance nor a mode — so what is it?

It is an *attribute* of the substance, something which manifests the properties of the substance, but only in the framework of *one* manifestation. Thus space manifests unlimited existence in the

2 "The existence of G-d and his essence are one and the same" (*Ethics* 1, 20).

framework of space — it is unlimited in extent (infinite) and unbounded in the number of modes which it includes. In the framework of this particular manifestation, ideas do not enter, because ideas do not take up space — so what kind of existence do ideas represent?

They cannot represent absolute substance, because if absolute substance were Idea, then Idea would have to be manifested through space, which is, after all, an attribute of the absolute substance. Idea cannot represent more than an attribute of the absolute substance, and, not having a place in the attribute of space, Idea must represent a different attribute of the absolute substance — an attribute in which the particular ideas are modes and their number must be infinite, as are the modes of space, that is, there is no measure to the number of ideas which can be thought.

Of course, these two attributes are not the only ones through which the absolute substance can be manifested, otherwise the substance would be limited in the number of its existing expressions and would thereby not be existentially unbounded. The absolute substance must therefore be expressible in an infinite number of attributes, although we know only of two, space and Idea.

Now this infinite number of attributes all manifest one and the same being, which is so far unitary, that it is even indivisible, i.e., the absolute substance cannot consist of parts: for if the absolute substance should consistent of parts, the parts would have to represent either unlimited beings or limited beings, but these parts cannot represent either unlimited beings or limited beings. Why not?

They cannot represent unlimited beings, because what is unlimited does not permit the existence of something else outside itself, and if even one part should be unlimited, it would not permit the existence of the other parts. But they cannot be limited either, because limited parts can never come to anything which is unlimited (the parts comprise the being of a thing, and if the thing is limited in its being it cannot, obviously, be unlimited).

But if the absolute substance is indivisible, then every one of its attributes must be indivisible, because an attribute is, after all, that through which, in the framework of a given manifestation, the property of the substance is appropriately manifested. Space must also be indivisible, and the divisibility which we take space to have can be only an illusion of our imagination — an illusion which is repudiated by deliberations [kheshboynes] of our mind.[3]

F.

It is superfluous to say that Spinoza's absolute substance is so perfect, so full of being, that it is able to cover Descartes' idea of a perfect being and then some [nokh mit a smitshik] — Descartes, clearly, never dreamed of a perfection which includes infinitely many attributes. And from the idea of an absolute, unlimited substance, Spinoza arrives easily at the idea that everything that comes from the mind must be true.[4] How is this?

If existence manifests itself simultaneously in an infinite number of attributes, it must be concluded, that what manifests itself in one attribute must manifest itself in an infinite number of attributes — i.e., in all the other attributes — and what exists in the mind must perforce exist also in space and in all the other attributes, and must therefore be true.

But at this point the old question arises: if so, where does falsity come from? Second, a new question surfaces [shvimt aroyf]: just as we must suppose that everything that exists in the mind exists also in all the other attributes, we must also suppose that everything that exists in any of the other attributes exists also in the mind — so why, then, do we not cognize that which exists in all the other attributes, besides space? And why do we not cognize even everything which exists in space?

The answer is [iz der terets]: in the absolute mind there does exist everything which goes on [tut zikh] in all the attributes. But the

---

3 Cf. Note 3, Proposition XV in the first part of the *Ethics*. We will see later, that the mind is for Spinoza the source of true cognition, while the imagination is the source of false cognition. When, therefore, what follows from pure thought is in opposition to our imagination, the imagination must be repudiated as an illusion.
4 "There is nothing positive in ideas, in virtue of which they can be called false" (Part II, Proposition 33, in Nathanson's [Yiddish] translation of the *Ethics*.)

human mind, which is one of the infinite number of modes of one attribute, and is thus limited, cannot manifest more than one mode of another attribute, that is, only the idea of one human body. In other words, a person knows only what is happening in his body. And this limitation of our mind is the source of all our errors, every falsity. How so?

Since a person knows only what is happening in his own body, every one of his representations must represent only that which happens in his own body and every new representation of his must represent only something new, i.e. a change, in his own body. For example, when a person sees the sun at a certain distance from him, this means only, that his body is impressed in a certain way, and that in his mind this bodily impression is manifested by the representation of quick radiation at a certain distance.

When we realize, subsequently, that this representation is false, that the distance between us and the sun is much greater than we imagine while looking at the sun, this does not mean that the person's mind does not correctly represent the thing which makes the impression on his body, but it means that the impression on his body does not represent correctly the nature of the external thing which made the impression; and since the person's mind represents only the impression made on the body — and not the external thing which influenced the body — it must therefore represent the external thing only according to the impression on the body. Therefore it will represent it thus even if we come to know that it is not real, that the representation is only an illusion, because as representation of a bodily impression it is always true. The root of falsity, therefore, is that a person's mind represents only the impressions in his body and not the external objects as they are essentially, i.e., that a person's mind is limited to a few ideas.

Now, what is the reason for the incorrect representation, by the bodily impressions, of the nature of the external objects which cause those impressions? The reason is, that the nature of the bodily impression is not entirely owing to the external object, but also to the impressed body. The bodily impression can therefore only partly represent the nature of the external object which makes the impression. Not only that, it is even true, that what impressed itself on our bodies might by now not exist at all; its past impression, however, might not yet be erased, and might subsequently be awakened by an association, which is tied to and carried along [mitgeshlept] with our impressions.[5]

Now, these very associations are responsible for the falsity of our dreams. While awake, the associations cannot deceive us, because we have, at the same time, other impressions, which indicate the appropriate place of the associations. For example, when an association evokes a deceased person in the mind, or any other person not near us, we see immediately that he is not near us; on the other hand, in sleep we lack the wakeful impressions and therefore we must accept the associations at face value [far gut gelt].

A third source of falsity is that our mind has the power to grasp only some of the details of complicated objects. Of a man, for example, the mind grasps only the height, color, and a few other characteristics which are common to all men and are therefore, easy for it to take in. On the other hand, the mind omits many characteristics in which men differ. This causes us to take for identical, things which in fact are different. And this leads us, furthermore, to make invalid deductions.

Thus we see how all sorts of falsity stem from this, that the mind's cognition is insufficient, or as Spinoza calls it, "inadequate." In the case when the cognition of our mind is "adequate" it cannot in fact be false.

When is it adequate? When the faults that we have listed here vanish [faln avek], that is, when the object of cognition is identical in all respects — in each of its parts as in the whole; in our bodies as in

---

5 Associations are of three sorts: (1) Association by similarity, as, for example, when the photograph of a person reminds us of the person himself. (2) Association by relationship, as, for example, the idea of one brother makes us think of the other one. Association by causality is a special case, as when hunger reminds us of bread, or bread reminds us of the baker. (3) Association by proximity — which can be proximity in space, for example, the idea of our mother evokes the idea of the shtetl where she lived, or the idea of milk brings with it the idea of whiteness; the proximity can be also in time, as, for example, in a summer hotel, the ring of the bell evokes the idea of going to eat.

the objects external to our bodies. Such is mathematical cognition, for example, where two times two has the same proportion, as two times two million, and a pound of feathers has the same weight as a pound of lead.

The best of these adequate cognitions are those which are so simple, that we cognize them quite directly — as the cognition that *idea is thought*, or other such definitions or logical deductions. Cognizing these cognitions entirely, we cognize also at the same time, that they are entirely correct, while in complex mathematical calculations we cognize only the correctness of the formulas. To distinguish between the better sort and the worse sort of the adequate cognition, the better sort are called "intuitions." The inadequate cognition are further called "opinions," i.e., cognitions that manifest only what is in the cognizing person.

G.

From the few points that have been elucidated here, we see that Spinoza was not a realist, because space as indivisible unity is certainly not the real space that we entertain. Indeed, Spinoza says this himself, in Note 3, Proposition XV, of the first Book of the *Ethics*. And if so, all the abovementioned difficulties for Spinoza's metaphysics vanish, because the objections we had to Spinoza the realist do not apply to Spinoza the nonrealist.

Thus the nonsense of taking space and mind as two manifestations of the same being vanishes, because this (alleged) nonsense stemmed from taking space as what we represent it as being, but since space is not what we represent it as being, it can easily manifest the same being as that which idea manifests. This does not mean that Spinoza takes space to be a kind of idea, that he was an idealist of Berkeley's type. If this were so, space would be not more than a mode of thinking. But since space is a separate attribute, it cannot have anything in common with thought, and must be so distinct from it, that were we to be acquainted only with space, we would not know even of the existence of thought. Now what does it mean to say that space and thought manifest the same being?

It means that both are only two different languages [leshoynes] in which the being informs our consciousness of its existence. It does this through thinking and though representation, because with both existence must be accepted.

The existence which must be acknowledged in the two different languages may be limited or unlimited. Spinoza seeks to prove that this particular existence must be taken as unlimited. That is all he is after in his four proofs of the existence of a perfect being.

In the first proof Spinoza argues in the way cited above: since the absolute substance must be *"causa sui,"* it must possess in itself a property of existing, it must exist only, that is, exist without limit.

In the second proof, Spinoza argues in the same way, except from the negative side: accepting substance as existing excludes immediately every principle of nonexistence, i.e., of limited existence; and since it is naturally unlimited, nothing can exist external to it, and there can be nothing, therefore, that could limit it.

Thirdly, he argues that if we were to suppose that there is limited existence, but not unlimited existence, the outcome would be that limited existence has existence in and of itself, while unlimited existence does not.[6] And because this is unthinkable, that means, that in the "language" of thought our consciousness is informed that there exists an unlimited existence.

In the fourth proof he argues the same thing a priori, i.e., without using the fact that we know that limited existence exists. He begins immediately with the deduction: because the idea of unlimited existence implies existence, then when we think about unlimited existence we must think that it has within it existence, i.e., that it exists.

This is, actually, the old "ontological argument" which the Eleatics employed: "That which is, is," i.e., existence means that it exists, but here it is substantiated on the basis that thought by itself, as one of the "languages" through which existence announces itself, is enough to confirm existence. "To say, that we have a true idea but we do not know whether it represents being, is the same as though we

---

6 When Spinoza says that existence has power, this has to mean that it exists, because all powers are in fact with it only modes of existence.

were to say, that we have a true idea but we do not know whether it is true."[7]

In this way, the logical blunders that we had found in Spinoza's proofs for the existence of a perfect being vanish, together with many other logical objections to these proofs — objections which we cannot here dwell upon.

H.

From what has been said here, it can be seen quite clearly that Spinozism is an indivisible system, a system in which the premises are so bound together that we cannot easily remove one of them and carry it somewhere else — as Buechner would like to do with the premise of two manifestations of the same being.

The premise that space and mind are two manifestations of the same being is with Spinoza tightly bound up with his nonrealistic standpoint, that space is not that divisible space which we represent to ourselves, and is in fact something which we are quite unable to represent to ourselves — because all our representations take in the divisible space — are the materialists ready to accept the same nonrealistic standpoint with respect to force and matter? Are they ready to agree that matter is something that we cannot represent to ourselves?

In addition, assuming that force and matter are manifestations of the same being, the materialists must also suppose, that even the space that matter takes up is not space, but something that we cannot represent to ourselves, because force or motion do not occupy space. Are the materialists ready to go so far?

We should not forget either, that it is none other than the materialists who continually boast that they do not submit themselves to obscure ways, that all their premises are comprehensible — is there, now, a greater incomprehensibility than the premise, that force and matter, or verb and substantive, represent the same being? Could

---

7 See the Note to Proposition VIII in *Ethics*, Book I.

one have a greater obscurity than that which very premise casts on the being of matter and space?

Above all, the materialist must also respond to the following hard question: if matter is something which is unknown and which we cannot represent to ourselves, then how does he know that it manifests the same being as force? Does he reason in Spinoza's manner, from the idea of existence? In other words, is he a rationalist — does he rely on ideas and not the senses?

Of course, in the matter of relying on the senses, a materialist cannot yield in the slightest. After all, sensualism is the basis of materialism; a materialist asserts that he believes only in the evidence of the senses. A materialist would do better, therefore, to disavow this particular Spinozist premise, which in any case adheres to materialism like oil to water [vie arbes tzum vant; lit., like chickpeas to the wall]. He will probably say that this Spinozist expression is only a flourish by Buechner, which should not be taken literally. He will point to many places in the same book where Buechner himself explains otherwise the relation between force and matter.

We need not go far. Buechner begins his book with a quotation from Moleschott, which reads as follows: "Force . . . is inseparable from matter, is one of the eternal properties residing in it." A little later, summing up the quotes from the materialist big shots [karpn kep] which he adduces, he writes as follows: "On these grounds, the abovementioned inquirers define force only as a property of matter. More precisely expressed, force can, or must, be defined as a state of activity or movement of matter or of the smallest particles of matter or as a the capacity for the above, more correctly, as a manifestation of the ground of a possible or actual movement."[8]

---

8 I have quoted the passage in its entirety, because it shows Buechner's haziness when it comes to logic. In this passage we find no less than four definitions of force: (1) a state of activity, (2) a movement of matter, (3) a capacity to move matter, (4) a manifestation of an unknown cause. Now the first definition is a simple tautology which explains nothing. The second and third of these definitions explain numerous things, one explains the effect of force and the other explains force as a cause. The fourth definition is further in conflict with the others, because according to it, force is something that is unknown.

These quotations speak explicitly of force as a property of matter. In the preceding chapter we already saw how far the assumption of *property* is poison both for materialism and for atheism. Presently we shall see what remains of these "isms" when we make that assumption.

—••◄◆►••—

Chapter Six

Force as a Property of Matter

A.

If force is to be [zol zayn] only a property of matter, then matter itself must be outfitted [bakleit] with all the powers that we experience in nature — it must be taken to have the power to move, attract, repel, fashion all the creatures that can be found in our little world, at least, from the bacteria to *Homo sapiens,* with the highly developed intelligence of an Aristotle, a Rambam (Maimonides), a Vilner Gaon (R. Elijah ben Shlomo of Vilna [Vilnius], 1720-1797), etc. It must be credited also with the power to reward good deeds with good and evil deeds with evil, because in nature there is such a system, or at least such a tendency.[9] This means that matter itself must be deified, so wherein lies the atheist achievement?

A materialist will surely reply, that what the materialists accomplish for atheism lies in their knowing how to limit both the action of force and its substratum, the source from which force emerges.

First, concerning the action of force: in religion, force is tamed; religion leaves open the possibility of miracles or free will, where force suddenly changes its usual direction. On the other hand, in materialism, in which force is taken to be a property of matter, there can be no change unless matter becomes different from what it was; in the same circumstances it remains the same.[10]

---

9 This has already been discussed. Here we will add only, that even if we suppose that the system of reward and punishment is not that precise, that not always is good rewarded with good and evil with evil, this means only that this power is limited, or that it does not follow the determinate order of causality that other powers follow. But it is impossible to deny altogether the existence of such a power, unless we also deny the possibility of any morality.

10 A property must characterize the substance and therefore cannot change before the substance has become different from what it was, because otherwise the result

And concerning the substratum of force: in religion the possibility is left open for an immaterial substratum for force, while in materialism, in which force is merely a property of matter, there can be no immaterial substratum for force. Even more, nothing immaterial can exist in the first place [iberhoypt], because something that has no force, no effect, not even the effect of resistance which we must attribute to matter, is not real and cannot exist.

These two premises are in fact the basis for materialism. Bertrand Russell says this as well, in his introduction to the English translation of Albert Lange's *History of Materialism*: "The two dogmas which make up the essence of materialism are: first, that only matter is real; second, the rule of law."

There is no doubt that these two premises are atheistic through and through. But since these premises, in fact, rest entirely on the foundation that force is only a property of matter, let us first get a feel for [a tap ton] this foundation, to see how logically consistent it is.

B.

The premise, that force is a property of matter appears to us very simple [poshet], and thus satisfactory. We are, after all, accustomed to thinking in the terminology of properties: sugar is sweet, because it has the property of being sweet; a living being wants to live, because it has a property of wanting to live; similarly, matter is movable, attracts, repels, because it has the properties of doing these things. When we consider the matter a little deeper we see that the matter is not so simple, and has an "impressive" [vazhne] logical difficulty.

In the preceding chapter we already noted, that having a property means existing in a certain way — when sugar has a property of being sweet, it is sweetness. But sugar has other properties: it is also

---

will be, first, that the same substance will be the same and different; second, that none of these properties will characterize truly what the substance is, and thus none of them can be counted as a property of that particular substance. If sugar were bitter, remaining however identical in substance, then neither sweetness nor bitterness would manifest the property of (being) sugar.

white, solid, etc. Is sugar sweetness and also [say] whiteness and also solidity? Are these diverse things, one thing?

This question is not new; it is at least as old as Plato's *Parmenides*. Plato attributes this question to Parmenides' disciple, Zeno, who specialized in finding logical difficulties. In the modern period, it was elucidated [aroysgebrakht] at great length by the English logician, F. H. Bradley.[11] Both Zeno and Bradley exploit this difficulty against realism, against the theory that our cognitions are not only ideas in the mind, but they indicate really-existing objects external to the mind. The reply Socrates gives to Zeno is also from the Idealist standpoint and thus realists cannot make use of it.

So how may a realist cope [an eytze gebn] with the difficulty? The best advice is, in my opinion, to point to the fact which we already noted, that the combination of diversities in a unity occurs in all of nature and it would be a wonder if properties should be an exception in this regard.

Among properties, therefore, or between substance and properties, a kind of bonding as between atoms in an element, or between impressions in a cognition, must govern. And because a bonding like that requires a bonding power, then besides the properties and the substance, another power must be accommodated. The result: the premise of "property" cannot help the materialists enough, because even if force were only a property of matter, nevertheless the existence of another power would have to be acknowledged, one which bonds force and matter together.

It will probably be said, that this bonding power can inhere [lign] in matter itself. But if so, then this power itself must be acknowledged as a property of matter, and as such it would, on its part [fun zayn zayt], again require a bonding power, and so on ad infinitum [on a shier]. Thus, the conclusion is [azoy kumt oys] that the response to the logical difficulty of properties in general that we have proposed [forgelegt] is inadequate [toig nit], when force is regarded [ven es handlt zikh vegn] as a property of matter and if besides force and matter nothing is allowed to exist.

---

11 Cf. *Appearance and Reality*, Chapter 2.

C.

This is only one logical difficulty with the postulate [yesod] of "property." Another logical difficulty can be found in the diversity of force. What is called force is, in reality, a general name for innumerable [on a shier] different powers and properties which are exhibited in innumerable individual things, powers and properties which are often so diverse as to be contradictory. Are they nevertheless properties of the same matter? Is matter both attractive and repulsive, both black and white, both sweet and bitter, both dead and alive, both clever and foolish [narish], both good and evil, etc.?

This very question, of course, tormented [gematert] the ancient materialists, who took the logical point of view very seriously [shtark gerekhent]. Their response was that the diverse properties have to do with the quantity and form of matter: a bigger piece of matter has not the same properties as a smaller piece of matter; something which is spherical is qualitatively different from something which is pointed. But this response cannot satisfy us logically; quantity and form cannot replace quality. The quality of bread cannot be other than it is, the bread can be bigger or smaller, spherical or pointy. This is particularly so, when the issue is [ven es handlt zikh] qualities, which are so remote [vayt] from one another, that they are contradictory.

Another Greek philosopher, Anaxagoras, attempted to dislodge this difficulty by postulating a kind of qualitative atomism. According to this postulate matter is supposed to consist of distinct particles [pitselekh] of matter with distinct qualities — one material particle is supposed to possess the quality of sweetness; another, the quality of whiteness, and so forth [keseder].

According to this account [kheshbn] some parts of matter should possess only the property of attraction; and some, only the property of repulsion. The attractive parts should attract only; and the repulsive parts, repel only. In this way, built-up bodies must consist only of attractive parts, because the repulsive parts cannot come together. All the bodies we see (since we see only built up-bodies) should therefore possess only properties of attraction, so how is it that we also see bodies with repulsive properties? Why do we see, for example, that the parts of all bodies are not compressible so far as to leave no interstitial spaces?

Incidentally, it should be noted here, that even Anaxagoras dared to accompany this postulate only as far as the gates of consciousness. Knowing his own consciousness first hand, he must have realized that consciousness is too important to be acknowledged only as a bit of matter [pitzele shtof] in him.[12] He must therefore have added that besides matter and its properties, there must exist also an immaterial being, a consciousness or "intelligence."

But besides all this, Anaxagoras' postulate of qualitative atomism is for us obsolete [alt gebakn]. We know, in fact, that matter consists at most of three different types: electrons, protons, and neutrons (I say "at most" because after all it is very probable, that these three types themselves should not be distinguished in quality, but only in quantity, meaning their density).[13] In that way, each qualitative atom would have to account for at least a third of all the powers that we experience, and that's much too much [a hibsh bisl tsufil].

D.

If the logical difficulties were not enough [a halbe tsore], the materialist postulate has to bear an epistemological burden, a difficulty which has to do with cognition of this very postulate. It is simply incomprehensible how, on the basis of the small bit [klayn bisl] of cognition that we possess, the materialist undertakes to assert that force is a property of matter, and aside from this substratum of force nothing exists.

---

12 When we acknowledge A as a property of B, we thereby already nullify [mevatl zayn] the existence of A and recognize only the existence of B — we declare that A has so little being, so little reality, that it can exist only as annexed to B, but not by itself. Of course, it is very difficult to acknowledge particles of matter as more consequential [khoshev] than consciousness with all its branches which reach all the way to the forty-nine gates of understanding.

13 [The author's point survives the glaring inadequacy of his account of particle physics, even as of 1948. –Tr.]

In order to cognize of *what* force is a property, we must get to the bottom, the root, the source from which it flows. But we are very far from such a fundamental cognition [gruntovner derkentenish] of force. In fact we have not even a superficial [oyberflekhlikhe] direct cognition of it. All that we cognize is alterations in things, of which we must take force to be the cause. A person does not even cognize his own force, except by its effects; a sick person at times does not know whether he can turn over, or whether he can move his limb, until he attempts to do so. A healthy person supposes, that he can do these things, because he knows that he did them just this moment, and he has no ground to think that he is different in this respect from what he was earlier.

But even in this indirect way we cognize force very little. Thus, we do not cognize the forces of things which are too small or too far. Just so we do not cognize force, when it is too much or too little, as, for example, when something moves too rapidly or too slowly. We do not cognize force either, when it does not cause a change in relation to us. Meanwhile [beyne lebeyne, from Araramic byny lbyny] the result is [kumt oys] that we have no knowledge whatever of the preponderance of force — so how can we have the chutżpah [khutzpe; for those with the chutzpah to question the translator, chutzpah is in the *OED*] to make pronouncements [aroyszogn] about force that demand a fundamental cognition of it?

A similar fate awaits [punkt azoy mit] the other part of the materialist doctrine [yesod], that besides matter and its properties nothing else exists. Our cognition concerning existence, too, is quite [shtark] limited — limited, in any event, in accordance with [loyt] the measure [mos], the space, and the time of its existence; something too small or too far in space or in time is excluded from our cognitive sphere. And even that which is, in fact [shoyn], in our cognitive sphere is cognized by us very little as well; everything we acknowledge thereby is a thin veneer [oybershte shal; lit., scarf, shawl]; about anything a little deeper, we cannot make any inference.

We conclude [azoy kumt oys] that what we cognize is no more than a drop in the sea of infinite existence. How then [iz vie azoy] can we on that basis [durkh dem] determine the limits of existence?

E.

The materialists will undoubtedly [avade] say, we can do this very well [gants gut] with the help of induction, which requires us to make a rule [klal] out of observed instances [bamerkte protim]. What does that mean [vos heyst]? Since everything we observe is matter clothed in force, we are logically required [mekhuyev al pi logik] to make a general rule of this and suppose that everything that exists is nothing but matter clothed in force. In like manner we suppose gravity to be a general rule, because gravity governs everything we observe.

The materialist doctrine [yesod], however, cannot be built up even with the instrument of induction. This can be illustrated best with the following example:

When one visits a new land, and so far as he goes he encounters white people only, the most he is entitled to suppose is that the land he has traversed is populated by white people only (I say "the most," because "lo ra'inu aynah ra'ayah" [Hebrew, Mishnah *Eduyot*, lit., "Failure to observe something is not an observation," i.e., that you have not seen something is no proof that it does not exist]). But he cannot generalize from this to the (part of the) land which he has not seen. How then, do we, in fact, make a general rule of gravitation, that it governs things which we have not yet observed?

When we see that an object falls to earth, we observe immediately both the character of mass [kerperlikhkayt] and also the property of gravitation. And if mass were the only character of the object, we would know at the same time also that gravity is associated with mass, i.e., that all bodies are governed by gravitation; but because the object has other characteristics, we must first eliminate them first — it must be shown that the other characteristics are not the cause of gravity. And that is all induction does here; it proves that gravity does not follow from the other characteristics of the object, because gravity holds even for objects which lack these other characteristics.

For example, when we observe, that water falls to earth, we cannot yet make a generalization that a mass [kerper] falls to earth, because we can surmise that the particular properties of water make it fall. Similarly, when we observe that a stone falls, we can surmise that the particular properties of the stone make it fall. But when we observe, that the stone, *and* the water, *and* other things fall, we realize that it is not the individual but the general properties of these things that cause the fall. And since we discover that mass is the only general property of all these things, we conclude that mass is the cause of their fall to earth, i.e., everything that has mass and is located in the earthly zone will fall to earth.

All that induction accomplishes is, therefore, to sieve out [oystsuzipn] the essential [iker] from the peripheral [tofl]. Somehing we have never observed at all cannot be the object of inductive inquiry.[14] This is particularly so, when this particular "something" is a thing which we are entirely incapable of observing, which we cannot perceive at all with our senses. It is as though [do zet es oys vie] a blind man were to make an induction that no color exists.

The difficulties with materialism are thus innumerable [on a shier]. Let us just [ersht] reverse our course [aroysdreyn dem dishl, lit., turn the wagon shaft around] and see what materialism has to offer [aroystsushteln, lit., put out] in its favor [gunstn]. This we will examine in the next chapters.

---•‹◈›•---

---

14 The only real accomplishment that used to be ascribed to induction was the rule of causality, that from the same cause follows the same effect. But there is a view [svore] that even this we discover initially through experience.

Chapter Seven

False Arguments for Materialism

A.

Earlier we cited Bertrand Russell as saying that two postulates make up the essence of materialism: "First, that matter alone is real, second, the rule of law." There are three arguments in favor of these postulates: one argument for the first, a second argument for the second, and a third argument for both postulates simultaneously.

The first argument is drawn [vert getsoygn] from the impossibility of representing to ourselves the existence of an immaterial being; everything we can imagine must be something that takes up space, corporeal. Nay more, it appears to us, that what does not take up space cannot exist at all. In other words, it is not only that such a being is unknown; rather, we *know* it does not exist — so what sense does it make to foist [ontsuhengen] the concept of existence on something which contradicts it outright? How can we entertain the existence of something which we know explicitly does not and cannot exist?

The second argument is drawn from the authority of the applied sciences. Those sciences are based upon the rule of lawfulness, which is expressed by the rule: same cause, same effect. Riding piggyback [ongeshpart oyf di brayte playtses] upon the sciences, the materialist feels himself secure against all possible attacks through logical argument, because the sciences are quite well protected against such attacks; they can point to concrete successes which cannot be refuted by even the best logical arguments.

The third argument the materialist draws from simplicity. Simplicity is a sign of knowledge; when somebody talks in a way that is easy to understand, it is a sign that he knows what he is talking about. Furthermore, simplicity is an instrument for creating knowledge; through simplicity one is in a position to transmit to others what one knows. And since the materialist is the only one who operates with simple concepts, concepts which come from experience and which everyone possesses, he is the only one who knows what he is talking about and who is positioned to spread knowledge all over the world. The other theories, by contrast, which postulate things which we have never experienced, and of which we cannot frame any clear concept, grope constantly in the darkness and disseminate dark shadows of ignorance throughout the world.

B.

We will first take the first argument, which is the most significant of the three. It is certainly true, that we cannot present to ourselves the existence of something which does not take up space. But this does not yet mean that we cannot know of such an existence. Presentation is not the same as knowledge; presentation is a kind of knowing which results from seeing and feeling. But there are other kinds of knowing, and an unimaginable thing can quite well be known through some other type of knowing.

Take the knowledge which comes from thought, as for example, knowing a cause by way of an effect: when I discern a group of people I know that some cause brought these people together, although I do not present the cause to myself at the time. Similarly, I know that I am mortal, although I have not at any time presented it to myself, but have concluded it from a syllogism, from my knowledge that all men die. In the same way I do not use any presentation in complicated mathematical calculations.

Similarly for knowledge that comes from our inner sense, which brings us to feel pain, love, hate, anger, fear, etc. No one would, of course, say, that hunger, for example, is a presentation of something that takes up space.

Presentation is therefore limited to that knowledge which comes from outer sense. But even among those senses the majority give knowledge without presentation: hearing, smelling, and taste are not presentations of something which takes up space. True, we connect these perceptions with some material cause. But this originates only from experience. In the perceptions themselves there is no such connection; a sound does not take up space, and smell and taste are quite analogous to the feelings of inner sense.

Inter alia, there thus remain no more than two senses that give us knowledge by presentation: the sense of sight and that of touch. But we must with the cognition of these very senses entertain also something immaterial, because presentation itself is consciousness, and consciousness is immaterial. All we can say is that a presentation compels us to suppose, that, external to it, there exists also a material object — an object which is, just as presented. Of course, however, such a compulsion does not nullify the existence of the immaterial presentation itself.

C.

Even here, there is an attempt to declare presentations, feelings, and thoughts as mere physical motions, motions of bodies: an electric current runs from the nerves to the brain, it is sometimes a presentation, sometimes a feeling, and sometimes a thought; it depends only on what nerves it runs through and to what part of the brain it comes; that is all.

And it is indeed known that when a person has presentations, feelings, and thoughts, his nerves and brain lose part of their electric charge and, simultaneously, the temperature rises in those places — a phenomenon which accompanies every movement. In consciousness as well, an animal having a complicated nervous system and a proportional brain weight stands higher on the ladder of progress, i.e. since its body possesses greater capability of nervous motion, it possesses thereby more capability for presentation, feeling, and thinking. Again, conversely, it loses this capability, when certain parts of its nerves and brain are damaged.

The human body, therefore, must be only a complicated machine, a robot with buttons, wheels, and springs, which are called receptors, conductors, effectors, synapses, and other technical names. What happens, however, when we press a button on this robot, and it is left in motion? Then some kind of [epes] presentation, feeling, etc., springs forth.[1] Is, however, this presentation or feeling only motion or is there more than movement — movement plus consciousness?

Nay more, there must be even something more than consciousness and motion, because when someone should know exactly the motion which occurs during a presentation, or a feeling, he would not, by this only, know the presentation or the feeling itself [gufe]. A doctor may know what goes on in and around the tooth during a toothache, but by this he does not obtain the actual feeling of a toothache, which the patient has at the time.

The main part [ikker] of every cognition — the presentation, the feeling, and the thought itself — is therefore incorporeal. And as Descartes already proved, the existence of this main part is more certain than the existence of anything else, because even if we could doubt the existence of what our cognition shows us, the existence of the cognition itself is certain.

D.

Finally, one must also mention the fact, that just as we cannot present to ourselves something that is immaterial, so we cannot clearly think something that is material; when we try to analyze it in thought, insoluble difficulties pour forth.

First of all, we have the difficulty that we have already mentioned, that of possessing qualities, which means to entertain multiple and diverse beings as one being. Aristotle even tried to solve this through an artifice, by connecting together all the qualities of a body under the unifying concept "form" which we have no difficulty in entertaining together with body as one existence; conversely, every body must surely have a form. This artifice,

---

1 This assumes the theory of "interaction," that the motion of bodies causes the presentation. Assuming, however, the theory of "parallelism," that a motion of bodies can only cause another motion of bodies, not a presentation, then there would be entirely no connection between the existence of a presentation and the movement of bodies.

however, cannot satisfy us, because as form it is possible to entertain only the passive appearance of a body, but not its active properties.

Next there are the difficulties connected with the fact that the divisibility of corporeal matter, like space, cannot be taken to be either finite or infinite.

On the one hand it stands to reason that corporeal matter, like the space in which it is found, must be divisible without end, because each part, however small, must possess six different sides: eastern, western, northern, southern, above, and below; and diverse sides means diverse places for matter and places for space, of which each one must itself have six different sides, and so on.[2]

On the other hand, we can argue, however, the opposite, that both matter and space are not infinitely divisible — both because the very concept of infinite divisibility is impossible and because it is impossible to experience infinitely divisible matter:

First, we cannot understand how infinite divisibility is possible in the first place: infinite divisibility means pure complexity, i.e., that simple elements are entirely excluded. On the other hand, we cannot avoid the conclusion that what is complex must have as a foundation the simple elements of which it is compounded, and without these simple elements there cannot be a complex.

Furthermore, we cannot understand our daily experience: every step we take we traverse a piece of space and all its parts from the beginning to the end; and if this piece of space were infinitely divisible — if there were no end to the number of its parts — the result would be that we arrive at the end of something that has no end.

---

2 This point may be better understood when it is set forth particularly concerning space: every part of space must come into contact with other parts, therefore, the six sides of each part of space must be contiguous with six other parts of space, which cannot touch the same place, because different things cannot at the same time take up the same place. Each part of space must therefore posses six different places, i.e., six different spaces with which to come into contact. And since corporeal matter is identified spatially — what occupies a different space is a different piece of matter — it must be divisible so far as its space is divisible. See *Selections from Aristotle*, ed. W. D. Ross, selection 32.

The first of these difficulties are adduced in Kant's Second Antinomy. And the only answer that Kant has to it is, that space, and thus corporeal matter, do not really exist in the first place, and neither, therefore, do their divisibility or indivisibility.[3] Of course, this answer will not satisfy the materialists.

The second difficulty is clearly expressed in the first of the four well known arguments of Zeno — over which the human brain has been tormenting itself [matert zikh] no less than [a kaymolon fun] around two thousand three hundred years. Every philosopher who lived during this long period racked his brain [gebrokhn dem kop] searching for a reply to them, because everyone certainly felt that his philosophy is not complete if Zeno's questions remain unanswered.

Indeed, there are two answers which many philosophers have grasped at [ongekhapt] — the reply which Aristotle gave formerly, and the answer with which Bertrand Russell favored us [mezake geven] recently. We shall see whether these arguments of Zeno are refuted successfully by Aristotle formerly or by Bertrand Russell today.[4]

———••◦❖◦••———

---

3 Kant cites this as evidence for his theory of "phenomenalism," according to which time and space are derived from a person's own cognitive faculties — the human cognitive faculty has the property of framing some cognitions in time only, and others in both space and time. Naturally the result for us is that existing things must themselves be spread out in time and in space, just as for someone who looks through blue glasses everything is blue.

4 The next chapter discusses an abstract matter, and the dialectic [shaklevetarye] demands a slightly more difficult style. The reader will therefore have to exert himself a little more, he will have to toil over many of the sentences. He will consequently, however, be rewarded with more spiritual pleasure. He who is not interested in so abstract a matter may skip the following three chapters, without excessive loss to the main topic under discussion.

Chapter Eight

Unsuccessful Attempts to Refute Zeno's Argument Against Infinite Divisibility[1]

A.

In his first argument, Zeno attempts to prove that motion is impossible, because in each movement a space, which is infinitely divisible, must be traversed [aribershprayzn], which is impossible. Consider: before you traverse a bit [brekele] of space, you must first traverse a half of the bit, and before you traverse the half, you must first traverse a half of the half, and so on.

To this Aristotle replies with the argument, that just as space is infinitely divisible, so is time. This reply can be explained as follows: since the proportion between an infinitely divisible time and an infinitely divisible space is the same as between a finitely divisible time and a finitely divisible space, and since the latter presents no difficulties for the possibility of moving from one place to another, neither does the former. Simply put, this means that in an infinite time we should be able to demonstrate the traversing of an infinite space.[2]

The error in this reply lies on the surface: if the difficulties in comprehending motion in an infinitely divisible space were taken from the proportion between space and time (because in such a space there cannot be enough time to go through a motion), then they would fall away as soon as we understood motion, under the same

---

1 Zeno's arguments and the answers to them turn on the problem of infinity which one hits upon often in mathematics. Bertrand Russell's answer comes, indeed, in a book entitled *Principles of Mathematics*. Knowing the importance of these problems and not being himself proficient in mathematics, the author showed the present chapter to the esteemed professor, Y[ekutiel] Ginzburg, editor of *Scripta Mathematica*, to his complete satisfaction.

2 Cf. the thirty-second selection of the abovementioned book, *Selections from Aristotle*, ed. Wittgenstein D. Ross.

proportion of space to time, in a finitely divisible space. But here the difficulties stem not from the proportion but from the nature of the infinite — the infinite has a nature such that it is impossible to traverse — so how does it help us here that the same difficulties would fall away under the same proportion in a finitely divisible space? The finite is not the same as the infinite; it may very well therefore be, that a circumstance of finitely divisible space and finitely divisible time might allow the possibility of motion, while a circumstance of infinitely divisible space and infinitely divisible time might not.

B.

Aristotle's reply was not accepted by the serious thinkers of all times — although there were always to be found, and one can find today, many who ruminate over this answer.

Thus we have seen that over two thousand years later, Kant found in Zeno's paradoxes support for his theory of phenomenalism. And thus says Fuller in his history of philosophy: "These paradoxes, although they appear so fantastical, have remained unsolved by mathematics and logic for twenty-two hundred years."

But Fuller thinks that today, after the twenty-two hundred years, we have shown how to solve these paradoxes because today "we can apprehend space as we cognize it."

What happened? In 1903, Bertrand Russell published his great work, *Principles of Mathematics*, which showed how to expand our power to apprehend.

I must confess, however, that my power of apprehension has remained as narrow as before, and that, therefore, I have not been worthy of understanding Russell's solution of Zeno's paradoxes.

C.

Let us consider the solution of Zeno's first paradox, which is found in the forty-second chapter of *Principles of Mathematics*. Russell there makes a distinction between an "extensional" totality and an "intensional" totality; between one such as can be defined only by running through the parts, and one such as can be defined without enumerating the parts. For example, we cannot define a hundred unless we can somehow enumerate all the units which are included therein; by contrast, we can very well define the concept of an animal (just as every class concept) without enumerating every single animal which falls under that concept.

A totality of the first sort which may have an infinite number of parts we can indeed not apprehend or define, because an infinite number of parts can never be enumerated.

This distinction is certainly a valid one. But it cannot help us in explicating how it is possible to apprehend the totality which consists of an infinite number of spatial parts, because this totality is of the first sort — not the second. What Russell designates as a totality of the second sort is actually not at all a totality which includes an infinite number of parts, but rather, by contrast, something which is included in every one of the parts.

Consider the "class concept" — how does it come about? Through our noticing a number of things which are in certain details alike and in certain details different — we take only the part in which these things are alike and this is our class concept for these things. Life, for example, is only a part of the characteristics of man, animal, bird, worm, etc., but it is the class concept of all these things because it expresses the part in which all these things are alike, i.e., the part which is included in every one of these things.[3]

---

3 Because the class concept is included in each of its individuals and it is therefore affiliated with all of them, it appears as though it embraced them all and as though they were all included in it. This is, however, an illusion from which it is easy to be liberated. Consider: all men have heads — a head is therefore something which accompanies every thought of a human body; but on the other hand, nobody will say that the head includes the entire human body, to say nothing of all human bodies.

That the class concept is only a part of each of its individuals can be shown logically in the following way: a class concept can serve as a predicate for each of its individuals. The concept "man," for example, can serve as a predicate for each man: Reuben is a man, Simon is a man, etc. The function of a predicate is to introduce the characteristics of the subject with which it is connected and therefore

Through the class concept, therefore, we do not apprehend all the individuals which fall under it and which will fall under the class. All that we thereby apprehend is a small number of particular characteristics — so how can it be be compared to our apprehension of space, which must include an infinite number of parts?

D.

It would appear that Russell himself felt that the analogy between a class concept and a piece of space is not so smooth [glat]. So what does he do smooth out the analogy? He patches it up using as an example the number one: since we can apprehend the unit, even though it can be divided into infinitely many parts, so can we apprehend a segment of space, despite its divisibility into an infinite number of parts.

You don't have to be a Mar, son of R. Ashi[4] to realize that there is a great difference between the infinite divisibility of a segment of space and the infinite divisibility of the abstract unit. In the former it is a question of [handlt zikh vegn] a concrete thing, of which the parts are included internally, so that dividing its parts by separation means actually breaking it. So here infinite divisibility means that it is possible actually to break it into an infinite number of parts, which together constitute the whole, i.e., that the whole must here be conceived as the sum of the infinite number of parts. This is exactly what Russell should have designated as an extensional totality — as

---

the predicate must present only those characteristics which are in the subject, because if it should present also other characteristics, we should then thereby ascribe to the subject also these other characteristics and not know, thereby, the correct characteristics of the subject. As a possible predicate of each one of its individuals the class concept must thus present only that which exists in each one of them. It can, further, not present all that is in one of its individuals because then this particular individual will be entirely similar to the class concept and it will thus not be an individual. Therefore the class concept can present only a part of each of its individuals.

4 [A Talmudic luminary; the Aramaic title 'Mar' means "master." –Tr.]

distinguished from a quality which consists of a number of degrees and is an intensional totality.

On the other hand, the latter (the number one) is a question only of symbols — the unit is a symbol for one thing and the parts are symbols for other things, other quanta. The infinite divisibility of one means, therefore, only that we are in a position to create, without end [on a shier], symbols — signs designating diverse quanta — this does not mean, however, that we have here an object which is the sum of endless parts.

Were the unity a sum of endless parts, or were it divisible in any respect [iberhoypt], then it would not be a unit, because it would then be a plurality [a rabim] and not a unity [a yokhid]; and unity is, after all, indeed the chief property of one, which distinguishes it from all the other numbers. Indeed [takeh], it is because of this specific property of one, and because of its difference from all the other numbers, that it used to be disputed whether one can be considered a number in the first place.[5]

E.

Besides the above, rejected, solution, there is the anti-realist solution of the "doctors" [doktoyrim] who believe only in operations — cognitive material which we cannot digest [iberkokhn, can also mean "cooked"] properly must be scraped out to the root and thrown to the dogs. In other words, all our cognition concerning motion, space, time — in a word, everything what is cognized by our senses must be declared illusory, existing only in the mind.

This was, actually, the purpose for which Zeno designed [oysgezukht] his paradoxes; to support the antirealist theory of his master [rebbn], Parmenides of Elea.

Parmenides held that everything that exists must be and eternally remain the same — it cannot [nit es ken] change, it cannot [nit es ken] be differentiated, it cannot [nit es ken] be divided, and cannot

---

5 The last sentence is based upon a remark by Prof. Y. Ginzburg, for which I am grateful.

take any form which brings with it the concept of disunity.[6] Zeno comes to his aid with proofs that some of the division and change that we observe is totally meaningless [ful mit umzin].

This solution makes the difficulty not smaller, but greater: if previously we found proud flesh [vildfleysh] only in part of what we cognize with the senses, Zeno now attempts to persuade us that the malady goes much deeper, and encompasses everything we cognize with our reason — except for the concept of unity, a very thin shell [shal, means also a plate, skin] — so how did it help when reason itself is entirely devoured [adurkhgefressn] by the malady?

The same holds for the other kinds of idealists — both those who hold that only ideas exist, states of consciousness, and those who hold that there exist some kind of monads [epes azoyne monadn] or spiritual organisms, which in our external cognition assume the material forms which we experience.[7] Similarly, if it emerges that everything the mind tells us is false — falsity coated [bashmirt] with nonsense [umzin] that floats to the surface [shvimt aroyf] in the idea

---

6 It cannot change, because change requires that that which exists at one time should in another time not exist, or, that what does *not* exist at one time should, at another time, indeed [ye, Lithuanian Yiddish dialect for yo, a sentence connective which does not exist in English, but whose doubling creates negation, as in "ye ye"] exist — but what exists cannot not exist just as what does not exist cannot in fact exist [nit ken ye ekzistirn].

And for the same reason it cannot be differentiated, because a difference requires that what exists in one thing should in another thing not exist, or, that what exists not in one thing should in another thing indeed [ye] exist, i.e., that existence should also be conceptualized as nonexistence and nonexistence should also be conceptualized as existence.

And what cannot be differentiated can thus also not be divided, because what is separated by division must have some internal difference (something different that exists, because what does not exist certainly [mimeyle] is not internal), i.e., it must have something internal that happens [vos tut zikh] by virtue of the differentiation. And if what exists cannot be divided, neither can it constitute many things. And if all that exists constitutes one thing, it cannot move, because movement cannot be the movement of one thing in another thing. And in this way all forms of disunity are excluded. This is the gist of Parmenides' theory.

7 Of course, this is not the place to dwell upon the philosophy entitled Idealism. Hopefully, we will meet this theme again.

of the infinite. Do not forget either that falsity itself is also a sort of nonsense (except if it has some kind of ground, i.e., if it is consistent with a system); falsity embraces the contradiction of representing that which does not exist as something which does, by this means [azoy arum] including existence and nonexistence.

The difficulties Zeno's paradoxes present cannot be made lighter by an antirealist solution, a solution which throws out the bathwater [shmutzige vasser] with the infant. If there is any solution, it must come from the realist standpoint — from the standpoint, that the things our senses perceive [bakenen unz], really exist, approximately as our senses perceive them. We will soon see how far a realist solution is possible. To this purpose we shall air the problems involved in Zeno's paradoxes.

—••⟨◆⟩••—

Chapter Nine

The Problem of Infinity

A.

In his four arguments, Zeno sets forth two problems: (1) the problem of infinity, (2) and the problem of constructing motion out of moments of rest. The problem of infinity we have already discovered in his first argument, in which he considers the difficulty presented by the infinite divisibility of space. In the second argument, he sharpens the same problem, adding the difficulty presented by the infinite divisibility of time.

He argues as follows: on account of the infinite divisibility of time, a faster moving thing can never overtake a slower moving thing: Achilles can never catch up to the tortoise. For since overtaking must, clearly, take time, and since in that time the tortoise must also move and displace itself further from the place which it had occupied, it follows necessarily, that every time Achilles arrives at the place where the tortoise was standing, the tortoise must have already moved on.

In a third argument, Zeno finds a contradiction in [the concept of] motion, associated with the unboundedness of velocity. He demonstrates, that a velocity can be faster in one way than in another. Consider three trains: A, B, and C. A and B run in opposite directions, while C remains at one place. The middle train, B, will traverse the length of A more quickly than it traverses the length of C; that is, running with the same velocity, B in one way traverses more space than in the other way.

This particular argument even looks very weak, and Aristotle had a simple refutation for it. He says, "The falsity of this argument lies in the assumption that a body takes the same time to traverse, with the same velocity, a body that is in motion, as a body of the same size which is not (in motion) — which is false."

And Aristotle is clearly right in this; when two bodies move toward one another, the velocity of both bodies must be ascribed to the motion of each one. In the example of Zeno's argument, therefore, B executes a motion relative to A with an entirely different velocity from that which it moves relative to C, and it is therefore incorrect to say, that the same velocity is both greater and smaller.

But this answer is only good against the argument in the form Aristotle gave it. There might be, however, another form of the same argument; a form according to which the difficulty comes primarily from the unboundedness of velocity.

First, it must be assumed, that everything that moves must occupy all the places of the path it traverses. And since occupying a place must take a minimum time, it must, therefore, further be assumed, there must therefore be a upper bound to the velocity of a motion, because the time which a thing takes to traverse a given path can be no smaller than the sum of all the minimum times it takes to "be" in all the places of the traversed path.

Now imagine two objects which move past each other in opposite directions, with the maximum velocity. Their (relative) velocity will be doubled, and the time it takes each object to traverse the other's space must then be cut in half — so where, then, will each of the two objects get the time to occupy the entire space of the other?[1]

In the fourth argument we find, finally, the problem of constructing motion out of moments of rest. Zeno argues there, that an object that moves must rest at the same time, that a flying arrow continually rests while it flies. For, since resting means to be at one place (Aristotle expresses himself, "at an equal space," which means, a space equal to the object in it), and since that which moves must indeed be at each moment in one place, it follows, that that which moves must at each moment be at rest.

---

1 [This seems to me to be an original argument, which I have not seen in the literature before. –Tr.]

B.

Let us first consider the problem of infinity, which has pride of place in the paradoxes. The problem arises in a double manner concerning space and time themselves — just as we cannot think of the divisibility of space and time as either finite or infinite, so can we not think of the divisibility of the entire extent of space and time as either finite or infinite. This can be shown in the following way:

Should we think of space and time as finite in their extent; then we must we must admit a boundary, a line with no space on the other side, or a moment before which there is no time. However, on the other side of every line of space we have to admit more space (every boundary in space must be admitted as a boundary between two parts of space) just as before each moment we must admit time.

Again, should we think of time and space as infinite in their extent, we should then run into the acknowledged, yet inordinate, difficulties concerning definite magnitudes, and definite relations, of space and time. These difficulties can be explained as follows:

Space and time admit of greater and smaller magnitudes: an inch occupies less space than a foot; a second takes up less time than a minute. According to a simple calculation, the same space must contain a greater number of inches than of feet, just as the same time must contain a greater number of seconds than of hours. But this calculation does not allow application to an infinite space or an infinite time, because in infinity the greatest number of every quantity is laid out, and thus an infinite space spans the same number of feet as inches, just as an infinite time spans the same number of minutes as seconds.

We meet the same logical difficulties concerning definite relations of space and time — the relations of higher and lower, earlier and later, etc. According to common sense it follows that an object which is higher has over it less space and under it more space than an object which is lower, just as an event which occurs earlier has a smaller past and a greater future than an event which occurs later. In an infinite space the higher and the lower have the same infinite space both above and below, just as in an infinite time, both the earlier and the later have the same infinite past and future.

Obviously, these difficulties are not being exposed here for the first time; almost every great philosopher racked his brains [hot gebrokhn dem kop] over them. Yet today some think that these pains are to no avail; they originate in past misunderstanding of what infinity is. It was the mathematician G. Cantor who first found the correct definition for the infinite, and thus solved all the difficulties.

How was the infinite understood formerly, and what did G. Cantor innovate? Formerly, the infinite was understood simply as something with no end; G. Cantor added a definition, which B. Russell explains as follows: "A collection of terms is infinite when it contains as parts other collections which have just as many terms as it has. If you can take away some of the terms of a collection, without diminishing the number of terms, then there are an infinite number of terms in the collection" (*Mysticism and Logic*, Chapter V, p. 86).

Briefly, this means that in infinity a part can be as big in number or measure as the whole: "For example, there are just as many even numbers as there are numbers altogether, since every number can be doubled. This may be seen by putting odd and even numbers together in one row, and even numbers alone in a row below:

1, 2, 3, 4, 5, ad infinitum.
2, 4, 6, 8, 10, ad infinitum."

C.

What are the defects of the former understanding of the infinite, and how do they fall away with Cantor's definition?

One defect of the past understanding was that there was only a negative conception of the infinite; one knew only what the infinite lacked — an end. Through Cantor's definition we ascertain the positive nature of the infinite, namely, that a part can have the same quantitative properties as the whole. And, by ascertaining the nature of the infinite we are thereby freed of all the difficulties attached to it — but how?

All these difficulties stem, indeed, from the fact that we discern in the infinite this very nature: each part of space or time can be divided in the same manner as the whole: Achilles goes through the same motion in a part of the time, as the tortoise in the whole time; when the two trains cross one another, each traverses, in one sense, only a part of the space which it traverses in the other sense; in an infinite extent of space and time, the inch and the second make for the same quantum as do those units of which they are mere parts (feet and minutes); the magnitude of an infinite space or time remains the same from wherever you begin to pull it, that is, it remains the same whether you add, or subtract, spatial or temporal parts.

These are all difficulties because we know that it should not be that way, that it does not agree with the quantitative nature of all other things. When we learn, however, that this is the nature of the infinite, and by this very nature is the infinite distinguished from the finite, the difficulties fall away. We then understand, when it comes to the infinite, it must indeed be different from all other things; since all other things are finite, and were it like all other things it would not be the infinite.

A second defect of the former conception is that the characterization of the infinite then current was so broad as to include things that are not infinite. Just so is the circumference of the circle, which is not infinite, although it has no end. Through Cantor's definition of the infinite, such a curved line is excluded, because the part has not the same measure as the whole, and when we remove something from such a curved line it becomes smaller.[2]

D.

These merits of Cantor's definition of the infinite bring Russell to such enthusiasm, that he declares this achievement to be "probably

---

2 [Actually Cantor's definition does imply that the curved line is "infinite" since it has an infinite number of points. The circle has finite *measure*, which Cantor was not talking about. Finally, there are sets of finite measure, which do not diminish in measure when parts of the set are removed. This is because there are sets of measure zero other than the null set. –Tr.]

the greatest of which our age has to boast." And our time is, for Russell, not to be dismissed. On the contrary, he "know[s] of no age (except perhaps the golden age of Greece) which has a more convincing proof to offer of the transcendent genius of its great men" (*Mysticism and Logic*, pp. 81-82).

This is not the place to take the measure of the geniuses of different periods. Nevertheless, if Cantor's definition of the infinite is the greatest achievement of our time, then our time has little, indeed, of which to boast. After all, it has long been known concerning the infinite that the part appears to have the same quantity as the whole. But while this used to be regarded as a "logical difficulty," Cantor has dignified it with the name "definition." His entire achievement is in renaming the difficulty — is this such a great achievement?

If only this achievement really removed the difficulties connected with the infinite — just as Russell wants to persuade us! But it does not remove them — even after we are told, that this is the very nature of the infinity, we cannot after all understand how such a thing is possible — how it is possible that the part should be as great in quantity as the whole, which includes, after all, the part plus something more.[3]

---

3 [In modern mathematics, there are two kinds of infinite numbers: infinite cardinals and infinite ordinals. A cardinal is an answer to the question: how many. Now, in the finite case we say that two sets have the same cardinal number, if we can match the members of one with the members of the other, for example, there are as many students as seats in the class, if each student has a seat and each seat is occupied by one student. Cantor's idea was to extend this criterion also to the infinite case, and by his criterion, part of a set (subset) could have the same number of members as the whole set. For example, it is easy to match the whole numbers one-to-one with the even numbers, or the points on a short line with the points on a long line. In the case of ordinal numbers, the question is not how many members does the set have, but how is the set ordered? For example, a set has an infinite ordinal number, if part of it, N, is ordered like the natural numbers: first, second, third, etc., but there is at least one set member which comes "after" all the members of N. With this kind of number, we DO remain with the traditional idea that the part plus something more is greater than the part, even with infinite sets, because when you add more elements, the ordering changes. Agushewitz thus misses the point of Cantor's analysis of cardinal numbers. On the other hand, his target,

It should not be forgotten, that these difficulties do not originate from the fact that such a thing [the infinite] does not agree with our experience, which is of the finite, but from the fact that such a thing is a contradiction and is unthinkable: that that which is more should also not be more. These are therefore difficulties which are connected with the very nature of our thought, independent of its object, and therefore remain, whatever the object of our thought, whether finite or infinite.

E.

Thus do we see that Cantor's definition has no power to abolish the difficulties connected with the infinite. It has not, therefore, the merits which are ascribed to it. On the other hand, it has great defects — better put, it is completely defective; it is totally inadequate as a definition of the infinite, because it lacks the chief characteristic of such a definition.

The chief characteristic of a definition is to express the essence of the definiendum, on one hand, to the extent that, when somebody does not know what the definiendum is, he should be able to find out using the definition. Thus, for example, should he not know what "even" means, he can find out when he is told, that it means a number, half of which is a whole number (not a fraction). It is difficult to believe, however, that somebody who does not know what "infinite" means could find out, when he is told that it means,

---

Russell, is not much better, because it is not at all clear that Cantor's analysis of cardinality has anything to do with Achilles and the tortoise! If anything, Zeno's paradox has to do with ordinal numbers, not cardinal numbers, because to catch up to the tortoise, Achilles has to execute a series of motions *in order*, and catching up to the tortoise happens, if at all, only after (in the order) the series is over. There thus has to be a number that comes after all of the natural numbers, which seemed to Zeno be absurd. The result of all this is that both Russell and Agushewitz are confused: on the one hand, there is nothing wrong with Cantor's theory of infinite cardinals; on the other hand, the theory does not solve Zeno's paradox, because Zeno's paradox is not about cardinals. In preparing this note I was aided by Prof. Carl Posy and by lectures of Prof. Saul Kripke. –Tr.]

"something whose part is equal to the whole." He would rather accept it as a strange puzzle, or as complete logical nonsense; it would certainly not occur to him that this means something that has no end.[4]

You see, if he were told that "infinity" means "not having an end," he would presumably understand this quite well. Even the fact that he has from this only a negative concept does not matter, because in the negative concept he will find the proper essence of the infinite, which is intrinsically negative. Positivity is connected only to an independent subject — the thing which is infinite is positive; but infinity itself, as predicate, as adverb, is negative. Nay more, it can be cut off from any subject, and then it is bare negativity; nothing is also infinite. To connect it to positivity it must explicitly be connected to a subject; one must speak of an infinite *thing* or an infinite *existence*.

Someone who understood properly the meaning of the words, "not having an end," would certainly exclude from this the circumference of a circle, because such a curve has an end, from wherever we begin, we can continue till the point from which we began; going further would just be doing the same again. The end of such a curve is therefore the point which bounds its beginning — although at first glance, the end of the curve is not determined, because the beginning is not determined.[5]

In order to highlight the distinction between a line that has no end and a line that has no determined end, it would have to be added, that the former is an extension of diversity. This characteristic occupies a place in the very essence of infinity and therefore you will find it in every sort of infinity. Thus, number is infinite, not because you can continually repeat the *same* number, but because you can continually imagine *new* numbers. Similarly, space is infinite, because you can

---

4 [As I wrote before, the concept of "having no end" pertains to the ordinal infinite, not the cardinal infinite, so Agushewitz is not correct. –Tr.]

5 [In modern mathematics, as I pointed out above, the circumference of a circle is considered (a) to have no *boundary*; (b) to have a finite *measure*; (c) to have an infinite *number* of points. –Tr.]

continually imagine new spaces; and similarly time is infinite, because you can continually imagine other times.

In what follows, we will see where this characteristic is derived from, as well as its relevance to the problems which we have found in Zeno's paradoxes; this will perhaps provide the key to some kind of solution to these problems.

———◆———

Chapter Ten

An Attempt to Shed Some Light on the Problems of Infinity and Motion

A.

In our earlier analysis[1] of the concepts of unity and diversity we found that each of them can be analyzed into four modes: homogeneity, composition, binding, and numerical unity [der unit] are the four modes of unity; heterogeneity, division, separation, and plurality are the modes of diversity. We note that we are indebted to these modes of unity, both for the ideas of the various sorts of infinity and for the difficulties these ideas involve.

Consider, for example, the infinitude of space and time. It is not difficult to realize, that the chief factor in this particular infinity is the first mode of unity, *homogeneity*. In accordance with this mode, on the one hand, we conceive everywhere the same space, and always the same time. On the other hand, however, the *heterogeneity* of magnitudes and relations (as was shown in the second section of the previous chapter) requires that space and time be conceived as bounded.

Or consider the infinitude of causality. This idea draws its pedigree from the familiar ancient Greek maxim, "From nothing, nothing comes"; any existent must therefore come only from a prior existent; that is, from a cause, and the cause itself must, further, owe its existence to another cause, and so on, ad infinitum. But where is the maxim itself derived from? Nothing else than from our idea of homogeneity, an idea which requires, in fact, that nothing should always remain nothing.

Similarly, the same idea requires, that what exists must always exist. A second ancient Greek maxim, therefore, used to accompany the first one, "That which exists cannot become nothing." And from

---

1 Cf. *Principles*, by Reuven Agushewitz.

this maxim is further derived the other aspect of the infinite regarding causality: it is an accepted maxim, that every cause must bring about an effect, and every effect must serve as a cause for yet another effect, and so on, ad infinitum.

The idea of homogeneity is thus the mother of the idea of the infinite with respect to causality. Correspondingly [punkt azoy], heterogeneity is the idea which *excludes* [derloz nit] this very infinity. How so?

First, concerning the fact of heterogeneity with regard to causality. It is not difficult to show that with causality one must admit heterogeneity, because the effect and its cause cannot represent the same thing.

The heterogeneity that must be admitted in causality comes in the form of change. A change must, further, mean an existence that is different from before, and therefore before every change there is a time at which it had not yet occurred. For this reason change cannot be admitted as something which has gone on in all times, but must have begun after some time.[2] And thereby it is perforce asserted that it has a beginning, that it is not infinite. And if change has a beginning, then ahead of all the effects there must be an initial effect, the cause of which must be an initial cause, consequently causality is not infinite.[3]

The infinite regarding divisibility originates, on the other hand, with the second mode of unity, *composition*. Thus must every region of space, for example, be composed of six sides. This kind of infinity

---

2 [This would appear to be an invalid argument. Though each individual change must begin after a time, change itself need not. That is, from the premise that for each change of a certain type there is a time preceding it, it does not follow that there is a time preceding all changes of that type. –Tr.]

3 This infinity can be refuted also by means of the definite stages of natural evolution: nature evolves by stages, first it achieves an earlier, then a later, stage of evolution. But if the process of its evolution should have no beginning, then nature in each epoch must have gone through an infinite number of stages and that which it achieves later it should have achieved earlier. It will be noted that this argument, which was employed by Kant, proceeds in the same manner as the argument against the infinity of space and of time — just as that one is supported by the diversity of relations, i.e., just as that one is derived from heterogeneity.

can, on the other hand, be excluded [upgefrekt] by the second kind of
diversity, by the idea of division, which compels us to accept the
opposite, that everything consists of distinct [upgezonderte] parts.

And if we look, we can find an infinite also in the other two
modes of unity and diversity: we just concluded in the preceding
chapter, that infinity must analyzed as the continuity of diversity.
But continuity is, precisely, the third mode of unity — *binding*. On
the other hand, through the diversity of continuity a perfect
separation is engendered [vert]. Kant, in fact, says in his *Critique of
Pure Reason*, that in a continuum [German: Fortsetzung] there are no
two parts, which are so near, as not to admit a part in between. And
separation is precisely the third mode of diversity.

The fourth mode of unity we meet in the infinity as a general
concept. Through this mode of infinity all the various infinities are
taken together to make a universal infinity. This is Spinoza's infinite
being, which logically excludes from itself every finitude, just as
living in general excludes death. This particular infinity, on the other
hand, can also be repudiated, because it must allow many attributes
and modes, which must be mutually exclusive and perforce bounded.
The impediment to this particular infinity comes therefore from
plurality, which is the fourth form of diversity.

B.

From this analysis it follows, that the whole business [gantse
mayse] of the infinite, with the entire complex of difficulties
surrounding it, is nothing but an illusion, which stems from our
disposition to admit both unity and diversity in things. I do not mean
by this to assert that there really is no infinite [loy hoyo veloy nivro],
that space, for example, must be finite both in extent and in
divisibility. One must not forget, that infinity is not located within
the bounds of our sphere of cognition [derkentenish], and we are not
able, therefore, to express any opinion, either positive or negative,
concerning it. I mean only that if it were not for the influence of the
modes of unity it would never occur to us to think about the infinite,
just as it does not occur to us to think that there is a market [yarid] in
Heaven. For us, accordingly, the infinite would not exist and the

infinite which exists for us is nothing more than an expression of unity.

The discovery of the conflict between unity and diversity in the problem of infinity sheds light also on the second problem which was exhibited in Zeno's paradoxes, the problem of constructing motion out of moments of rest. We see now very distinctly that in this problem as well, the difficulty originates from the same source. Here diversity is represented by motion, which is change — change of place. Again, unity is here represented by rest, which is unity of place.

And thus do we arrive at the spring from which all Zeno's paradoxes flow and all Kant's antinomies; it is the eternal conflict [vayisroytzetzu[4]] between the antagonistic twins [tzviling fun hipukhim[5]], unity and diversity, which must, unfortunately [nebekh], live together in a single bed [tzuzammenvoynen in eyn nare]. But is this cohabitation so remarkable [khiddesh]? Do we not, on the contrary, encounter it in every object of knowledge?

In order not to overextend ourselves concerning a matter which has been much discussed in another place, we will refer the reader to the already mentioned book, *Principles*, by Reuven Agushewitz, where it is shown how all the modes of unity and diversity take part in the development and formation of all objects. However, as a pair of examples we can cite facts which have already been mentioned. Indeed, we have already mentioned that all known material objects, such as the molecules, atoms, protons and electrons in every material body, are both bound together and yet separate. And thus we have also already mentioned the fact, that varied characteristics represent the very [mamesh] same thing (the same lump of sugar is represented by whiteness, sweetness, and hardness).

Yet not only the object of cognition [derkentnish], but also the cognizer [derkener] exhibits [merkt zikh] a strange combination and a strange collaboration of such grossly distinct [vayt upgezonderte] elements such as body and consciousness. We know, in fact, that

---

4 [This Hebrew term is the first word of Gen. 25:22. –Tr.]
5 [The metaphorical allusion is to Jacob and Esau. –Tr.]

every human sensation and action is a result both of the motion of bodies and of the determination of consciousness. In exactly the same way is cognition [derkentnish] itself a somewhat odd amalgam [epes aza min shatnez]. Here we see a house. Consciousness represents to us a chunk of matter which occupies a space of a hundred feet. It is not, however, plausible [shikt zikh nit], that the representation, as such, is real matter — because how did such a piece of matter entirely make its way into [areingekrokhn hak un pak], and become exhibited in, our consciousness? It is also not plausible, however, that it is pure consciousness — because how can consciousness take up space? It must, therefore, be something intermediate, a combination of both.

Thus do we see how in all things, modes of unity and diversity go together, and it would therefore be a wonder, if in space, in time, in causality, and in motion, should they not go together — so what's all the commotion [mah rash]? Why does it constitute such a difficult problem? Why are we so affected [nispoel] when the contraries of unity and diversity manifest themselves occasionally as contraries of the finite and the infinite, or of motion and rest?

C.

It will certainly be said: Splendid [nu], but what do we gain by linking the antithesis of the finite and the infinite, or of motion and rest, to the antithesis of unity and diversity; and what do we gain by discovering that the antithesis of unity and diversity is a universal problem [tzoras rabim]?

Well, there is, however, a great difference between the antithesis of unity and diversity, and the — ostensible — antithesis of the finite and the infinite, or motion and rest — a difference that stems from the fact that unity and diversity are cognized [derkent] directly, while the cognition [derkenish] of the finite and the infinite in the divisibility and the extent of space, time, and causality, as well as of rest and motion, are inferred logically. What is this difference?

A direct cognition reaches us completed [fartigerheyt], therefore we cognize [derkenen] it only as it is, but not how it comes into being, or where its details [einzehlheiten] come from. When we see the white color of sugar we do not cognize its origin; whether from a specific element of the sugar, or by a composition of all the elements of the sugar, or, indeed, from a composition which includes the elements of the sugar and also the nature of the eye. By contrast, a logical cognition we form ourselves and we must therefore know exactly the material from which each of the details of the cognition derive. And from this very distinction follows, that a contradiction in an inference must present us with a great logical difficulty, while a contradiction in a direct cognition need not perturb us. Why?

Everybody understands, that a contradiction is only genuine [giltig] when the two opposing cognitions come from the same source; it is only a contradiction when the same thing is cognized [derkent] both as existent and as nonexistent; it would not be a contradiction when one thing is cognized as existent and *another* thing as nonexistent, just as it is not a contradiction that two times two makes a different result than two times three. And, therefore, our direct cognitions are not susceptible to a true contradiction, because not knowing their source, we cannot know whether the opposing cognitions follow from the same source. In contrast, a true contradiction is possible in logic, where we know necessarily exactly the sources from which every drop of cognition originates.

As a matter of fact, this is the answer that Socrates gives Zeno in Plato's *Parmenides*: "There is no contradiction in [saying] that the same thing is both like and unlike, because the same thing can participate both in the Idea of likeness and in the Idea of unlikeness. It can be like in one respect and unlike in another respect." A contradiction would only be if the Idea of likeness should be cognized as Idea of unlikeness.

The contradiction between unity and diversity, therefore, falls away; dragging with it the contradictions between the other cognitions which follow from unity and diversity, for example, the contradiction between the finite and the infinite. Here the matter appears yet simpler, because, since infinity follows from unity and the finite follows from diversity, the two do not issue from the same source, and, accordingly [mimeyle], the contradiction between the two is null and void [botl].

D.

This answer does not appear valid for the second problem, that of motion and rest. Here the contradiction seems to be in the idea itself: motion consists of moments of rest; ergo, motion is rest. But when we contemplate the matter [men trakht zikh arein in dem] a little deeper, we see that even here the difficulty springs from an oversight with regard to unity and diversity, and that even here, this oversight is due to a distinction between reasoning about, versus directly cognizing, motion and rest. How so?

What must be determined first are the modes of unity and diversity that are represented in rest and motion. Well, at first glance, we find at once here the "unit" and "plurality" — by rest we understand [derhern] being in *one* place, while by motion is understood being in *many* places. But if only these forms of unity and plurality were involved, motion and rest would not present any problem, because motion would consist of moments of rest, just as every plurality consists of units — just as the ten consists of ones — so where lies the difficulty?

The difficulty is that there is another difference between motion and rest — a difference between the unit and plurality which is found nowhere else: elsewhere, we have in the plurality only what there was in the units. "There is nothing in the generality but what is in the instances" (*Pesahim* 6b, etc.); in motion, however, there is also change, which does not apply to rest. And this particular difference is what makes motion qualitatively contrary to rest, which is essentially the absence of change, and therefore it is impossible to say that the same thing should be both in motion and at rest.

But here the question begs to be asked: how do we know that a thing moves and rests at the same time, and not at different times? The assumptions concerning motion and rest which were cited in the previous chapter will undoubtedly be mentioned, namely, (a) that everything that moves must in every moment be at a single place; and (b) that this very [state] can also be called "rest." But these assumptions are not totally correct. Being at each moment in one place is not yet motion, and certainly not rest — and here is why:

Motion requires being at many places of which each one demands for itself a moment of time, and therefore motion must comprise more than one moment of time. Just so, rest cannot be satisfied with one moment of time, because when a thing rests, it must be at one and the same place, i.e., it must be now at the same place, which it was a moment earlier. Motion and rest must therefore both take up a plurality of time. But, after all, there is a difference between the two concerning the plurality of time that they take up. What is the difference?

Motion, in fact, takes up also a plurality of place and therefore the plurality of time is spread out over plurality of space, i.e., a moving object must in the later moment be in another place — a place regarding which the present moment is the first one (it is only a later one regarding a moment of being in a different place); a later moment of occupying the same place will not represent motion, because it will then lack plurality of place; by contrast, the first moment of being in any place whatever, can never represent rest, because meanwhile it lacks plurality of time, which rest also, in fact, must embody [arein nemen] (one cannot attribute to rest the time of being in different places, because rest necessarily is being in one and the same place).

Rest can therefore begin only at the *second* moment of being in one place. That is, when we are at one and the same place for several moments, the first moment is completely different from the others — the first moment is only motion and the other moments are only rest — and in this way the difficulty in the problem of motion and rest completely vanishes: whenever there is motion there is no rest, and when there is rest, there is no motion; these two contraries never take place at the same place at the same time.

This seems, so it appears to me, very clear, although great philosophers were confused about it. Where does the confusion, indeed, originate? Clearly, from not appreciating in thought the meaning of mere plurality in time — a plurality of time in which the object which takes up the time remains entirely in one place — and therefore it follows, that when an object is found at several moments in the same place, we make no distinction between the first moment and the other ones, and according to the principle of "majority rule," [akhrei rabim lehatoys] it follows further, that since the other moments are (those of) rest, for us the first moment is also rest.

E.

Earlier in this chapter we noted, that because we ourselves construct [tu'en] a logical cognition, we necessarily know its basis; i.e., we find its basis, necessarily, in the cognition itself. Every syllogism, in fact, contains not only the conclusion, but also the major and the minor (premises) which entail the conclusion. All men our mortal (major), Socrates is a man (minor), therefore Socrates is mortal (conclusion).

It is self-evident that this is not valid for *direct* cognition, which we receive complete; therefore, we never possess the ultimate ground of any direct cognition. We have, therefore, another difference between logical and direct cognition, and if we overlook it, we are likely to err and assume that direct cognition also includes its own basis, i.e., that *what* we see must already contain the ground of *why* we see it.

It is clear that from that error the materialists have taken nine measures and therefore they think, that with the senses we must admit also the ground for that which exists before our senses; therefore it emerges that what we cannot receive with our senses, cannot be valid as ground for that which lies before our eyes.

And from here stems the first argument of the materialists, which originates mainly from insufficiently differentiating between logical and direct cognition. In the coming chapters, we will see that the other two arguments of the materialists are no better than the first.

—··❧❀❧··—

Chapter Eleven

A Theistic Rule of Law is More Expedient for Science than a Materialist One

A.

The second argument of the materialists takes the same route as the first one; here, too, the materialist begins with assertions that are true but irrelevant [lit., bear the wrong address]. It is true, of course, that scientists have recourse to the postulate of lawfulness; certainly it is also true, that a postulate required by scientists cannot be denied — but then did the theist ever deny this postulate? Has he not consistently held, on the contrary, that the Lord [der eybershter] runs the world in a regular order, and that "He gave nature, his dominions, a law and a time, that they change not their functions."[1]

The issue here is, then, not the fact, but only the type, of lawfulness at issue: theistic or materialistic lawfulness. We first ascertain the differences between these two kinds of lawfulness. Then we will see which of the two ought better to serve the needs of scientists.

B.

The differences between theists and materialists in the matter of lawfulness are to be found in their differing answers to the following two questions concerning lawfulness in nature: what is its origin? And, how far does it extend?

---

1 These words are part of the Blessing over the New Moon [kiddush levanah], found in *Sanhedrin* 42a. The same thought is also expressed in the reply, "The world takes its natural course," [Hebrew: `olam ke-minhago noheg] (*Avodah Zarah* 54), which our Sages once gave to a Roman philosopher; cf. also *Bava Bathra* 16.

As for the first question, theists hold, that lawfulness is a positive achievement of the Active Power: this Active Power ordained that the heavenly bodies should always follow their set course, that the earthly bodies should always be bound to the earth, that the positive and negative or the opposite sexes should continually seek out one another, so that the changes of death, birth, etc., should go on always. In contrast, the materialists hold that the lawfulness of nature is nobody's achievement, but follows immediately from the principle that what exists has no power to change of itself, and whatever follows upon something once must perforce follow upon it always.

This dispute, concerning the first question, is related to the dispute concerning the second: if lawfulness follows automatically from the fact that existence cannot change of itself, then it depends upon nothing and it must encompass all that exists, existed, or will exist. According to the materialists, lawfulness is necessary, absolute, universal, and eternal. According to the theists, in contrast, lawfulness depends upon the Active Power, which has ordained it and which therefore extends only so far as this Power has ordained it.

Let us now inquire after the theoretical and practical virtues and drawbacks connected with these different views concerning natural lawfulness.

C.

First, concerning the dispute over the source of lawfulness in nature. At first glance, it seems that the materialists are right. Reason indeed yields that, of itself, a thing should not be able to become different. Why? Because becoming different must mean, in fact, one of the following two things: either that something which existed must cease to exist, or that something that did not exist must begin to exist, i.e., that either existence should become nonexistence or nonexistence should become existence. But it seems as though both must be impossible, for how can something become the opposite of what it is?

And if lawfulness should be allowed in nature in and of itself, we no longer, accordingly, need to have recourse to a World-Designer and the postulate of a World-Designer is perforce superfluous. And if superfluous, then logically forbidden. The logical rule of simplicity governs this case: namely, if a thing can be explained in a simple manner, then it should not be explained in a complicated manner, a manner which demands a greater number of hypotheses.

For this reason, scientists, rather, lean toward the standpoint of immanent lawfulness. Very popular among scientists, therefore, is the reply that Laplace once gave Napoleon — when Napoleon asked Laplace why he left out the hypothesis of a World-Designer, he answered that he has no need for that hypothesis.

This tendency ruled also in philosophy in its infancy [dan ven zi iz nokh geven in di vindelekh]. On this position we find agreement among such otherwise much opposed philosophies as the extreme idealism of the Eleatics and the extreme materialism of the ancient atomists. Upon this assumption, similarly, Parmenides erected his theory that change is impossible: "That which is, is; and that which is not, is not." This was also the main foundation of Democrates' theory: "From nothing, nothing comes, and what has existed, cannot become nothing."

However, this tendency has not been maintained in philosophy for a long while. The weight [royv minyen un royv binyen] of philosophical opinion from the first turned toward the assumption of a World-Designer. Why? For the very reason of simplicity, because the assumption of a World-Designer is immeasurably simpler than the assumption of immanent lawfulness. This appears so clear, that it is a mystery why not everyone realizes it:

When the order in nature is ascribed to a World-Designer, a single, entirely sufficient assumption is being made: that there exists a power that organizes nature. Certainly this assumption leaves many things unclear; certainly we have many questions about the created order — it appears to us, that were it left to us, we would have done much better. But the questions do not come from our assuming that the World-Designer is unable to create in nature the order we experience, but, on the contrary, from our assuming that He is able to create in nature all possible orders.

That is, the assumption of a World-Designer is so broad that it is enough to cover not only the actually experienced order of nature, but also all possible orders. In contrast, the assumption of immanent [mimeyledike] lawfulness is too narrow to cover even the unique actual experienced world and we must therefore continually plaster it over, continually creating new assumptions with which to cover the holes which continually pop up.

Required first, is the assumption, accordingly, that each piece of matter that we experience is a queer hybrid [epes a min murkov] of substance and power, of corporeal matter and incorporeal energy. To this must be added that it is an incongruous power, which both attracts and repels. The genesis of new powers requires, further, the assumption of "emergence," that change in the external form of matter gives birth to powers which had not existed previously. Add to this, above all [ve-al kulom], the strange emergence of consciousness and the interaction of mind and body, which can be taken so little for granted [passn zikh azoy veynik arayn in der mishpoche fun memeyledikeit], that after all the labor [maternishn], and all the attempted hypotheses [hanokhes], their very existence is for us a mystery.

D.

The same goes for the second dispute, over the extent of lawfulness in nature. At first glance it seems as though scientists must feel more certainty and more comfortable [bakvemer], when the laws on which they rely are necessary and absolute; not dependent upon the whim, so to speak, of a World-Designer. But the truth is not so. Scientists would only gain, and gain much, both in security and convenience if they would only rely upon lawfulness ordained by a World-Designer. How is this so?

Concerning certainty, I have no desire to reopen an old wound, which science received from the arrows of the skeptics, who hold that an immanent lawfulness is logically unsupported. But one thing must here be mentioned, that if one can, finally, overlook the arguments of the skeptics concerning lawfulness in general, one cannot do the same with regard to lawfulness in the specific sciences, which call for the assumption, not only that from the same cause the same effect follows, but also that things which appear alike must possess the same properties.

First of all it is difficult to understand the necessity of the assumption — why *must* similar substances possess the same properties? After all, the bond between a substance and its properties is regarded as contingent, rather than necessary; we can very well imagine that an atom of oxygen, for example, should not bind with two atoms of hydrogen. Whence, alongside the atoms of oxygen which possess such a property, there could very well be atoms of oxygen which do not.

But let us even concede that substance determines its properties and that what is alike in substance must perforce be alike in its properties; this is still no proof, that which seems alike to us is, in fact, completely alike. Our faculties of knowledge are not so perfect as to enable us fully to rely upon them; even with the aid of the most exact instruments we are not in any position to observe what goes on [tut zikh] in the atom. One atom can therefore possess unobserved details by which it might be distinguished from another, similar, atom, and because of which it might also exhibit altogether different properties — so how can a scientist infer with certainty from one like thing to another? And how can even an ordinary mortal [posheter bosorvedom] go on with his daily activities, which demand a large measure of this kind of scientific certainty — how can a man, for example, rely with certainty upon his previous experience with mushrooms, which are similar to these which he is about to eat now, without being afraid that perhaps the other ones are a little different from these, and that although the others sustained him these will poison him?

What can free science from the clutches of this kind of skepticism? Only the assumption that lawfulness in nature is derived from an order created by a World-Designer. If we make that assumption, then we need not fear that in important matters we are deceived by our experience, because the same order which requires lawfulness in the essence of things, requires as well that we should be able to discern that very essence — if we were not in a position to distinguish food from poison, that would create exactly the same disorder as when the things themselves should sometimes nourish us and sometimes poison us.

In order to have certain knowledge, the assumption of a World-Designer must therefore be accepted. This does not mean that those who do not accept this assumption suffer from uncertain knowledge, because all profit from the order in nature, even those who do not believe in it. In other words, the order of nature brings it about that we do not in science philosophize too much or indulge in skepticism, that we accept our experience as sufficient.

So much concerning certainty. But the same goes for convenience — lawfulness which depends upon Order is more convenient for the scientists if only because it sometimes opens a little door [tirele] for an exception, because the exception is sometimes necessary, indeed, for the need of order, or for a better order, as in the case, for example, where the exceptions are needed for the goal of progress. In contrast, no exceptions whatever are allowable in an absolute lawfulness, which must take in everything that exists, existed, or will exist. For a scientist who relies upon this kind of lawfulness, such exceptions must, therefore, present extraordinary difficulties.

And certainly no one will deny that in experience we come across such exceptions: they bring about problems in almost every science; and there is even a current proverb, that every rule has an exception and the exception proves the rule. Thus it emerges, that from every viewpoint it is more expedient for the scientist to adopt the standpoint of lawfulness through Order.

E.

The dispute over necessity versus contingency extends also to the realm of the will. Those who assume that everything that occurs in nature had to be the way it is, hold that even a person is no exception in this regard: everything he does he must have done, in the way he does it — he who does good must have done good, and he who does evil must have done evil.

Conversely, those who believe in free will hold that there is no such "must." From the standpoint that a natural law follows from a

World-Designer, and therefore there may be exceptions to the law, they maintain that man is precisely such an exception, that according to the requirements of a higher order (morality), man must possess a certain measure of autonomy over his deeds — his deeds must not be completely predetermined by the compulsion of natural law. Those who assume this standpoint are called, therefore, "indeterminists," while those who adopt the first standpoint are called "determinists."

We must concede that indeterminism is in fact in opposition to the possibility of an exact science concerning human will, or concerning the other branches of science where we have to take into account the influence of human will. That is, if psychology, sociology, or economics were to represent exact sciences, they would deliver a death blow [gegeben a toyt klap] to the idea of free will. These branches are, however, far from representing exact sciences. They do not even manifest the possibility of ever [ven es iz] representing them. Why?

Because a science of some thing requires a cognition not only of what the thing is, but also of that which makes it what it is. The observation that such-and-such medicine cured Reuven does not make for a science unless we know as well why such-and-such a medicine cured Reuven's illness. When we do not know why such-and-such a medicine cured Reuven's illness, we do not know, in addition, what it cured, which element of the medicine, or whether it was, in fact, cured by something else.

In order that psychology should, in itself, represent an exact science, we should need to be in a position to discern, not only the effects manifested by our will, but also their causes. But psychologists themselves concede that unknown causes operate in the soul of man — causes having to do with each one's special heredity or perhaps even with the fortuitous working of cosmic rays — so how will we ever be able to construct an exact science of psychology?

And if an exact science of the field of psychology is not possible, then it is certainly not possible in the field of sociology and economics, where we must reckon with the influence of individual human wills. Most of the prophets of these fields have proved to be false prophets. And therefore the determinist cannot be helped by piggybacking [anshparn oyf di playtzes] on these particular sciences.

It is evident that what has been said here is insufficient to give an account of the standpoint either of determinism or of indeterminism — in particular, the standpoint of the latter, because its weakness is in the logical direction and the remedy must therefore lie in a logical clarification. The matter of determinism and indeterminism will therefore be discussed separately, in the next chapter.

———••⟨◆⟩••———

Chapter Twelve

Determinism and Freedom of the Will

A.

Those who accept determinism do not deny to humans the power of choice. Just as the indeterminists, they believe that each person is free to choose and to do what is good for him. So what then do they believe [vos den]? They hold that that very fact speaks for determinism: since a man does only what he chooses, and since he chooses only that which appears, in his eyes, to be the best for him — the outcome must be, that what he did must have appeared in his eyes to be the best for him and thus he had to choose it, which means that he could not have done other than what he did.

The determinist holds that this logical conclusion applies to the best just as with the worst and silliest deed. One who commits a murder in order to rid himself [poter tsu vern] of a little noise [tuml] which his victim used to make, had to do it, because it seemed to him at the time [beshas mayse], in his eyes, to be best for him. Of course, he will later have regrets [kharote]; he will find out, that his deed is associated with punishments which are far worse than a little noise and therefore this particular deed was not worth doing [nit geloynt]. But this he could find out only later; at the time he did not have the punishments in mind, and therefore, at the time, he had to hold that what he did was more expedient for him.

But is it possible to overlook the electric chair or the other well known punishments meted out to a murderer? This, one says, is quite possible for persons on a low level [madreyge]. They are in this respect like animals, who are moved mainly by the present and very little by the future. The punishments for murder, which belong to the future, could not occupy any place in their deliberations [kheshboynes].

This is actually what we usually say concerning a murderer or a lecher [baltayve] — that he was blinded — what does that mean? It means simply, that he did not have at the time in mind anything else — something which could combat his lust.[1] Therefore this kind of blindness occurs more often with crude men who are closer to the level of an animal. Refined persons are not usually blinded so much by lust — why so? Because they stand on a more progressive stage of existence, their being is fuller and more active (in Spinoza's expression), they give off sparks which make contact with what is far removed in time — in short, these persons have in mind at any given time [beshasmayse] the gains and the losses of the future, they therefore better can assess whether their deed is expedient or not; [in the words of the Mishnah,] the "wages of sin against the loss thereof."

A third class of people is on even a higher level of existence. The existence of these people is so full and so active that it flows to the length and the breadth; it comes into contact even with that which is removed in space; such a person is moved even by the gain and loss of others. Of course, these people must take into account in their deliberations their altruistic or ethical feelings, and the result of these deliberations must be different from that of the other two classes. On the other hand, the deliberations of of this class, too, must lead to a determinate conclusion, which must be executed — just as in the

---

1 This standpoint is taken by our Torah, which demands that a criminal must be warned when he commits the crime, in order to bring into his mind the full harm [shod] associated with his deed. This thought is explicitly expressed by one of our Rabbis [tanoim] who therefore holds that "A scholar [haver, talmidkhokhem] needs no warning, because warnings are given only to distinguish between inadvertent and deliberate actions." The majority of our sages go even further. They hold that this standpoint of our Torah applies even to scholars. Even more, they hold that the human mind can be so caught up in lust, that he may not be in any position even to take heed [derhern] even of an explicit warning; a criminal can therefore not be punished with the Biblically ordained punishment unless he states explicitly that he knows the punishment associated with his deed and is doing it anyhow. Of course, the result of this standpoint is that it is impossible to punish a criminal, and in order to defend society our sages had to administer to criminals a passive measure — prison [kipe]. Later we will see why this does not contradict the standpoint of indeterminism, which is assumed in our religion.

other two classes, the egoists; there is no difference in this particular between those who rule, and those ruled by, their harmful impulses.

According to determinism, man is no exception to nature — what issues from him is as determined [bashtimt] as a physical effect, which issues from its cause, and if we knew well enough a person's character (his impulses and purposes) and his power of calculation we could quite well predict his decisions, just as we can predict a physical effect, when we know the cause. And just as in physics, where two equal and opposite forces neutralize one another, to the extent that neither of them is in a position to bring about an effect, so too in psychology, an equilibrium between two equal and opposite tendencies will never allow a decision. For example, if a person should be equally hungry and thirsty, and he is located at equal distances from food and drink, he will not be in a position to make a decision to move in one direction or another and he will inevitably remain in one place until he dies from hunger or thirst.

B.

The determinist knows quite well that his theory is not so easily swallowed, that it has difficulties on various sides — from epistemological, moral, and pragmatic standpoints. He holds, however, that he can contend [an eytze gebn] with these difficulties easily. What are the difficulties with determinism?

First, it is difficult in any case [stam shver] to believe that everything we do is something we must do as we do it. Take, for example, someone who sits on an easy chair smoking a cigarette. Look how he exhales the smoke in different ways: through the nose, the mouth, in different coils or in one column. Now just [aderabe] try to persuade him that when he blew the smoke in different directions he had to do it that way, he could not have blown the smoke in one column, as in fact he did a moment later.

Still less will he believe you, when you tell him the story [mayse] of Buridan's ass and you tell him that he himself would not behave differently, that he also would die from starvation or from thirst, unable to move from his place, because of indecision over whether to eat or drink. He would certainly be offended. He would say that he is no ass [ayzl]; he knows quite well that staying in one place is worse than anything. He knows, too, that it possible to do both [efsher le-kayem shneyhem; this Hebrew phrase is used by some medieval rabbis (rishonim) to set forth an exception to the usual rule that one who is occupied in doing a commandment is exempt from doing another one] that he has the option [breyre] to satisfy both his hunger and his thirst by going first to one and then to the other for sustenance [lebns mitl]. Which first and which later? He doesn't know meanwhile. He is however sure, that in such a case he would, when it came to it [beshasmayse], have to decide on one side or the other.

These are difficulties from the epistemological standpoint. There are greater ones from the moral standpoint: if we assume that he who does evil or good was compelled to do what he did, he should not be punished or rewarded for his deeds, because a man is not responsible, and he gets no thanks, for deeds he is compelled to do. Nobody would blame another for a blow inflicted when the latter was thrown upon him by a gust of wind. Similarly, no one feels grateful to the official who doles out government aid for the poor or a pension for old people. More yet: deeds which a man is compelled to do are not even thought of as *his* deeds: we say not that the official paid out the pension, but the state; the official is taken only as an instrument through which the payments are made — so how can a person be punished or rewarded for deeds he did not even do?

In reply to this it may be said that the principle of punishment and reward rests entirely on the basis of utility: it is useful for society to punish a criminal, in order to protect itself against the damage it is likely to suffer from his crimes, because the punishment has the effect of a whip to hold the criminal in check; the punishment serves the criminal himself as a counter-motive to reconsider his decision, against the motives which incline him to commit the crime. Just so it is useful for society to reward good behavior, in order that people should seek to do what is good for society.

This would be fine if punishment for evil deeds and reward for good deeds were only dry, mercenary [meykekh-umemker-dike] facts, to be disbursed [oystsoln] the way the owner [balebos] disburses wages to his workers, or the way a borrower [original has: malve, apparently an error] pays interest. But the matter is no so: good and evil evoke special feelings — feelings of praise and love toward the one who does good, and feelings of hate and contempt toward one who does evil — and what sort of justification is there for these feelings? Why should we praise somebody for deeds which he had to do, and which anybody would have done in the same circumstances? And further, why should we hate somebody else who is himself, unfortunately [nebekh], only a victim of circumstances?

On the other hand, there is a danger that these very calculations can have their own effect, and cause much harm to society; persons who adopt the determinist standpoint will cease to blame the criminals. Why should somebody feel remorse for a murder when he knows that he could not help himself, and he is therefore only like an outsider, a spectator who, likewise, could not help? And because this blame which we cast has the effect that next time the criminal is more likely to refrain from committing the same crime, the result is that determinism is likely to interfere with an effective war on crime.

The harm is increased by a psychological factor: a person employs more effort over something which he believes he can accomplish than over something which he doubts he can accomplish. The reasoning [seykhel] is simple: in the first case he is sure that the effort that he employs is not wasted; in the latter case he is not sure, and therefore he is afraid to invest [arayntsubrokn] too much effort. The result is, therefore, that one who believes in free will, and who is certain that he has enough power to combat every evil instinct — he will certainly more readily do, than he who believes that his power to combat the evil instinct is somewhat limited by the determinate amount of effort that he is in a position to exert and that perhaps it is predetermined that he will not be able to combat these evil instincts.

Inter alia it emerges that determinism is liable to do great damage to society and that the idea of free will is therefore necessary for the way of progress. These are the difficulties that determinism faces from the pragmatic standpoint.

C.

The determinist, however, will not be overly impressed [nispoel] by these particular difficulties; for these questions [kashes] he has good answers [teyrutzim]. What are they?

(1) As for the difficulty [kashe] from the epistemological standpoint, every determinist knows how to repeat [ibertsukhazern] the answer Spinoza once gave to it: "Men think that they are free, because they are conscious of their wishes and appetites, while at the same time they are ignorant of the causes by which they are led to wish and desire, not dreaming what they are."[2] In other words: because we do not know the causes of our wishes, we think that they have no causes, that they are free wishes.

In another place he says the same concerning our actions: "For instance, men are deceived because they think themselves free, and the sole reason for thinking so is that they are conscious of their own actions, and ignorant of the causes by which those actions are determined. Their idea of liberty therefore is this — that they know no cause for their own actions . . ."[3]

According to this answer by Spinoza the result is that the smoker who let out the smoke in different coils was at that time [beshas mayse] compelled to do it by a determinate cause and he could not, therefore, have done otherwise. Merely because he has forgotten the cause — or perhaps never was conscious of it — he thinks that his present action was uncaused and he therefore could have done otherwise.

The same exact answer Spinoza gives to the query, whether a man would emulate Buridan's ass, if he found himself in the same situation. He says the following in the Note to Proposition XLIX, Part II of his *Ethics*: "I entirely grant that if a man were placed in such a state of equilibrium he would perish of hunger and thirst,

---

2 [I have used the Hafner library translation of the *Ethics* in giving this quote, from the Appendix to Part I of Spinoza's *Ethics*, rather than translating the Yiddish version. –Tr.]

3 [Part II, Proposition XXXV, Note. I have again used the Hafner edition for the translation. –Tr.]

supposing he perceived nothing but hunger and thirst, and the food and drink which were equidistant from him."[4]

Certainly this seems to us a little awkward: certainly we would conclude that a man, a rational being [bards], would in that situation find a way out [volt zikh gebn an eytze]; he would be able to do the trick [kunts] which children do when playing: they cast lots or count themselves. But this means only that a man would presumably [mistome] never find himself in such an asinine situation: he would certainly look for some cause [epes an urzakh], which would determine him to one action or another — the action which is predetermined by nature from that cause, which is likely to come into his mind at the time. But should a man really find himself in the situation of Buridan's ass, he would at that time not be aware of any cause which could determine him to one side or another. Then he would really have to cast lots.

(2) Determinists have a similarly good response to the difficulty from the moral standpoint: why do we love him who does good and hate him who does evil, although both are due to circumstances compelled to do what they do? The answer is [iz der teretz] that these feelings are derived not from reasoning but from the societal instinct — an instinct which usually is not defeasible by reasoning — what does this mean?

Just as we possess instinctive feelings which have the function to protect our personal survival, so too we posses instinctive feelings with the function of protecting the survival of society: we have, therefore, feelings which compel us to cultivate whatever is useful for society; the first are our feelings of hate and contempt for those who do evil and the second are our feelings of love and esteem for those who do good. The fact that a man must do that which he does does not alter the effect that his deeds have on the survival of society and therefore on our feelings.

But are we not inclined to forgive a sinner, when we discover that special circumstances compelled him to commit the sin? Do we not cease loving and admiring somebody when we discover that the good

---

4 [Translation from Hafner edition. –Tr.]

he did did not come from a wish to serve society? So why in those cases is the effect on our feelings changed, although the effect on societal survival is not?

The answer is [iz der teretz], that in such cases the deeds themselves are shifted from one category to another — we discover that those deeds do not belong to the category of deeds for which we possess instinctive wishes to punish or reward, but they belong to the category of neutral deeds, which are not relevant [noygea] to our social instincts. Why is this? Because sin which is committed under special circumstances is not at all harmful for society, because special or unusual circumstances usually do not exist and the sin is usually then not committed at all. Similarly, when one does good, but not for a social motive, for example, when a doctor "accepts" a high fee for treating a patient, then he is in any case rewarded for his deeds and therefore they do not belong to the category of deeds for which our social instinct compels us to reward.

(3) As for the pragmatic difficulties, the determinist is hardly in a stew over them [makht zikh bikhlal a knapn tsimmes]: it might be [ken zayn] that it is better to believe in free will, but the issue here is not what pays but what is — that it pays to believe in free will does not make the will free. Aside from this, the determinist can point to the merits [mayles] of believing in determinism, and in his eyes these merits are far greater than the drawbacks [khesroynes].

One of these merits is precisely that it introduces an element of reasoning in a place where formerly instinct reigned; it gives humanity the opportunity to have its voice heard where the beast in us had the sole say. How so? When we know that the criminal himself is nothing but a failure and that he could not in his situation help himself, we have more understanding for him, and our conduct towards him is based more upon reason than on the passions of the moment. We understand that we must punish him and sometimes even eliminate him, just as a gardener must weed out harmful plants from the garden; but at the same time we must also have compassion for him, and look as far as possible to sweeten the bitter medicine [tropn] which we are forced to administer.

Another merit, which is much more important than the first one, is that believing in determinism reveals for us the ways and objectives of education: if human wishes and actions follow from their causes as surely as physical effects follow from their causes, then they should be able to be brought forth in the same artful way as physical effects, and thus in the future it should be possible to bring forth generations of angels; all that we need is to be acquainted enough with the causes from which good wishes stem and to produce those causes, i.e., to create a perfect psychology and a perfect eduction.[5]

On the other hand, the determinist holds that the drawbacks of believing in determinism are in practice much smaller than they appear in theory, because in practice he who believes in determinism will condemn crime and will struggle to prevent it no less than he who believes in free will. Why? Because freedom of the will is an illusion and like every illusion it never ceases to operate even in him who knows that it is an illusion; just as the sun appears near and small even when we know already that it is very far and very large, so will we feel and act as though our will were free, even when we know that it is not.[6]

D.

Of course, the determinists do not content themselves with defense, but go over to the attack; they point to difficulties connected with indeterminism. These difficulties are primarily logical; indeterminism appears quite nonsensical, when we try to formulate it explicitly [im aroysbrengen min hasofe el hakhutz]. Here is why:

Indeterminism can be stated in two ways: (a) Either we suddenly receive new ideas or wishes — ideas or wishes which are not a continuation of the old causal lines; or else (2) The causality of some

---

5 Today's determinists reject Schopenhauer's hypothesis that a bad character cannot be made over. They believe, indeed, in eugenics, in the heritability of character, but they hold that appropriate circumstances can improve, bit by bit, even a bad character. See the chapter concerning freedom of the will in Cunningham's *Problems of Philosophy*. [Cunningham, G. Watts. *Problems of Philosophy. An Introductory Survey*. New York: Henry Holt, 1924.]

6 See the Note to Proposition XXXV, Part II, of Spinoza's *Ethics*.

of our old ideas and wishes can be extended, more or less, so that we can accomplish with them something more than we have already accomplished — in other words, we always are in a position to exert ourselves a little more and overcome [goyver zayn] the evil inclination [yeytzer hore], i.e., the wishes which impel us to do evil or refrain from doing good.[7]

There is a great difference between these two ways in the matter of freedom: according to the first way, freedom is not *our* freedom — the receipt of a new idea or wish does not turn on us; we are only a passive medium in which an idea or a wish intrudes [khapt zikh arayn] like a transmigrating soul [gilgul] and compels us to act according to its dictates. By contrast, freedom is our freedom; we ourselves at the time [beshas mayse] must be active and everything turns on us ourselves.

These two ways are both blocked by the same rule of causality, which requires that every effect must follow from a cause and from every cause must follow the same effect. According to this rule both ways are necessarily impossible — it is not possible for a new idea to originate of itself, nor for more to follow from the idea than from what has already followed.

Possibly the logical difficulties with the first way are not so great as what some determinists think, because there is no real contradiction between assuming that something can come from nothing, i.e., that what has not existed at one time should not exist in another time.[8] But on the other hand this particular way must be rejected because we meet therein all the difficulties which have been presented here in connection with determinism — difficulties which cannot be defeated in the way the determinists defeated them.

First we have the difficulty from the epistemological standpoint: precisely the actions which we take for free are taken as though they followed from our exertions and not from an external source, which does not demand from us any activity. We should not forget that free

---

7 See the chapter on willing in William James' *Psychology*, particularly p. 455, where he says, "In the experience of exertion we feel as though we could do more or less than what we actually do in one moment."

8 This has already been discussed at length in my book, *Principles*, pp. 174-192.

will is taken to be the same thing as self-rule, which certainly requires exertion.

Then we have the difficulty from the moral standpoint: if a man's good and bad deeds follow from ideas or wishes, which intrude themselves on him fortuitously, then it is not just [yoysherdig] and even useless to judge him according to his deeds, because he who is today compelled by some fortuitous idea to do a good deed can tomorrow be compelled by another fortuitous idea to do a bad deed, and vice versa.

The same from the pragmatic standpoint, we find here all of the drawbacks and none of the benefits which are connected with determinism. The result is, that an indeterminist who rejects determinism because of the above difficulties can certainly not accept indeterminism of the first "way," which manifests the very same difficulties, magnified — why would anybody barter a shoe for a slipper [oysbaytn a shukh oyf a laptshe]?

Nothing remains, therefore, for the indeterminist but the second "way." But this way seems to be logically impossible — how can we make a bigger effort than what we make? The indeterminist has the following dilemma [mimah nafshokh]: if we can, and it is expedient, to make a greater effort to do something or to oppose something, why, then, do we not make the effort? If, on the other hand, it is not expedient, why would we ever make the effort?

Perhaps it will be said, that it is expedient to make the effort, but we do not make it, because we do not *know* that it is expedient. But then we cannot make the effort, because out of ignorance we will have to assume that the effort is not expedient, and we will therefore have to act as though it is not expedient.

But could it not be that if we were to suspend judgment temporarily [abissele upvartn mit unser bashlus] we would discover the truth, that it is indeed expedient? The answer, however, is, that this itself requires effort and therefore we have the same dilemma all over again: if it is expedient to make the effort, we must make it; if not, not. The second "way" thus also fails to achieve an indeterminist philosophy.

E.

As it now appears, the determinists are quite robust [ayzn shtark] both in their self-defense and in their offensive against indeterminism, and therefore they believe, in fact, that they have their complete victory in their pockets. We should remind them of one thing that they have not kept in mind, however — a thing which has a double action, one which undercuts [upshvakhn] their self defense and shatters [tsebrekht] their offensive. What is it?

In order to have a net determination, all relevant factors must be determinate; if one of the factors is indeterminate, so is the whole. $1+2+x=3+x$, but if we don't know the value of x, we don't know the value of the total. The outcome is that if all our actions follow from a determinate decision, which is a weighted sum of what is and what is not expedient, the magnitude [mos] of expediency and inexpediency of each factor must be determinate — otherwise no determinate decision results.

This does not mean that in order to make a decision, we must know exactly the magnitude of pleasure or pain that each action can cause for us. Certainly it is enough that we should know in general that this action is more expedient than any other, even if we should not know how much more exactly. But some kind of comparison between actions we must make in our calculations and therefore our actions must be comparable — this is an absolute requirement for the possibility of calculation.

We have no difficulty with this requirement if our calculations take account only pragmatic motives — expedience and inexpedience. Here everything can be evaluated and certainly will be evaluated, either instinctively or with deliberation [yishev hadas], by finding out the advantages [mayles] and drawbacks [khesroynes] of each action. What happens [vi iz uber] when the calculations must take into account moral motives — which are independent of issues of expediency — how is it possible to compare such motives with pragmatic motives?

For example, when the issue is whether to go to the theater after a hard day's work, then we can quite well calculate a decision by representing to ourselves its advantages and drawbacks and seeing what overweighs what. When he imagines, on the one hand, the pleasures of seeing nice sights, of laughing, and of escaping [oyston zikh] from the daily grind [vokhendikeit — this is hard to translate, since the author appears to see the theater as nothing but a poor substitute for shabbes]; and, on the other hand, the effort of driving to the theater while exhausted, coming home late, and having to show up for work tomorrow without a good night's sleep, then we can pose the question clearly: is it more expedient to pay this much pain for that much pleasure?[9] The answer will then come of itself [mimeyle] because somewhere in the mind or in our feelings there sits an accountant who occupies himself with this sort of addition and subtraction — the arithmetic of expediency. When it comes to profiting from a falsification, one who avoids falsehood out of moral motives will have to turn to two different departments: to the department of expediency and to the department of moral obligation, and from each department he will receive a different answer. Which of the two answers should prevail? What sort of calculation should determine the answer?

F.

A determinist will surely say that the answer will be determined by the importance of the department from whence come the different answers, or, rightly put, from the importance which each department has for each individual separately: one who takes greater account of the department of pragmatic issues will perforce accept the answer that comes from the pragmatic department; another who takes greater account of the department of moral issues will perforce accept the answer that comes from the moral department.

This reply would not be bad if in such cases the deliberation each time were short and easy, because since from each department the

---

9 [The way the author poses the question, I want to go to sleep right now — he seems, however, insensitive to the issue of decision under a description, i.e., that the same action can be described in many ways, and these alternative descriptions may well be relevant to their expediency. –Tr.]

verdict [psak halokhe] comes immediately, without vacillation and without calculations, and because each person has already decided in advance which of the departments is more important for him and in whose favor the verdict will be (according to the determinist, Schopenhauer, this is already decided for each individual at his birth), there need be no deliberation over the verdict. But the facts are otherwise [iz ober di zakh nit azoy]; very often such a decision requires much effort and much time — when we demand of someone, under threat of death, that he betray his friend or his idea, he will certainly ask for time to deliberate and in that time his brain will work very rigorously [shtark] until he comes to a firm conclusion. What happens during that time? And in what does the effort consist?

It will perhaps be said that the time and the effort are filled up with a battle between the advisors [yoyatzim] of the different departments; during this time a heated discussion goes on in which each side sets forth his arguments. The end of the discussion, the decision, can be determined in advance, by the character of the men in whom the discussion takes place: in one, morally inclined, the Good Inclination will prevail; in another, pragmatically inclined, the Evil Inclination will prevail.

But even this appears a bit difficult: what does a calculation between moral and pragmatical values even look like, when they are incommensurable. We could, nevertheless, say that in the case under discussion, the moral values alone are calculated, because life itself has a moral value as well and one is therefore not required — and is even morally forbidden — to sacrifice one's own life except for morally overriding motives.

For us Jews even this is a weak reply, because a Jew must not make these particular calculations by himself — our Sages, of blessed memory, already made them for him; in *Sanhedrin* 74, it is precisely determined when a Jew must give up his life and when not. A scholar [a yid a talmidkhokhem] who is morally inclined, therefore, should not have to deliberate when he faces such a trial [nisoyen]. The facts, however, are different; not only did Jews like that often deliberate (for example, R. Amnon, author of the poem "*Unesaneh Toykef*" of the Yom Kippur liturgy, who asked for three days to deliberate before giving up his life as a martyr during the Crusades), but some could not withstand the ordeal. And there is no doubt that among the Marranos there were often to be found very good Jews [fayne yidn], who even after their failure [durkhfal] fought like lions once again.

Even concerning these cases some will find excuses. Particularly those who seek to underrate the moral attributes of the Jews will certainly argue that in these situations of deliberations before martyrdom the time was occupied by crass calculations, weighing rewards [khelek livyosen, lit., the piece of the Leviathan promised to the righteous] in the next world [oylemhabe] against temporal existence [khayesho'e] in this one. But if this could be said concerning the time of the deliberation before an ordeal, this is no answer whatever to the efforts of those enduring the trials [ba'ale nisoyen] — the efforts which are the apex [smetene] of every lofty moral action, and about which both the Midrash and the best of world literature speak so much.[10]

It should not be forgotten, either, that to exert effort means to add something; when someone exerts himself during a battle or when carrying a heavy weight he adds force [kraft] which he had previously reserved, or which is generated at the time through certain glands. Therefore, the concept of exertion does not apply [khal] to activities of a thing which cannot at the time of the event add anything — for this reason we cannot say that a wind or another inanimate being exerts effort. For the same reason the concept of exertion does not apply to our wishes if at the time we cannot add anything to them.

G.

But perhaps the determinist can also admit this premise of adding a wish? Perhaps the determinist can say that although a wish can at

---

10 As an example in world literature it suffices to mention Tolstoy's "Resurrection." For our sages, again, the only absolute might is "Who is mighty? He who conquers his own lust."

the time be added to, this particular addition is itself predetermined, i.e., this particular addition must under such and such circumstances, have been added?

Let the determinist admit this premise, he will then necessarily run up against [onshtoysn oyf] a manifest [ofenem] contradiction; if we must add to a wish, we must wish to add to it, i.e., we must wish to will more than we will; and if we wish to will more, then we wish it already, and we need not add any other wish.

True, the indeterminist cannot avoid this contradiction either. But the indeterminist at least is located on a terrain which he can more or less defend against this terrible weapon, while the determinist is not located on such a favorable terrain. Now, in what respect is this so?

The difference between determinism and indeterminism lies chiefly in how they interpret [oystaytshung] the rule of causality: the determinist is sure that the rule of causality can be interpreted only as having necessity and universality; every effect whether a wish or a power, human [medaber] or otherwise, can therefore following only from a sufficient cause [grund], i.e, a cause which already had in itself everything what is in the effect, and the effect is not more than a combination of what was in the cause uncompounded. By contrast, the indeterminist does not regard himself as such an authority [halt zikh nit far aza mumkhe] on the interpretation of the rule of causality; he holds that our cognition is insufficient to give the rule of causality such a far-reaching exegesis.

The indeterminist can therefore allow quite well [gants gut] the postulate, that in some realm or other [epes a gebit] causality may not rule in complete authority [bekhol toykfo], that in a conflict between expediency and moral obligation there can be added a little wish [a bisele vuntsh], created at the time. The determinist cannot on any account [beshum oyfn] allow such a postulate; from the determinist standpoint, every bit of wish must follow automatically from the given causes and the possibility of drawing forth a wish through exertion is consequently excluded.

H.

But does not reason justify [git rekht] the determinist? Does not logic require us to assume that there is a sufficient ground for every effect and when there is such a ground the effect necessarily follows? Can we then, concerning our moral actions themselves avoid the query: what makes it the case that we should draw out this or that particular wish, why should we exert our effort? What then will the indeterminist reply to this question? How can he contend with [git zikh an eytze] the logical requirements of his own reason?

These are questions which cause the indeterminist initially quite a headache [fil kop veytog]. But after he considers the matter more deeply these questions cease to torment [matern] him; he is no longer overawed [nispoel] by these logical demands upon his reason. Why? Because just as there are illusions of the senses, so too are there illusions of reason, and he discovers that these logical demands in their fullest extent, have indeed all the signs of illusions. Now, what are the signs of an illusion?

One sign is what we find mostly in our dreams: a dream presents a cognition which we know that under the existing circumstances we should not be in a position to cognize — for example, while lying in a bed in New York I dream that I am speaking to my brother who lives, surprisingly enough [gor], in the Land of Israel. The same goes for the logical demands upon our reason; we are presented with a cognition concerning the universality of the rule of causality, while we know that our reason cannot be in any position to draw a conclusions like this for every corner of the universe.[11]

---

11 It appears that the determinist is completely blind to this limitation of our reason and this is the origin of his exaggerated gnosticism: it is also the origin of Spinoza's opinion that he knew the ways of heaven just as well as he knew the streets of Amsterdam [Tr. note: This is an allusion to the Talmudic sage and astronomer Samuel, who knew the ways of the heavens just as well as he know the streets of his home town in Babylonia, cf. *Berakhot* 58b]; the origin of Schopenhauer's self-deception, that he had detected [dertapt] in the will the true noumena, the thing in and for itself that Kant had held that with our reason we will never discover; and

Another sign of illusion is a contradiction between one cognition and another, so that one of them perforce must be an illusion. We have this case, for example, in our cognition of the sun which represents it as a disk a few feet large, while other cognitions show us, that the sun is very large. This is true also for determinism, which is in contradiction with our cognition of indeterminism — our feeling of freedom of the will and with our "calculus of incommensurability" between expediency and moral obligation, and the exertion of effort when the comparison is nevertheless made.

A third sign of illusion allows us to choose between contradictory cognitions, to determine which of them is ture and which an illusion. What is this sign? A true cognition has its ground in the cognized object itself, while an illusion has its ground in something else. For example, the cognition that the sun is very small has its ground not in the sun itself, but in the distance from the sun, because everything appears from afar smaller than it is. This we have also with the cognition of determinism — determinism has a subjective ground, one which comes from our own reason. How so?

The function of our reason is to inquire concerning the continuity of effects — from what something follows and what something leads to. This is, therefore, the only thing that our reason can take note of, for a discontinuity reason has no "eyes." Furthermore, for everything reason approaches, it must proceed with the hypothesis [deye] that there is a continuity of effects, for otherwise, there is nothing there to inquire. For this reason [meyhay tayme] it must proceed as well with the hypothesis that this continuity is determined — from the same cause must follow the same effect — because only a determined continuity allows inquiry. For example, should ice follow from heat as well as cold, then we would never be able to know where ice comes from. Accordingly [kumt oys], our reason must approach everything with a determinist prejudice; in other words, the ground for assuming determinism lies not in the cognized object but in our own reason [seykhel].

---

finally, the origin of the materialist certainty that there exists nothing but what the senses can perceive.

I.

But if all the signs show that determinism is an illusion, why have most philosophers and scientists not discovered it — indeed, they happen to be inclined to the belief that *indeterminism* is the illusion![12] Are not the philosophers and scientists the biggest experts [hoypt mumkhem] on exposing illusions? Not only do they catch exaggerations, they inquire concerning illusions even in cognitions which have hardly [knap] any signs of an illusion. So why, as a matter of fact, are they not in a position to recognize here (in determinism) such manifest signs of illusion?

The answer [teretz] to this difficulty [kashe] is, actually [grod], not hard to find — this error originates in the slightly deviant nature [abisl andersh fun umatum] of this particular illusion: in general, where there is a conflict between the senses and reason, we find the illusion on the side of the senses and the true cognition on the side of reason, while here it is actually the opposite, the illusion is located on the side of reason and the true cognition is represented by our feeling of freedom. And this deviance should have the power to mislead philosophers and scientists even more than other people, because philosophers and scientists are accustomed to take the side of reason always [shtendig].

This is an error which comes only from custom — one is accustomed to the role of reason in criticizing the senses and not the reverse. Another thing which can mislead is the following — when we philosophize or pursue inquiry, reason is alone in the field; the feeling of true freedom (not the freedom to calculate what is expedient) is never heard from at the time. Why? Because in order that a feeling should be heard from we must have at the time at least a

---

12 Of course, this is said only of most philosophers. A minority of philosophers has long exposed the illusion of determinism. So did the ancient Skeptics, and Kant came to the same conclusion. The problem [khisorn] with Kant, however, was that he stumbled into a web of weak postulates [shvakhe hanokhes] and weak proofs and in this mountain of copper, the bit of gold was lost [farfaln].

clear recollection of it — but how can we have a clear recollection of something that we do not understand, something against reason?

All this means, that when we treat the problem of freedom of the will, we indeed have not true freedom in mind — the freedom we experience while making an exertion to do what we ought to do. What kind of a freedom should we have in mind when we speculate concerning determinism and indeterminism? Only a fiction, a freedom, which is fabricated momentarily [beshasmayse]. This kind of freedom is in fact nothing but an illusion; worse, it is a speculation of something that we know of it only that it is against our reason.

A third cause for self-deception in the matter of freedom is that many people experience it very seldom themselves. We should not forget that free will is not a cheap guest; it stays in very expensive hotels [akhsanyes], in people who are located on a high moral stage. But concerning this we will have further occasion to speak.

J.

There is a final point which the determinists make a big fuss [vezn] — the point concerning induction. What is that? Indeterminism purports to present a phenomenon which we never meet up with in all nature; all in nature is strongly deterministic; everything follows the requirement of the law of causality — how can it be plausible that there is one thing which rebels against that very law, constitutes an exception?

First the fact must be mentioned, that there is a big doubt whether the law of causality really rules over all nature. As a matter of fact [grod], recently there are many scientists who doubt whether the elements of certain atoms actually submit to the law. And certainly they must have a good reason for this doubt of theirs. But even if we suppose that the causal law rules over all other things, from this it does not follow that man, too, and certainly not every man, is subject to it. A glance at the technique of inductive logic will show us that such an induction cannot be made.

The technique of induction consists usually in the formation of rules through observed instances. For example, we observe many instances where oxen do not bite people, so we thereby make a rule by induction, that oxen do not bite people. The logic of this technique is the logic of likeness: things that are alike must possess the same nature. It is not hard to show that this logic has the same source as the causality rule which requires that like causes bring out like effects.

The same rule requires, that like effects must follow from like causes — and this really is the logic of the complicated technique of induction, in the case where the matter of induction takes also into account differences and the rule is manufactured only by picking elements of similarity. For example, when we observe that different things fall to earth, logic prompts us to say that the effect of falling follows from something which is common to all these things. Once we discover the common element [tzad hashove], and connect the effect with this alone, we conclude subsequently with a simple induction, like the Talmudic argument by generalization [mah motzinu] — from this common element the same effect will always follow, and everything, insofar as it has that common element, will always manifest the same effect.[13]

In an induction, therefore, the conclusion is only by likeness. And if so we shall never be able to conclude by induction that what we have found elsewhere in nature will be found in the spiritual side of people, because the spiritual side of people is quite different from the rest of nature: man has reason, ideals, and other spiritual properties which the other things in nature do not have. And just as man is different in these properties, so can he be different with respect to causality.

K.

Perhaps the determinist will say that although a person *can* be different from all other things concerning causality, it is logical to

---

13 I say "insofar," because the conclusion of an induction cannot be extended [oysshpreytn] from the common element to something else with which it is related [farbunden], i.e., that if a thing should include other elements apart from the common element, then we cannot conclude that the effect which is connected to the common element is also connected with these other elements. For example, we can conclude only that the body of a man is subject to gravity, but not his ideas.

assume that he is not different, because just as he can be different so might he be no different, and, because of the uncertainty, it is more plausible, rather, to say that he is no different from all existing things, or, at least, from most of them. This is what we say in general, where there is a doubt whether something is like or unlike most things — "majority rules" [akhrei rabim lehatoys] — so why should we not say the same concerning humans in the matter of causality?

It is, however, not difficult to show that the logic of the majority has also to do with likeness and that which is explicitly dissimilar is not subject to this particular logic. We can see this by considering a concrete example of majority and paying attention to how the logic works there.

Consider the following case: on a ship where most of the passengers are American it would be logical to assume, of every unknown passenger, that he or she is an American. Why? Since because in this detail, of being a passenger, the unknown instance is the same as every other one on the ship, and because on the ship there are more Americans than non-Americans, the unknown is more like the Americans than the non-Americans; if on the ship there were 100 Americans and only 10 non-Americans, then since the unknown passenger has an equal chance to be any of them, then he has a hundred chances to be an American and only ten chances to be a non-American, and the bottom line is, therefore, that the odds are ten to one that he is an American.[14]

---

14 It will perhaps be said that this particular example presents only one kind of majority, while in fact there is another sort — the majority of opinions, for example, when a conference adopts the judgment of the majority. This case is not the same, however, as the sort of majority which sets forth the relation of the other existing things to men and therefore it should not concern us if the case of majority opinion should be based upon another logical principle. But the truth is that it appears that even the case of majority opinion is based on the logic of likeness. Why do we accept the judgment of the majority against the judgment of the minority? Because since every person's judgment expresses that which he sees in the matter, and because the matter must have some appearance of — i.e., some resemblance to — what each person sees in it, the matter must therefore have more resemblance to what the majority sees in it. Therefore, indeed [tak'e], when an opinion does not express an appearance of the thing — for example, when it is a matter of an opinion of one who knows nothing concerning the thing but is trying simply to guess [glat

This is fine [alts gut] where we are dealing with something which is like the majority. But when we are dealing with something unlike the majority, then this logic falls away. For example, from the fact that the majority of the passengers on the ship are American, we cannot conclude that the furniture or the machinery on the ship are American.

L.

Another thing should be observed, that man is not just plain "different" from other existing things, but rather his difference carries determining signs of indeterminism: he is different in that he possesses the conditions for indeterminism — conditions which are lacking in other existing things whose nature we know more or less.

What are the conditions of indeterminism? First, what is required is the reality of different directions, a fork in the road. Then it is required that the relation between the different directions should be such as gives the possibility to determine which direction should more likely lead to the destination. Besides these two objective requirements there is also a subjective one, namely that the "driver" should not keep his eyes trained in one direction only, but should continually pause and look around in order to observe the different directions which present themselves to him.

These requirements are very well met by humans — particularly by one who is on a higher moral plane [madreyge], a person who sets himself high ideal goals which he tries to achieve.

First, such a person must have before him different directions, a direction of pragmatic interests and a direction of moral interests; on the one hand, he is pulled by the desires of a simple flesh and blood human being, and on the other hand he is attracted by some ideal which is found often enough in the opposite direction. For example, when you tell a Mussarite [musarnik, an adherent of a school of Jewish ethics, founded in the 19th century by R. Israel Salanter of

---

tref] — then it is of no value, and nobody will take such an opinion into account in deliberation.

Lithuania] about an exceedingly humble person [groysn onov], you will evoke in him feelings of admiration and envy, i.e. he will wish to be also one who flees from honor [boyreakh min hakoved]. But since he is not (yet) on this high plane, he will simultaneously crave a little honor [abissele koved] on the side, so altogether you will have in him a conflict [vayisroytsetsu, cf. Gen. 25:22] between two opposed desires.

But a conflict between desires can be found as well in men who are on a lower moral level. One who is interested only in pursuing pleasure can stand before the problem, whether it pays for him to spend so much money for one pleasure or another. But there it is a question only concerning the amount of pleasure — it is only a question of which direction can produce the most pleasure — and this can be determined only through the directions themselves; everything we need to do is only to calculate how many drops of pleasure will rain upon us in each one of the two directions. By contrast, the conflict between pragmatic and moral interests is a matter of weighing desires which are incommensurable — a truly humble person must flee honor, whether in small or great measure. In this way the second requirement of indeterminism is fulfilled, the relation between the different directions is such that the proper direction cannot be determined.

In the same way the third requirement of indeterminism-a person who is on a higher moral plane [madreyge] does not rush — [aylt zikh nit] to follow a desire, because he is accustomed to meditate over [nokhtsuklern] decisions, to "calculate the loss caused by fulfilling a commandment against the gain therefrom and the gain accrued by committing a sin against the loss therefrom" [Mishnah Avot 2:1, quoted in the Hebrew original]. Such a person has time also for the effort required by freedom.

On the other hand, it is certainly [avade] superfluous to demonstrate that other objects in the universe do not fulfill these requirements for indeterminism, and therefore it is nonsensical to conclude from these other objects that man as well is not indeterministic. It is as though we were to conclude that on our Earth there are no animals or plants, since we see [baasher bkhen] that on the sun, the moon, and most planets, the requirements for living organisms like this are missing.

M.

Finally, it will not be superfluous to dedicate a few words to the question of whether the belief in determinism or indeterminism is more socially progressive. We have already seen that there are arguments on both sides [mitsad hasvore ken men zogn azoy un azoy]; it is possible to speculate concerning the virtues of determinism and of indeterminism. It remains, then, to consult experience; perhaps there, rather, we will find an answer to this question.

How do we, however, consult [vendt men zikh tsu] experience? Take a poll? Investigate everybody's beliefs and character? Of course, we cannot do this "on one foot." There is, however, an easier way: there are philosophies and religions which have accepted determinism or indeterminism. We can see the fruits of these philosophies and religions, what effect they have on their adherents.

As for philosophies, it would seem, that we cannot find a better example than the case of the Epicureans and the Stoics, which arose almost at the same time, about 2,300 years ago. These two philosophical schools au fond [in toykh] were quite close — close in their physical theory and close in their ethics. Where they parted ways was in the question of causality and of freedom — the Epicureans were determinist, the Stoics believed that everything depends on the will.[15]

---

15 One will recall what has already been stressed, that materialism is based on two postulates: (1) that everything that exists must be connected with matter; (2) everything follows from the law of causality. The first postulate was accepted even by the Stoics — they, too, believed that everything that exists must be connected with matter and that our ideas originate in impressions on our brain matter, which is at birth a "tabula rasa," an empty slate. Just so is the moral theory of the Stoics similar to that of the Epicureans — the lifestyle recommended by Epicurus and Lucretius from the standpoint of expediency is also recommended by Zeno and the other prominent Stoics from the standpoint of perfection. However, the second

And what was the outcome of this difference? Everyone can find out easily enough by consulting [areinkukn] any encyclopedia or history of ancient Greece. He will see, that while because of its good influence, Stoicism has the reputation of the noblest pagan philosophy, the Epicureans at the same time earned the nickname, swine. Stoicism succeeded in putting out a line of first class thinkers and moralists, while Epicurism continually spawned lazy bums [poylentser], gluttons, and drunkards [zoylelvesoyve, Hebrew: zolel ve-soveh, cf. Deut 21:20].

As for religion, we find the same good example in the case of our cousins, the Arabs. There once was a time, which cultured Arabs certainly regard as their Golden Age; a religion which was modeled upon our faith (in distinction from Christianity, which puts less weight on good works [Hebrew: mitzvot ma`asiyot]) woke them from their primeval slumber and guided them to progressive activity in almost every realm. It did not take long till these former desert people surpassed [aribergeshtign] all the civilized nations of that time. But suddenly all of this came to an end. What happened?

In the Islamic religion the Ash`arite party, who believed in determinism, slowly came to power — in contradistinction to the Mu`tazalites, who believed in free will. Beginning in the twelfth century the latter party was persecuted in all parts of the Islamic cultural world: in Baghdad, in Egypt, and in Spain. And precisely in that period the Arabs begin to revert to their cultural desert — so deep was the effect of the difference between believing in determinism and believing in free will.[16]

---

materialist postulate is rejected by the Stoics, because matter possesses internal activity — it is a burning fire — and it does not need, therefore, external causes to elicit effects. One of the activities of matter is "binding" and we have, therefore, a unity for which matter is the body and activity (the art of creation) is the soul. This is the pantheism of the Stoics. However, for the Epicureans, for whom matter is internally passive and has no binding power, matter must perforce be constituted by discrete atoms.

16 Some believe that the sudden break in Arab progressive creativity has to do with the invasion of the Seljukes in the eleventh century. But first, the Seljukes took over only the Baghdad caliphate. Egypt was not only left untouched, but on the contrary, under the celebrated Saladin, protector of Maimonides, became stronger

Experience shows, then, and in vivid colors, that for human progress, it is more expedient that men should believe in free will.

N.

But what do we gain if the belief in free will is expedient for human progress? Does this expediency make any difference? Is a theory then "truer" if it is expedient to believe in it?

This is certainly a good point [shtarke tayne] concerning philosophy. The matter is quite different when the subject is religion. Here expediency makes a big difference — whether a religion is true or false depends in large measure on whether its postulates are expedient for human progress or not. How so?

We have seen earlier that religion consists of two parts: (1) belief in G-d; (2) belief in prophecy. The first has to do with the existence of an unknown Power; the second, with our relationship to this very Power: what he demands of us and the reward and punishment connected with these demands.

It is not difficult to realize that the question of determinism or indeterminism is not connected with the first part of religion, because since the first part does not take into account the relationship between us and the unknown Power, nor, then, does it take into account the relationship between our wills and this Power. For the believer there are, therefore, two ways open: he can assume that G-d determines every one of our desires, just as he can assume that He leaves room for freedom of the will;[17] thus, indeed, there are religions that include the belief in indeterminism as well as, respectively, determinism.

---

by far. Second, it is simply unreasonable that pious Mohammedans like the Seljukes would hinder the *mutakallimun*, the Islamic religious scholars. The sudden cessation of Islamic cultural creativity must have come from some malady in the theories of these very scholars.

17 Some argue that the perfection of G-d contradicts our power of self-determination, because if we had such a power, then this determination would depend upon us and not upon Him, so that something would be independent of Him, i.e., He would not have the power to rule over it; so that G-d would lack a certain power, and thus not be perfect. Some go even further, concluding from His

What causes a religion to adopt the former or the latter? This has entirely to do with the second part of religion, with its prophecy (later we will see what is meant by the concept of prophecy). And since the task of prophecy is to cognize or become acquainted with the commands of that unknown Power, the question of determinism and indeterminism is perforce bound up with the question, what are the commands of the unknown Power — if these commandments should presuppose belief in determinism, then a true prophecy must cognize determinism; and if the commandments presuppose belief in indeterminism then a true prophecy must cognize indeterminism.

We shall see later, that the commandments of the Unknown Power presuppose what is good for human progress. From this it follows, that if the belief in indeterminism is good for human progress, then a true prophecy must presuppose such a belief — it must cognize and aquaint us with indeterminism — because if not, it would not be presenting correctly the commandments of the Unknown Power and perforce not be a true prophecy.

O.

Others argue, however, that prophecy cannot presuppose belief in indeterminism, because the two are in contradiction [tartey desasrei]: prophecy means to foresee, i.e., to determine in advance what will be

---

perfection that He Himself is also not free, that He can do nothing other that what He does, because since He is perfect, everything that issues from Him must be perfect, everything that he does must also be perfect, and thus perforce he must do only that which He does.

Now [iz] concerning the first argument, it should be remarked that those who believe in free will suppose that the Master of the Universe desired that man should possess free will and that thus He created him. This means, that the freedom of men is derived not from G-d's negativity, from a privation [feln] of power but, on the contrary, from His positive power to create a free will and from His own will to let man be free. This reply already invalidates [makht shoyn mimele botl] also the second argument — even if God's perfection requires that He Himself must do everything he does, man can nevertheless be free because the freedom of man expresses a case of perfection. In any case, these particular arguments do not touch the first part of religion, but the second, prophecy, because how could we know whether the Unkown Power is perfect or imperfect if not for prophecy?

in the future, which is the opposite of indeterminism, of which the simple meaning [taytsh] is indeterminacy regarding the future. Prophecy and indeterminism give the lie one to another — so how is it possible that both should be true, nay more, that one of them should be presupposed in the belief in the other?

It must immediately be remarked, that the logic of contradiction requires only that opposites should not be represented as the same thing; it does not require, however, that they should not be represented in different things: it is a contradiction to hold that the same thing should both exist and not exist, but it is not a contradiction to hold that one thing exists and the other does not. Therefore prophecy and indeterminism can both be true, although the two are in contradiction, because they refer to different things — since indeterminism has to do only with free will, prophecy can have to do with anything that is not in the category of free will.

It should not be forgotten that what is not included in the domain of free will represents a very large territory, so large that there is plenty of room for prophecy. For example, there is enough room for prophecy to determine the commandments of the Unknown Power, a determination which should represent the highest task of prophecy. Similarly there should be enough room for prophecy to determine what is morally good and evil, a determination which should represent the essence of the commandments of the Unknown Power. Or again, there should be enough room for prophecy to determine the consequences of good or evil, reward and punishment. Finally, there should be enough room for prophecy to determine the ways that lead to good or evil, the ways of life [Hebrew: orhot hayyim].

It should not be forgotten what has already been mentioned, that free will is not a cheap guest, he lodges only with the special few [Hebrew: yehidei segulah]. In this way, prophecy can determine even what a man usually does, because his usual behavior is deterministic. Furthermore, prophecy can predict what will happen with a group [klal] — with people or with the world — because the small elite [Hebrew: benei 'aliyah] found within the group will probably come to nothing [botl vern] within it, so that the elite will not have the power to reverse the course [kireven dem rod] of their society. On the other hand, from this point of view, there is no certainty in this sort of prophecy and even a prophecy concerning a group could be overturned — as was the prophecy of Jonah concerning Nineveh.

This particular example shows quite clearly that we are dealing here not with ignorant hypotheses [boykh svores], but with the viewpoint of the Jewish religion. I believe that it is not necessary here to cite Jewish texts to establish the fact, that according to the Jewish religion a prophecy concerning men or people can be overturned [botl vern] — as in the Talmudic expression from *Sanhedrin* 89: "Perhaps he had regrets." On the other hand, we do see fit to cite the famous Midrash of the Jerusalem Talmud (*Makkot* 2:6): "They asked wisdom, what is the punishment for a sinner? She answered: 'Evil will pursue the sinner.' They asked prophecy, what is the punishment for a sinner? She answered: 'The soul of the sinner shall perish.' Finally, they asked G-d, what is the punishment of a sinner? G-d answered, 'Let him repent, so that he be forgiven.'"

This will have to suffice [mit dem veln mir yoytze zayn] concerning the baffling [harber] problem of determinism and indeterminism, as we go over to the third argument of the materialists, which will be treated in the next chapter.

———•⟨⟩•———

Chapter Thirteen

Concerning the Simplicity of Materialism (Refutation of the Third Argument)

A.

To have difficulties means to represent something which is hard for us to understand, something which is the opposite of simplicity. And since materialism, in fact, has difficulties — as has been demonstrated in this treatise — it can no longer be as simple as it pretends to be. This already refutes, actually, the third argument of the materialists — the argument from simplicity.

But on the other hand we cannot make do [yoytzey zayn] with this brief answer to the argument from simplicity, because we cannot, indeed, deny the facts upon which the pretense of materialism to simplicity rests: we cannot deny that the concepts in the philosophical treatises of the materialists are much clearer than those in the philosophical treatises of the nonmaterialists, just as the language used by the former is more popular and thus more comprehensible than the language used by the latter — from where, then, does this simplicity originate?

It would, however, not be difficult to prove that this simplicity of the materialists does not originate from more or better cognitions, but, on the contrary, from fewer or worse cognitions. It is like the simplicity of someone who looks at a little water without a microscope. Not seeing the dense mass of various microscopic creatures [bruimlekh] lingering there [dreyen zikh dort], someone like that certainly thinks that he has an accurate and simple cognition — a bit of clear water that is good to drink and nothing more. The same goes for materialism. Its simple cognitions and its simple interpretation [oystaytshn] of what exists originate from not discerning, or pretending not to discern, the dark shadow of metaphysics, which threatens [olel, Hebrew: `alul] to spread darkness in the philosophies of those philosophers who do discern it.

What is metaphysics? And why is it enveloped [ayngehilt] in a dark shadow?

B.

In nature, two sorts of beings are acknowledged: consequences [folgn] and principles. For example, each piece of matter can be decomposed into parts, i.e., the piece of matter is composed of parts bound together and thus results from the binding of the parts; the piece of matter is therefore a consequence, while the parts and the binding force are its principles. The same goes for our feelings. For example, when we inquire after [zukhn tsu dergeyn] the ground of our moral feelings, we are inquiring after nothing other than the principle of these very feelings and, consequently [mimayle], these feelings must be taken to be consequences.

Now [iz] in this very treatise we have already spoken both of the infinite divisibility of matter and of the unknown power that binds it together, demonstrating that with our senses we cannot arrive at [dergraykhn] either principle — we cannot arrive at the indivisible parts of which a piece of material stuff is composed, nor can we find out anything about the power which makes the stuff bond together or separate in definite ways. This leads us to the conclusion, that with our scientific instruments we can never fathom nature from its principles.

Nay more, even if someone were to tell us something about the essence of nature we would be in no position to conceive it [masig tsu zayn], just as a blind man is not in a position to conceive the nature of color. To demonstrate this, it is sufficient to mention the fact, that all our concepts are shaped [oysgeknotn] from material which we receive through our senses, i.e., from material which expresses only the nature of the consequences. Our minds have no concepts with which to receive or cognize, in a determinate way, the nature of that which is not a consequence.[1]

---

1 Concepts are ideas which we have ready in our minds and through which we determine the nature of our perceptions [bamerkungn]; this perception is red, this is a book, this is hunger, etc. These ideas are themselves perceptions; but by being

C.

But if the place where the roots of existence are found is so concealed from us that we cannot have any conception of what is going on there [vos dort tut zikh], then how do we nevertheless obtain some information from there? How is it possible to have any communication at all [ven es iz] with the closed off realm of metaphysics and what can be the means of such communication?

There are two possible means: (1) Directly, by an extraordinary sense with which one may be in a position to penetrate a little deeper than what is usually possible with their senses;[2] (2) Indirectly, by investigating the nourishment which the trunk and branches draw from the roots — for example, we can infer unity in the principle through finding regular collaboration in the consequences.

Both means, however, have the drawback, that we gain from them no cognition which is relevant to the actual nature of the first principle. Even for the flashes of intuition which perhaps we can receive in the direct way, we cannot find concepts to package them, and for the present they must be dressed in the flesh and the bones of that which can be comprehended but which does not conform to them

---

reiterated more than the others, they become more tightly bound to our mind, which keeps them in storage for the purpose of determining the others. For example, the perception *red* is reiterated more than others, because it represents the common element in many different perceptions: blood, wine, roses, and everything that is colored red. Similarly, *book* is that which represents the common element in books of varying size, forms, and colors. Hunger is another perception which repeats itself quite often. The names of concepts are associations, words which are connected in the mind with these perceptions.

2 It is certainly not necessary to show that the power of perception is not equal in all men, that some penetrate much deeper with their senses than do others. We see wherever we turn [oyf shrit un trit] how the power of observation and of empathy of one man goes much further than that of another — how one is naturally more of an artist, more of a psychologist, more morally inclined, etc. Further, we find men who lack entirely a given sense. These are, of course, the exceptions. But, similarly, there can be exceptions who possess a given sense in more than the usual measure; it is therefore not entirely out of the way to speak even of the possibility of select individuals [Hebrew: yehidei segulah] with a sixth sense. Meaning, that one man's metaphysics is another's physics.

at all.[3] The convolution and the darkness [di blonzhenish un di tunkelhayt] of mysticism stem precisely from here. Far worse is the indirect way, in which the nourishment we arrive at is from the beginning entirely clothed in the nature of the comprehensible, i.e., the nature of the consequences.

On the other hand, however, both "ways" are quite useful, because by their means one does get closer to the wellspring of sustenance in the field of the sciences and therefore we can better find out the true nature of this nourishment — better find out the requirements of the first principle and the means through which these requirements can be more readily fulfilled (concerning this we will later have occasion to speak).

D.

As we see, the ways to metaphysics can lead both to darkness and to light, and we must be very cautious when we set out on these ways. But the materialists are great cowards [groyse pakhdonim] and fear to go where caution is indicated. They reject altogether, therefore, the ways of metaphysics and they deny even that there are such ways, or, even more, that there is even such a field as metaphysics, declaring as they do that not only the consequences but even the first principles fall in the realm of the sciences.

According to materialists the outcome is, therefore, that the chain of principles and consequences go no further than the limits of our understanding — and here is the secret of their "simplicity." They begin their story [bereyshis] with a conceptual principle, with a completed, moveable, material stuff, which moves until it brings forth all possible combinations and forms and until the movements are transformed into all sorts of energy and even into thought, because mind is also not more than a sort of energy which is

---

3 So laments the prophet: "Woe is me, for I am struck dumb, for I am a man of unclean lips" (Isa. 6:5). And so determines the famous Mishnah in Tractate *Hagigah*: "It is forbidden to study the mysteries of the Divine Chariot ... except to a wise scholar who can understand them by himself." See also Bergson's *Introduction to Metaphysics*.

deposited from the nerves in the same manner as bile is secreted from the liver or urine from the kidneys.[4]

This example is not very apt; everyone can realize that there is no analogy here [Hebrew: ein ha-nidon domeh la-ra'yah]: in the case of the liver and bile, or urine and the kidneys, only material stuff is involved, which separates itself from other material stuff, while in the case of brain and thought, something immaterial is involved, which comes from matter. Here the question, therefore, arises — how does matter bring forth the immaterial? Where does matter get it from? By creating it ex nihilo? Aside from this the cases of liver and bile, nerves and urine, are themselves not so comprehensible: here, too, the question begs to be asked: how does it come about that the liver or the nerves, like the other organs of the body, work precisely according to a pre-established plan?

These are only negative difficulties, difficulties which originate from not understanding why what is, is the way it is, difficulties which serve only to refute the pretension of the materialists to simplicity. But there is also a positive difficulty here with the cosmogony [breyshis] of the materialists; if we assume that right from the beginning there has existed a movable material stuff, having the potential to evolve in the way it has evolved according to causality, then reason demands precisely that it should be other than what it is, because the things and events of the present should have already existed in the past, rather than at the time they do exist. Here is why:

The time of an effect depends upon the time of the cause — if the cause should exist earlier, than the effect should also; in order that an effect existing now should not exist earlier, its cause must not exist before a given moment. The same can be said for the cause itself, its time can be determined only when the time of its cause is determined, and thus for the cause of the cause, and so on until the first cause. That is, in order that an effect should exist no earlier than the present

---

4 Cf. the chapter on thought in *Force and Matter*, where the following is stated in the name of Karl Fagt: "Thoughts stand in the same relation to the brain as bile to the liver or urine to the kidneys." Naturally, Buechner agrees with this.

moment, then the first cause can exist no earlier than a given moment. And since the first cause must exist eternally, i.e., before any given time, then every effect must also exist before the time which it exists.[5]

E.

This particular difficulty is not being discovered here; metaphysicians have been racking their brains [gebrokhn dem kop] over it a long time already. Yet on the other hand, they have found only two possible answers. What are they?

One possible answer is, that the first cause is not something from which effects follow by causality, but it is a power which creates freely. This power could well have existed before any given time, while its creation could have begun at any given time — and thus the above difficulty falls away.

This is the answer of religion. And, of course, this answer is not acceptable to the materialists, because the principle which creates freely must be found in the realm of metaphysics, which they deny. What remains is only the second possible answer, which attempts to defeat the difficulty by avoiding entirely the idea of a first cause.

According to this answer, the chain of causality and consequences has no beginning or end (if it has no beginning then it is simpler to depict it as endless), but like the curve of a circle, it continually turns from below to above and from above to below — from earth to water, to air and to fire, and then again to air, to water, and to earth; from inanimate, by many transformations, to rational animal [medaber] and then back to inanimate.

It appears at first glance that this theory of cyclical evolution should cover both the shadows of metaphysics and the wish for

---

5 Let us say that it must take quite [gor gor] a long time till the zig-zag of causes and effects should lead from moveable matter to the evolution of a man in his present stage — let us say it should take a trillion years. Then moveable matter must have existed at a time before the trillion years (because it did not come into existence at a specific time ex nihilo) and man in his present stage would have had to exist earlier.

simplicity, because according to this theory it emerges that the chain of principles and consequences does not begin at the boundaries of our understanding, but does not transgress them either. It is no wonder, therefore, that many materialists and atheists seized upon this theory on various levels. In the next chapter, we shall see if this theory is so satisfactory is it seems at first glance.

Chapter Fourteen

Cyclical Evolution — Heraclitus

A.

The idea of cyclical evolution is by now quite old; we find it already in the writings of Thales the Miletian, who was the first of the group known as the Ionian philosophers, with whom one usually begins the history of ancient Greek philosophers. Thales held that water is the source of all existing things and that all those things are, with time, transformed back into water.

Thales' disciple, Anaximander, even attempted to explain why this evolution occurs. According to Anaximander, this evolution occurs because the various compounded qualities continually separate and unite like with like.[1] It is similar to what happens on a ship carrying passengers from different nations — certainly the members of each nation will gradually find out about and associate with each other, so that separate little groups will be formed — this is the way differentiated things continually come to be.

Of course, this account is still quite a naive one, which smells strongly of anthropomorphism. Besides, it appears to cover only the rise of differentiated things but not their passing — their eventual return to the undifferentiated mass in which the separate qualities must once again blend together, as the idea of cyclical evolution requires.[2] This account, therefore, leaves a blank which must be filled in.

---

1 Cf. the three chapters about Anaximander in *Ancient Greek Philosophy* (Yiddish), by Reuven Agushewitz.

2 In *Ancient Greek Philosophy* an attempt was made to explain this by the fact that even antithetical qualities present some degree of likeness — cold is a lower degree of warmth and existing things, even contrasting ones, have their existence as common properties. This account is even better than the other one, though it is rather forced, because it means after all a change in the natural striving — first this

However, it did not take long until the theory of cyclical evolution received its correction by a explanation which filled in the blank. The murky theory of Heraclitus explains already both the rise and the passing of all things — a rise and a passing which are both bound up with an original principle, which the philosophers before Heraclitus never noticed. What is the principle? And why did nobody until Heraclitus notice it?

B.

As has been already shown, our reason inclines more to unity and to diversity; it takes the standpoint that that which is, must be for all times, unless some cause changes it. This was the merit of Heraclitus, who recognized change as the principle of existence, something that goes on even without a particular cause.

This is actually the essence [toykh] of Heraclitus' philosophy. The rest is not more than explanation and justification — explanation of how change must be advanced as a principle of existence; and justification in the face of objections to advancing it.

Concerning explanation, first an answer must be given to the question of the source of change — did change exist from the beginning, or did it arise later? Heraclitus did not strain to find the answer to this question: change could not have arisen later, because being the mother of generation (generation can come only through a change) it must exist before any generation. Change must therefore represent an original principle.

What is the nature of this principle — is it connected with something material or is it an immaterial power? Of course, Heraclitus — trusting his intuition and presuming that the paths of Heaven were as clear to him as the paths of Ephesus — could not admit the principle of change as an immaterial power, which is outside the limits of human understanding [hasoge]. He had therefore

---

striving is concerned with separating from that which is less alike, but subsequently it is concerned, on the contrary, with uniting with it.

to admit this principle as a property of something material [epes a shtof] — but of what [fun vos far a shtof]?

This he could easily [shoyn] find by induction from what is observable by sense — although he probably [mistome] believed that he drew this also from his intuition. Now in what kind of substance do we apprehend the property of change? In fire; where there is fire, there is ongoing change — what burns continually changes. Fire must therefore be a substance which has existed from the beginning and which is the source for everything that comes into being and passes away.

When was this beginning? It could not have begun at a particular time, because then before that time change could not have taken place, and change would have had to be admitted as generation (which has been shown to be impossible, since change must be the mother of generation); it can also not be admitted in an unspecified time, because then all that exists in the present would have to be shifted to an unspecified past (as we have shown in the preceding chapter). Heraclitus' answer to this was the cyclical evolution, which has no beginning. "In the curve of a circle, the beginning and end coincide."[3]

And thus it emerges that fire is, according to Heraclitus, both the beginning and the end of all things that change — they must come from fire and perish in fire. And since all things change, "Everything flows, nothing stands," fire must be the beginning and the end of all things, "All things are exchanged for fire and fire for everything, just as goods are exchanged for gold, and gold for goods."[4]

---

3 This quotation, like the others from Heraclitus, are taken from *Source Book in Ancient Philosophy*, by C. M. Bakewell.

4 The cycle of change, for Heraclitus, goes from fire down to air, water, earth, stone, etc., and from stone back to earth, water, air and fire. This path he certainly observed in experience. Take a burning candle. You see that particles of tallow become continually thinner and livelier until transformed into fire, while the fire does not grow because parts of it become transformed into air. The volcanoes also show how parts of air become water and parts fire. On the other hand the fact cannot be overlooked that in modern science heat is identified with energy and thus [azoy arum] Heraclitus was the precursor of the scientific way, which posits energy as the source for everything existent.

C.

The objections from coming into existence and passing away, therefore, fall away, because if change is a principle and needs no cause, it must occur spontaneously and continually — things must spontaneously and continually come into being and pass away, "One cannot step into the same river twice." But here other difficulties join us. What are they?

First of all, it is difficult to understand the entire matter of such a principle of change: let us concede to Heraclitus that original substance had, in fact, a property of alteration. But however it changed, it would have had to become another substance with other properties — so it would have to lose the property of alteration together with the other old properties — so why should the original alteration continue to occur? Why should it remain an eternal property of all existing things?

Heraclitus, it appears [vayzt oys] himself sensed this difficulty and he attempted to reverse course somewhat [dreyen dem dishel abissl tsurik]. He argues that alteration is not something that touches the nature of original substance: "This universe, the same as all . . . has always been and will always be an eternally living fire." It touches only the relations or forms of the substance. How so?

First, with regard to change which takes in the distinctions of beauty and ugliness, good and evil, just (what should be) and unjust. It is very easy to prove that these distinctions are not more than relative distinctions, because what is beautiful to one can be ugly to another and one man's good can be another's evil: "To G-d all things are beautiful, good, and just; people think that certain things are unjust and some just."

Next, with regard to change which takes in the distinctions of coming into being and passing away — birth and death. Heraclitus argues, that these distinctions too are no more than relative distinctions, because what is dead for one is born and living for another: "Fire lives the death of air and air lives the death of fire; water lives the death of earth and earth lives the death of water." In the essence of substance, therefore, there is no difference between death and life — death is there in essence also life and life is there in essence also death.

And if the distinctions between coming to be and passing away fall away, then the distinctions between different states and different events also fall away: "And as the same thing there exists in us living and dead and the waking and the sleeping and young and old: for these things have changed round are those, and those having changed round are these."[5]   And further: "G-d is day night, winter summer, war peace, satiety hunger; he undergoes alteration in the way that fire, when it is mixed with spices, is named according to the scent of each of them."[6]

D.

Here, therefore, we have an answer why the property of alteration must remain eternally, because this particular property is connected with the essence of original substance — an essence which remains always the same and therefore must possess the same properties. But this answer is self-contradictory [ubgrefrekt (= upgefrekt, the Yiddish prefix "up" is rendered "ub" in the author's dialect throughout) miney uvey]:

If alteration is a property connected with the essence of original substance, then alteration must occur in its essence and not only in its forms; the substance must become different in its essence and it must consequently lose its essential property of alteration. But besides this there are great difficulties with Heraclitus' principle of change even if we were to concede that this principles does not touch the essence of the original substance, but only its forms, because according to this principle, all our intellectual [gaystike] properties would be made impossible. Here is why:

If we assume that everything continually changes and what existed at one moment has already by another moment disappeared, then [iz] how can we account for self-consciousness, which, after all,

5 [Fr. 88. –Tr.]
6 [Fr. 67. –Tr.]

implies that the same "I" maintains its existence over a time which comprises many moments?

And how can we understand the existence of memory, in which the same representations and the same ideas, must constantly persist [ongehaltn vern]?

And how is it possible to fulfill a wish, something that requires that the same object which exists in the mind [fav der forshtelung] should exist later in reality at the time of the fulfillment?

Above all, how is thought possible, which consists, after all, of many particles which follow one another in succession — are these particles thought by different thinkers, thinkers who die and are born at the time of thinking the thought?

These objections [kashes] to Heraclitus' principle of spontaneous [mimeyledike] change are not original with me [zaynen nit do ersht oysgefunen gevorn]; they have been known since Plato took this [Heraclitus'] theory to task [oyfn tsimbl] in his *Theaetetus* and *Cratylus*. All who have read Plato's dialogues must have come across them [gemuzt fun zey visn]. And, in fact [dokh], we do not find the least reply [epes a teretz] to these objections in any of the philosophers who adopted, in one form or another, the theory of spontaneous change.[7]

But surprisingly [gor] in recent times the well known Henri Bergson attempted to reply [gebn a teretz] to these objections [kashes]. In the next chapter we will see what Bergson has to say about this and whether his reply is adequate [a teretz maspik].

---

7 One must admit that Plato's arguments did not entirely fall on deaf ears, because before Plato, Heraclitus' theory, it appears, was the chief tone-setter for ancient Greek scientists. The *Cratylus* cites Socrates as stating that the names of the highest concepts, according to the old scientists, are designated in accordance with the theory of universal flux.

Chapter Fifteen

Creative Evolution — Henri Bergson

A.

Henri Bergson's name is still fresh in our memory. He took the philosophical world by storm not so long ago. He attempted to open a new philosophical fountainhead and for a time was considered the greatest modern philosopher. It will not be superfluous, therefore, to present the Yiddish reader something of a synopsis of Bergson's theory, at least insofar as our topic of continual change is concerned, or, as it is more generally known, continual flow.

Bergson does not deny that his theory of continual flow goes against reason [legt zikh nit oyfn seykhel]. The blame for this, however, he placed upon [aroyfgevorfn] reason itself — reason itself has not evolved to apprehend real life, nor does it possess the necessary means [keylim] for such apprehension; the concepts which reason uses to grasp presentations are not sufficiently refined for this.

All this Bergson tried to prove by an inquiry into the nature, the history and the functions [oyfgabe] both of our intelligence [seykel] and of our concepts.

B.

First, concerning our intelligence — what is our intelligence? Where does it come from? And what is its function?

It is an instrument, created by life, by means of which to wage the life struggle — the struggle that life carries on to rule dead matter and to clothe matter with its nature. What kind of struggle is it and how is it carried on?

Life is by its nature restless [tsapeldig], always impulsive and always seeking to progress, to outdo [iberyogn] itself. Near life is, however, dead matter, which is, on the contrary, immovable, phlegmatic. Life seeks to penetrate this dead matter in order to animate it, transport it with its impulse.

Life has created various instruments for this purpose. One of these instruments is instinct, which we find in the arthropods and which achieves its highest expression in the insects. Another such instrument is intelligence, which life began to use later in the period of the vertebrates, and which achieves its highest expression in man.

Why did life first attempt to make use of [broykhn] instinct and afterwards intelligence?

The reason is that instinct has an advantage but also a drawback: the advantage of instinct is that with it we get directly to those means [mitln] which are regularly employed in the life struggle. The entire bodily machine of the creature of instinct is so established that it should make use of such and such means in such and such circumstance. This saves the creature of instinct the trouble of seeking the appropriate means, and saves him from errors and inaccuracies in exploiting the means, This virtue is, however, outweighed by the drawback that instinct allows only one means to be employed in any one situation.

Why is this? The entire bodily machine of the creature of instinct is organized [ayngeshtelt] for the use of such and such means in such and such situation; it is good only for a particular means, in a particular circumstance; the employment of another means would require a reorganization [ibershtelung] of that particular machine, i.e., a changeover of the body of the creature of instinct. Allowing only one means leaves the instinct helpless in unusual circumstances, so changed that the old means are no longer appropriate.

Life, therefore, later tried out intelligence, which is an instrument of indirect identification of the correct means for waging the life struggle — by inquiry, by testing [ibertapn] various means until coming to the right one. This has the virtue that it gives intelligence an opportunity to switch means when the situation requires it — therefore it has the drawback that it lacks the effectiveness and accuracy of instinct. Intelligence suffers necessarily, as well, from errors and imprecision; from sometimes dwelling upon an incorrect means or employing a means in an incorrect measure and not in the correct way.

C.

This is the history of intelligence; from which it follows, first, that intelligence is made not for theoretical functions, but for the practical ones, to find what is useful in the life struggle. Second, it follows that the cognition of intelligence comes about only through deliberation — just as the dog with his paws and snout, so do we, with our understanding and intelligence, take up an object and turn it about on all sides in order to consider its usefulness and to find a way to bite into it.

Again, it follows that with intelligence we grasp only that which persists, what does not change during the time we are taking it into consideration. That which flows, which continually moves and changes, we cannot grasp with our intelligence.

Therefore, by intelligence we can never grasp the nature of motion. For us, motion is rest in many places; when we say that something moved, we mean that it has been or rested in all the places of a specific space — but how is it possible that motion should be made out of resting?[1]

Therefore, we cannot with intelligence grasp the nature of life, whose continual goings on through time are also as fluid and changeable as motion. Aside from this, we should not forget that intelligence was "created by life, in definite circumstances, to act on definite things, how can it embrace life, on which it is only an emanation or an aspect?"[2]

And therefore we cannot with our intelligence grasp the nature of our souls either, which is a personification of life, a spark of life which has been superimposed upon the little bit of matter of which

---

1 See Zeno's fourth argument, which was cited in the ninth chapter of the present volume.
2 Cf. the introduction to *La Evolution Creatrice*, translated into English by Arthur Mitchell under the name *Creative Evolution*.

the human body is composed and which, in a certain way, transports [mitraysn] the matter into its impulsive course [gang].

On the other hand, intelligence feels at home regarding lifeless matter, which is possible to embrace and to examine — therefore intelligence is greatly successful in the sciences of inorganic matter. And this is actually its function, to investigate the nature of lifeless matter in order to know how to turn it toward the service of life. In other words: the sciences are also only instruments for practical purposes, and all the scientist does, is only to figure out in advance how to do later what is useful.

D.

So much regarding intelligence. The same goes for our concepts — an inquiry into our concepts shows that they too are only for practical cognition and they too are not suited for that which is purely alteration.

First, regarding the practical character of concepts. This we find when we investigate their history. When we check out [gibn a tap] the pedigree [yikhes] of concepts we see that they are a small part of our experience, retained by our memory: we have seen many books and in each book we have observed many properties; what remains in memory is only the general form of a book, with which we gauge our future experience — that which can be clothed in that form is a book.

How did this form merit [zoykhe geven] being the only thing left in memory? This has everything to do with its usefulness. How so?

Actually, we should have remembered our entire past; every impression which passed through our mind at any time should have remained with us our whole lives — why? Because as long as we live we endure [doyeren zikh] and in enduring the past cannot be cut off from the present: "Pure duration is the form which the succession of our conscious states takes on when our ego is allowed to live while refraining from dividing its present state from its past states."[3]

---

3 Taken from Bergson, *Time and Free Will* (p. 100), translated by F. Z. Pogson.

But why do we recall only a small part of our past, while usually forgetting the greater part? Because our consciousness illuminates only that which can bring benefit, because "The chief office of consciousness is to preside over actions and enlighten choice." Only a small part of our experience can bring benefit — the ideas of the near past can bring benefit, which we must join with the idea of the present in order to build a complete thought. For example, in order to know the meaning of a sentence we must know also the first words of the sentence. Also, the universal forms which bound our partial cognition can bring benefit, as, for example, when we see only the surface of a book our memory gives us immediately an image of the entire book. "Consciousness, then, illumines, at each moment of time, that immediate part of the past which, impending over the future, seeks to realize and to associate with it. Solely preoccupied in thus determining an undetermined future, consciousness may shed a little of its light on those of our states, more remote in the past, which can be usefully combined with our present state, that is to say, with our immediate past: the rest remains in the dark."[4]

It remains in the shadow because it is more likely to bring harm than benefit — because "Of what use are these memory-images? Preserved in memory, reproduced in consciousness, do they not distort the practical character of life, mingling dream with reality? They would, no doubt, if our actual consciousness, a consciousness which reflects the exact adaptation of our nervous system to the present situation, did not set aside all those among the past images which cannot be coordinated with the present perception and are unable to form with it a *useful* combination."[5]

---

4 [For clarity, I have cited here more of the passage than the author has. –Tr.]
5 The last three quotations come from Bergson's *Matter and Memory*, tr. Paul and Palmer, pp. 182-196. Bergson provides a synopsis at the beginning of his *Creative Evolution*, which goes as follows: "In reality, the past is preserved by itself, automatically. In its entirety, probably, it follows us at every instant; all that we have felt, thought and willed from our earliest infancy is there, leaning over the present which is about to join it, pressing against the portals of consciousness that would fain leave it outside. The cerebral mechanism is arranged just so as to drive back into the unconscious almost the whole of this past, and to admit beyond the

The upshot [poyel yoytze] of this is, that concepts owe their right to exist only to their usefulness; otherwise, they would remain in the shadow, i.e., unconscious, together with the entire bundle [pak] of experiences of the past. And profitability is the only thing which we seek to draw from our concepts: "To try to fit a concept on an object is simply to ask what we can do with the object, and what it can do for us."[6]

E.

From this it also follows that our concepts are not suited for that which continually changes, because since they come from the memory, our concepts must present something which has already been cognized in the past, and thus [mimeyle] they are not suited for something that is always changing, which must be different in the present from what it was in the past.

Nay more, since concepts represent universal forms of things, they can take in only what is alike in those things — and not what is different in them. For example, the concept "book" takes in only what is alike in all books, but not their difference in size, language, and content; just as the concept "human" can take in only that which is alike in humans, not their differences in sex, race, and color. Therefore our concepts cannot take in the true nature of life, which is in continual alteration, and therefore we cannot ever conceptualize that nature.

---

threshold only that which can cast light on the present situation or further the action now being prepared — in short, only that which can give *useful* work."

The distinctions Bergson makes between this "automatic memory" and "motor memory" — memory which comes to being through memorization — certainly cannot harm the practical character of memory, because motor memory comes definitely [gevis] only because of utility; we memorize only something which seems to us to be useful.

6 Taken from Bergson's *An Introduction to Metaphysics*, tr. T. H. Hulme, p. [35. My page reference is to the 1913 Macmillan edition of Hulme's translation. Incidentally, Agushewitz both misspells Hulme's name (though this may be a printer's error) and slightly mistranslates the passage. –Tr.]

In order to conceptualize the true nature of life, we would have to have an entirely different sort of concepts, we would have to have concepts which should be made to order specially for each object of cognition [bashtelt far yeden kentenish obyekt bazunder] — concepts which should be suited, each one, for not more than one object of cognition, and which should give the specific nature of that object.

F.

In Bergson's version, therefore, the theory of continual alteration has found its repair [tikkun] — here we have an answer to all our objections [taynes] against the theory.

First, we have here an answer to the objection, why change occurs continually, why change does not occur in such a way as to lose the property of change itself. The answer is, that this has to do with the nature of time, which is continual change, continual growth — the present grows continually upon the past. Everything that is active in time — everything that lives — must therefore also grow continually, become larger, as the activity of the present is added to the activity of the past.

We have as well an answer to our objections, how continual change is consistent with the unity which is associated with our mental properties of consciousness, memory, will, thought, etc. The answer is that change which occurs continually in time has the attribute of duration, which is a unity par excellence, because the past grows into present, so that the present has within itself the entire past.

Even this is not so easy to understand, but you know very well already, that the blame for this rests with our intelligence, absorbed as it is for practical reasons in corporeality, which itself possesses not the real unity, since in matter the parts exist simultaneously one alongside the other. Therefore, unity is there only a connection [tsunoyfgeshtukevete], an association — like, for example, things which have a number of identical properties are taken together under one concept. Such associations help the intelligence analyze the nature of matter and therefore it lies in its task to make use of them. On the other hand, intelligence cannot draw any practical use from the true nature of unity and therefore cannot understand it.

We even have here, therefore, in advance, an answer to difficulties which one might at any time find against this theory — because what is a difficulty? Something that is difficult to grasp with the intelligence — but we already know that our intelligence need not grasp everything, that it is like a sieve in which are contained only the possible kernels of hard matter, while the liquid reality leaks out.

G.

Everything appears [dukht zikh] good, everything secured [bavorent]. Yet there are objections to this theory which cannot be removed even by such precaution [bavorenish] — difficulties which recall the arguments of the Sophist, Gorgias: (1) Bergson's fluid reality does not exist; (2) even if it existed we would not be in a position to cognize it; and (3) even if we were to cognize it we would not be in position to share the cognition with others.

To go from the light to the weighty, we will begin with the third argument, that a cognition of a fluid reality cannot be shared. Trying to prove this would well be called belaboring the obvious [brekhn in ofene tirn, lit., breaking into open doors], because Bergson himself concedes that not only can such a cognition not be transmitted to others, but even for himself it cannot be formulated, i.e. one cannot make for oneself definite ideas of it.[7] And this is the ABC of Bergson's theory, because to make for oneself definite ideas of it one must, indeed, conceptualize it, possess concepts, which should be appropriate for such a cognition — but Bergson continually instructs us [einkneln mit unz] that our concepts are not suited for a cognition of that which is continually in flux.

From the third objection, we will move to the second one, that even if such a thing should exist, we would be in no position to

---

7 Cf. the end of his *An Introduction to Metaphysics* where he speaks about how the form of a metaphysical theory is spoiled when theory is taken over by disciples. And then he concludes (p. [76 in the Macmillan ed.]), "And the master [Agushewitz translates: rebbe] in so far as he formulates, develops and translates into abstract ideas what he brings, is already in a way his own disciple [Agushewitz translates: talmid]."

cognize it. And with that objection, too, we will rely upon Bergson's own words — does not Bergson say himself that with intelligence, as with the other instruments of our intellectual faculties, we are in no position to cognize such a cognition. The same goes for our senses, which are certainly made (like the snout and paws of a dog) only for practical cognition.

The only out [tirele] Berson leaves open for such a cognition is through an intuition (some kind of internal sense, an instinctive perception) which we would be able to cultivate [oysbildn] for such cognition, by thoroughly cleansing ourselves, for this purpose, from the practical dross [khometz]; we ought to see that when this intuition activates its "eyes" we should then be interested only in cognition for its own sake [lishmo], in cognition for the sake of cognition, and not for the sake of action [maysim]. But, in fact, this intuition is nothing more than a ludicrous [lekherdiker] bag, which should not be able to retain pure theoretical cognition. Why is this so?

This is so because to retain a cognition, one must indeed retain that which one has cognized in the past, i.e., one must have memory. Without memory, we would have only so much cognition which can give us a moment of the present — a moment which should represent with itself the smallest part of the infinitely divisible time and should therefore be imperceivable. Bergson says this himself: "The truth is that every perception is already memory."[8] And memory, according to Bergson, is controlled by by our consciousness, which permits it to be used only for practical cognition. Therefore, the outcome must be, that even when a privileged intuition has access to pure theory, it cannot take away from there any cognition, because in the moment when it cognizes something it must get a fillip in the nose from consciousness and must immediately forget it.

And this leads us, further, to the first argument: if we are not in a position to cognize that which is in constant flux, we then have no ground to assume that such a thing exists, because to assume that something exists, we must think about something, we must perceive

---

8 Cf. *Matter and Memory*, p. 96, where it is stated: "Practically, we perceive only the past, the pure present being the invisible progress of the past gnawing into the future."

it with our mind — otherwise we will be thinking of existence without an object, of the existence of nothing.

This does not mean that to say that we must be in a position to cognize everything that exists — on the contrary, it is more reasonable to assume [es legt zikh gikher oyfn seykhel], that our cognitive sphere is limited and that there exist things that we cannot even conceive of, just as a blind man cannot conceive of color. More, as was demonstrated in the beginning of this volume, we cognize quite explicitly the existence of a power of which we are not in a position to conceive. But we saw there also that precisely because this power is over our conception, we have no right to determine its nature, to say that it is in flux or rigid, or that it is a principle or a consequence, etc. And just so Bergson has no right to determine the nature of the unknown reality by characterizing it as in continual flux.[9]

H.

But let us even suppose, that Bergson, with his intuition, reaches the pure theoretical reality and he succeeds there even to embrace the nature of continual flux. He can nevertheless after all not know whether he has reached the very top of it [same dek], or whether there

---

9 At the beginning of his *Creative Evolution* Bergson even attempts to prove continual change as a fact, and these are his words: "Let us take the most stable of internal states, the visual perception of a motionless external object. The object may remain the same, I may look at it from the same side, at the same angle, in the same light; nevertheless the vision I now have of it differs from that which I have just had, even if only because the one is an instant older than the other. My memory is there, which conveys something of the past into the present."

I have to admit, that I cannot understand how in such a case my vision in one moment is different than in another. We suppose quite the opposite, that my vision remains the same even when I look at an object from different angles, and in different lighting, as long as the difference is not too big [shtark]. So, for example, the green grass looks entirely and always the same color, though the same light does not fall everywhere upon it. Rather than diversity, the memory introduces similarity in my internal states. And I believe that this is the experience of most people, among whom are found in any case Russell, Broad, and other modern philosophers. Cf. *The Problems of Philosophy* by B. Russell, as well as *Mind and its Place in Nature* by C. D. Broad.

is over this reality not something different which is its cause or creator. In other words, our cognition can show us only that a certain thing exists, but not that that thing is all that exists or is the principle of everything.

This reminds one of the tale [maysele] of the blind men who were permitted to feel an elephant. One felt the elephant's foot, and thus assumed that the elephant is like a pole; a second felt its side, and assumed that the elephant is like a wall; a third felt a tusk and assumed that the elephant is like a skewer [shpiz]; a fourth felt the trunk and assumed that the elephant is like a snake; a fifth felt the tail and assumed that the elephant is like a rope. And so each of them took away a different conception of the elephant's appearance.

No commentary on this tale is necessary — everyone understands the relevance of it with the gnosticisms that go by the name idolatry, materialism, and pantheism, deism, vitalism, etc. What is required here, however, is to add an appendix [tusgebn epes a hoysofe] to the tale — an appendix which should reflect a little better this relevance — namely, that it is possible that the blind men should not reach the elephant itself at all. Rather, they should only touch the water that he releases from his trunk or feel his warm breath.

I.

But here the question of simplicity again comes around. How so? Simplicity requires that if a thing can be explained with fewer premises, one should not seek an explanation with more premises; if therefore Bergson's "élan vital" is in position utterly to explain the course of nature, we should satisfy ourselves with it alone, and therefore presume that this is the principle of everything — for why should we rely upon the extraneous premise that there is a higher principle over it?

But the truth is, that Bergson's theory is in no position to explain the course of things in nature; it is faulty [hinkt unter] already when it comes to explaining the relation [shaykhes] between the most general elements in nature — the flow of life and material substance.

What is the relation between these two elements — do they each represent a different fundamental principle or is one derived [shtamn zey up] from the other?

The first of these two premises reminds us of the old, faded [ubgebliakevetn = upgebliakevetn] dualism, no longer modern. But on the other hand, this premise would better suit Bergson's theory — why? Because since these two elements are for Bergson so dissimilar — one is continually active and the other passive — it is implausible [shikt zikh nit] that one could be derived from the other.[10] But Bergson had before him a difficulty which a fundamental dualism is not able to eliminate. What is it?

The principle of activity must in fact be the source of existential energy; and when one says that it has in it the property of continual growth, this must mean that energy continually grows, the amount [mos] of it is continually growing — and how is that consistent with the accepted rule, that the amount of energy remains always the same?

The only answer that Bergson could find to this objection is that energy is converted [farvandelt] into something else. And as outside of energy there exists only matter, it thus remains, for him, that energy is converted into matter, i.e., matter is derived from energy. The relation between energy and matter is, therefore, for Bergson, entirely different from that for Heraclitus — instead of energy being a property of matter, it is, for Bergson, the principle from which matter is derived.

---

10 Professor Perry did, in fact, assume that Bergson's theory is in essence a dualism: Cf. *History of Philosophy*, by Alfred Weber, *Philosophy Since 1860*, by R. B. Perry. Dualism has difficulties even with the uniform order we discern in nature — the uniform order that we discern, for example, in animals, in which in the middle years life continually conquers matter, and from then on, on the contrary, it is conquered, and weakened. But this difficulty can be met by a proportion of forces [koykhes] when through continual growth, life spreads itself out over too much substance, then must it begin to be conquered by the greater mass of substance and become lost.

J.

This by itself [shoyn] makes Bergson's theory a far remove from simplicity — of course it is hard for us to understand how immaterial power is converted into material substance. But that does not yet amount to anything [oysgemakht]. The chief difficulty is derived from another distinction between Heraclitus and Bergson: for Heraclitus, energy is only a power of alteration — alteration which occurs from above to below just as much as from below to above; it can lead to a regress just as to progress, to shrinking as well as growth — while for Bergson it is a power that must lead to growth, because it continually adds created life of the present to existing left of the past. But if so, the question poses itself: How does it come about that energy suddenly makes a descent, being transformed into dead matter? How does it come about that the natural, continual upward course of energy is suddenly cut off [ibergehackt] [?] and instead of becoming more life, it dies away completely?

This very question must have pushed Bergson even more on the way to unity. He seeks to reply to it through the premise that life is not much different from matter — both are movements: "Life is a movement, materiality is the inverse movement."[11] Or, "Life is tension and matter is extension."

Fine [gut]. But why should life suddenly pass over from the natural motion to a retrograde motion? Here Bergson had no other choice, it seems, than to have recourse to the premise of resistance — the natural movement of life is arrested by some kind of resistance. And because besides life there exists only matter, matter indeed, must be that which arrests the natural course of life: "The impetus of life... consists in a need of creation. It cannot create absolutely, because it is confronted with matter, that is to say with the movement that is the inverse of its own" [p. 265].

---

11 Cf. *Creative Evolution,* p. [263 in the Macmillan ed.]. The interpretation [taytsh] of this is, that life is growth and change, which can only follow, while matter continually moves, but it exists at the same time. The following quotations come also from there, from the same chapter, which speaks of the creation of matter.

But here once again such a question comes up: if matter is created by life's being arrested, driven off the natural path [derekh hayoshor], and if matter is again that which arrests the natural course of life, then matter had no need of being created, because before it even began to be created, it did not exist and could not have arrested the natural course of life — so how is the genesis and consequent creation of matter to be explained?

Bergson's theory is therefore far from being able to explain all, and in any case is not satisfactory from the standpoint of simplicity, because it is the opposite of what we chiefly look for in simplicity. How so?

What we chiefly look for in simplicity is the assent of the intelligence. And since Bergson himself adds that the "élan vital" is not conceivable by intelligence, the intelligence cannot give its assent — for how can intelligence assent to something it knows not?

In this way we see that the attempt to win simplicity through eliminating the idea of an unknown principle has on the theoretical domain led to no good. In the next chapter we will see that in the practical domain the same attempt has brought us, as well, much damage; it has served to ruin our morality.

———•‹◆›•———

Chapter Sixteen

Simplicity and Morality — The Ethics of the Materialists

A.

Simplicity in logic has one meaning — a cognition concerning which one need not think much is simple.[1] The simplest cognitions, are, therefore, those we receive directly from our sensations of seeing, touching, feeling bodily pleasures and pains, etc.

Of course, not thinking is easier for us than thinking and therefore we have a special bias [naygung] for simplicity; one would like to believe [es vilt zikh gloybn] that everything that exists must be something which is simple for us; therefore we are more inclined to suppose that everything that exists must be something that we can see or feel, and therefore we are also more inclined to suppose that everything that is good and bad has to do with bodily pleasures and pains.

We therefore see that materialism usually goes hand in hand with an inferior [niderike] theory of morality, a theory which grounds morality on feelings in respect to [mit] which we do not differ from the lower animals. But how far this simple morality limps we can see from the fact that the materialists themselves must prop it up continually with all new premises, premises through which they continually retreat from their previous position.

---

1 Outside the logical domain, simplicity has another meaning: when we speak of simple men or simple commodities, we mean that the men or commodities are of lower quality. It seems, however, that this particular meaning is a derivative one. We see this particularly in the case of men, because a simple man means the average man, one whose essence is easy to cognize, which excludes him from being, not only a genius [goen], but also a madman [meshuggener]. This use of the concept to characterize humans is presumably [mistome] taken over from other subjects.

Thus, Epicurus had to reject the naive hedonism of the Cyrenaics.[2] He had to realize that gorging oneself and guzzling [fresn un zoybn] and indulging one's lusts without limit [nokhgebn zikh tayves on a shi'er] does not pay even from the standpoint of physical pleasure, because it brings more pain than pleasure. Everything must, therefore, be done in the right measure and therefore one must know the right measure of all things. And this leads in turn to the conclusion [maskone], that knowledge is an element which must accompany all our actions, i.e., knowledge or inquiry is something that we need more than anything else; it is the most important moral factor.

We attain knowledge by becoming acquainted with facts of our own and others' experience. And experience teaches us, that a poor man eats with more appetite and thus has more pleasure from his poor meal [sude] than the wealthy man [gvir] from his rich meal. Luxury, therefore, does not engender [farshaft] any pleasure in one who is habituated to it. On the other hand, such a habituation is likely to cause suffering, because when we get used to luxury we then cannot do without it, and the occasional lack of it causes suffering.

We learn from experience also, that with regard to feeling good or bad, suffering is a greater factor than pleasure: when a man suffers pains, no pleasure can make him happy. Conversely [farkert], on the other hand [vider], when a man is healthy and has no worries hanging over his head (mental suffering) then is he perforce content and joyful.[3]

We also find out that mental suffering has more of a place than physical suffering, because we begin to suffer mentally at an earlier time, before the real suffering comes. So, for example, when we must undergo an operation, we suffer mentally already many weeks in advance, dreading the operation, while physically, we suffer only

---

2 Hedonism is the theory which grounds morality on physical pleasure.

3 Cf. the maxims of Epicurus, tr. Hicks, of Diogenes Laertius, in *Source Book in Ancient Philosophy*, by C. M. Bakewell: "The magnitude of pleasure reaches its limit in the removal of all pain." Here, however, one should have reminded Epicurus that precisely when a man feels nothing, he suffers from boredom.

during the operation; mentally we imagine every moment the entire suffering of the operation, while physically we have at every moment of the operation only a moment of suffering, because the suffering of the past is already over and the suffering of the future has not yet taken place, "he-'avar 'avar ve-he-'atid 'adayin" [Hebrew: "The past is past, and the future is not yet"].

The same example shows us also quite clearly that the greater part of our mental suffering comes from a false prejudice, we imagine suffering of which in fact we will bear only a very small part. That is not all. Often what causes us distress [agmas nefesh] is the fear of suffering which will mainly not come about. Such a distress is caused by the fear of death, which can in fact cause no suffering at all, because if we were in a position to suffer then death is still absent, but if death is present then we are not in a position to suffer.

If, therefore, we should be freed [loyz] of our false preconceptions, we should have true knowledge, we would become rid [potur] of the greatest part of our suffering. Such a true knowledge is, however, difficult to bring up [aroyftsubrengn] into the mind in real time [beshas mayse], because when the mind is taken up with the presentation of suffering, it has no capacity [koyekh] to think something else. It is therefore good for a man to have friends in whom he can confide his suffering and who should console him, help him gauge the true extent of his expected suffering.

Another means to protect oneself against excessive psychic suffering is not to commit crimes, because crime fills the mind with worry and fear: one who commits an overt [ofene] malfeasance has on his mind the suffering of the punishment which he therefore will receive; one who commits a secret [bahaltenem] crime must suffer in his mind the fear that he will be found out [tomer vet men es oysgefinen].

The chief requisites [foderungn] of Epicurus' morality are, therefore: to avoid getting used to luxury, to avoid criminal behavior, to root out false preconceptions, to make the effort [mi] to study in order to acquire [ayntsushafn] as much knowledge as possible, and above all [vial kulom] to acquire friends.[4]

These requisites are actually quite far from what the Cyrenaics held that a person must do, but at base [b`iker] the two moral theories are the same, because Epicurus holds as well that all that a man must do is to acquire as many pleasures as possible, and as few pains. He merely keeps better books, directing [heys] us to forgo [reading farboygn as farbaygeyn] a pleasure sometimes, when it can deprive us [baroybn] us of a greater pleasure or bring about more pain than pleasure; and to incur pains, when they are likely to spare us greater pain or bring upon us more pleasure than pain.

B.

It is superfluous to say that Epicurus' moral teaching stands immeasurably [gor nit der erekh] higher than Aristippus'. And therefore it had, in fact, much more success; for over six hundred years it was considered [gegoltn] as the code of the law [shulkhen orukh] for a quite substantial [gants hibshe = hipshe] group of materialists (although they attempted to fulfill only a part of it, being lazy students [lernen hot men zikh gefoylt]), but in the end they had to realize that even this moral theory was full of gaping holes and they had to patch them up. What are the holes?

First of all, this particular moral theory is incapable of accounting for [dekn] the extent of our moral feelings: we feel that we must help a sick [elendn; probably with the German meaning] man even when he is on the verge of [er halt shoyn] death, there being no hope that we will gain [epes gevinen far zikh] by helping him. Similarly, we feel that we should not cause such a person distress [tsar] although we ourselves would not lose anything by so doing. Now, where does such an obligation [darfn] come from? Where, in Epicurus' egoistical moral theory, is there room for compassion [rakhmones]?

---

4 This is also Epicurus' maxim, which we find in the same place: "Of all the means which wisdom acquires to ensure happiness throughout the whole of life, by far the most important is friendship."

Second, there is no place in this moral theory for our feelings of justice: if everything a man need do is only that which is expedient from the sensual standpoint (direct or indirect), there is no ground for saying that the stronger must not seize something he needs from the weaker. It is true that the stronger can himself suffer from injustice, because he also can be robbed. But this does not yet mean that therefore it is expedient for him not to do an injustice, because he can suffer an injustice even if he had not committed one himself.

It will perhaps be said that Epicurus forfended this, by proving that it is not expedient to commit crimes because of the consequent suffering from fear of punishment. But if even Epicurus is completely correct in this, he cannot explain away [farentfern] our feelings of justice, because for him the relation between injustice and punishment is just the reverse from the way we feel it: we feel that the punishment comes because an injustice has been done, while according to Epicurus an injustice is done because of the coming punishment.

And it is superfluous to say that between the two there is a great distinction, because we can in fact sometimes perpetrate [opton] the greatest evil [rishus] without fear of punishment. Genghis Khan certainly did not expect to be punished for his cruelties. The greatest evildoers [rishoim] in the history of mankind, the Nazis, were confident that they would rule over the entire world and would never have to give an accounting for their atrocities [maysim tatuim]. Epicurus' moral theory would have given them a sanction [hekhsher] for their horrifying crimes.

But more, since they have a sanction for these crimes, we also can no longer punish them — because how can one punish someone for something he was permitted to do? Also, we should not forget that according to Epicurus the only ground for punishment is deterrence: "Natural justice is a pledge of reciprocal benefit, to prevent one man from harming or being harmed by another." And if so there is no ground for the punishment of the sort of crimes we usually do not believe will be punished: the punishment, regarded as a coincidence, will not prevent the reoccurrence of the crimes.

Incidentally, one of the greatest admirers [strengste onhenger] of Epicurus' moral theory admitted as much. The English Epicurean,

Thomas Hobbes, says explicitly, that according to the natural egoistical character of men "nothing can be unjust."[5] Hobbes goes even further. He holds that in accordance with human character even friendship is more a disadvantage [khesorn] than an advantage [mayle] because in a group conflict can more readily take place [gikher forkumen] owing to mutual insult [balaydungn] and recrimination [taroymes]: "Again, men have no pleasure (but on the contrary a great deal of grief) in keeping company . . ."

This means, that according to Hobbes, in an Epicurean egoist moral theory there is no place for the virtue [tugnd = German: Tugend] of friendship, which had added quite a bit of color to this moral theory, and of which, therefore, Epicurus breaks forth in praise.

C.

Of course, the Epicurean Hobbes did not seek simply [glat azoy] to throw stones at Epicurus' ethical theory. His intention was to correct it, to put patches on the holes. And what were these patches?

First, concerning the question of pity. Here Hobbes makes things easy for himself [git zikh laykht an eytse], by declaring pity to be a person's fear that another's misfortune [tsore] should happen to him: "Grief for the calamity of another is pity; and ariseth from the imagination that the like calamity may befall himself."[6] That means that pity is consistent with egoism; we all fear the same miseries [tsores], and because of that common fear we are perforce all partners in combating them.

Concerning the question of justice and friendship, in contrast [shoyn], Hobbes' answer is not so short and simple. Here we have to familiarize ourselves with his theory of mutual agreements and the absolute right of kings — a theory which he sets forth at great length. Insofar as it concerns us here, the theory can be explained briefly as follows:

---

5 This and the next quotation comes from Chapter XIII of Hobbes' *Leviathan*.
6 This quotation is from Chapter IV of the same book [*Leviathan*].

Nature demands of every person to do only that which preserves and strengthens his existence, and moves him therefore to utilize the means leading to this. A person discovers these means in two ways: directly, through sense perception; indirectly, through foreseeing by means of reason. Reason tells him (of course by learning from experience) that more than anything his existence can suffer from the hand of another person, who seeks to exploit him for his own need for existence. What counsel should he pursue [vi azoy zol er zikh an eytse gebn] against such an enemy?

There are two possible counsels: the way of war and the way of peace. One can defeat and destroy the enemy, or else one can conclude with him a mutual agreement not to do harm. Now the alternative of war and defeating the enemy is excluded, because in that way each person would have to wage war against everyone and defeat everyone, which is certainly impossible. There remains, then, only the alternative of peace.

Thus it results, that peace is an major means of self-preservation and nature necessarily requires of a person that he make use of this means, just as it requires of him to make use of the other means for the same end. Here we have already the basis for the natural requirement of concluding friendships, because friendship is, after all, also a form of peace, though with a positive line — peace is an agreement in which each obligates oneself only not to do harm to the other, while friendship is an agreement in which each obligates himself to help the other.

An obligation can have value only if the obligating party complies with his obligation; he may not repudiate it without the agreement of the other parties. In order that an agreement be valid there must therefore be a power which can compel each one of the parties to keep his word, and therefore one of the means for our preservation is to create such a power. Such a power will be created when several persons pool their efforts and build a joint power. A kingdom is just such a power, represented by a king or parliament. And the kingdom gives the basis for justice and injustice. How so?

Everyone has a power to determine to do what he thinks is good for his self-preservation. When he delegates that power to the kingdom, he consents thereby that the kingdom should have the power to determine for him to do that which it supposes to be good for his preservation, and thus he obligates himself thereby to do or not to do what the kingdom commands. It thus follows that when a citizen violates the laws of the kingdom, he is not doing his duty and commits an unjust act.

This does not, meanwhile, give the kingdom the right even to punish violations of its laws, because the power to punish oneself (to act against one's own preservation) nobody has, and therefore cannot delegate it to the kingdom. Yet this very right the kingdom need not take over from the citizens, since it has it automatically by natural right. How so?

By natural right, everyone may do everything that is necessary for his preservation, even to kill an enemy, if this is good for his own survival. In delegating his powers to the kingdom, a citizen merely renounces this natural right to the extent that the kingdom demands it of him. But the kingdom itself does not renounce this right and exercises this right to compel the citizens to obey its laws.

The kingdom has the same natural right when it punishes foreigners or revolutionaries, who do not agree to delegate their right to the kingdom. With regard to such people, the kingdom has no obligations, and it may, therefore, deal with them as did primitive man used to treat his enemies, upon conquering them. Nevertheless, even the kingdom is limited in the treatment of its own citizens. It may not punish the innocent, because it has received power in order to use it for the good of the kingdom, and punishing the innocent is not good for the kingdom.[7]

D.

It will undoubtedly be noted that this last point justifies the Nazi treatment of aliens, and this by itself shows how far Hobbes' theory conflicts with our feeling for justice. But his basis for punishing a

---

7 Cf. Chapters XXVII and XXVIII of the *Leviathan*, which speak of rights and punishment.

citizen is not much better; our feeling with regard to a just punishment demands that it should be based on something other than the possibility to do evil to another. To prove this, the following remarks will suffice:

If the justice of a punishment should be based only upon the possibility of doing wrong to another, it should not obligate the punished to accept even a deserved punishment. On the contrary, he is obligated by nature to defend himself, to oppose the punishment with all possible means. This means that if a person sentenced to death should think that by killing innocent people he would have a weak chance of saving himself from death, he would be justified, and even morally obligated to do so (because according to Hobbes, a man is obligated to do only what is good for him) — so why don't we accept [oyfnemen] this? Why do we feel the exact opposite, that by doing such a deed, the sentenced criminal commits a new crime against morality?

It will perhaps be said, that Hobbes already took care of that with his premise of a kingdom-covenant, which obligates every citizen to obey the laws of the kingdom, and thus not to kill innocent persons. But this reply is not valid here, because the entire matter of the kingdom-covenant, just as the entire matter of complying with one's obligations, is derived only from what is good for the preservation of a citizen and it is therefore required of him by nature; when, however, it results in evil for his existence then nature requires not to take account of all that, just as originally, it requires him to do every possible sin that facilitates his preservation.

And it should be noted immediately, that what is involved here is not a mere detail, but rather a great principle — Hobbes' justice is essentially different from what is usually accepted; we accept justice as absolute; what is just for me must be just for everyone and what is the contrary, must be unjust for everyone.[8] For Hobbes, by contrast,

---

8 There are various theories of justice and equality . There are also disputes how to interpret the principle that, for example, when we assume that the principle of justice and equality for all one can nevertheless dispute how this equality is to be expressed — whether in equal laws for all, whether in giving everyone an equal share in world production, or only in proportion to that which he contributed.

justice is relative — the kingdom does justly when it punishes me; and I do justly too, when I employ every possible means to avert the punishment.

What does this all show? That Hobbes' moral theory is unable to account for [dekn] our feeling for justice and that therefore these feelings flow from some other source. Likewise, his theory is unable to account for our requirements concerning friendship — requirements which far surpass [shtaygn vayt ariber] the terms of a reasonable, businesslike peace agreement between natural enemies.

Take love, which is only a higher degree of friendship. There is no doubt that a beloved would not be satisfied with the lover who showed only a businesslike interest — it is expedient for him to be associated with her because of passion or even money. What she demands of him is an altruistic interest, that the lover should wish for her preservation just as a mother wishes for the preservation of her child. But where is there a place for such a direct altruistic interest, when all our feelings are concentrated around the narrow issue [enge daled ames] of self-preservation, as limited as it is in Hobbes' theory?

This theory is also unable to give a satisfactory answer to the question of pity. Certainly we cannot deny that in our feelings of pity there is a certain part of association with the thought of our own suffering. But that this is not the whole story can be proved from Hobbes' own argument: if this were all, we should not feel pity over suffering which ourselves never had and which we could never have; the white men of our Northern states should not have been moved so

---

Similarly, then can also be smaller disputes concerning interpretations, like the ones which used to take place in our Sanhedrin, or today in the Supreme Court. For those, however, who suppose the same principle in the same interpretation, the same things should be just or unjust, i.e., even the party which is unjust should recognize the fact, if he is a man of truth and is able to see the truth. From this, the Talmudic dictum is derived: "Any judge who is called to justice and is found, in a fair trial, to owe money, cannot be a judge." [I translate freely from *Bava Bathra* 58b, rather than literally from the Yiddish.]

much by the descriptions in the book, *Uncle Tom's Cabin*, and they ought not have had to spill their own blood to free the blacks.[9]

E.

So we see that Hobbes' medicine proves not to eliminate any of the weaknesses of Epicurus' moral theory. The reason for this is that these weaknesses are derived not from an illness in one limb or another, but from a defect in the heart of this very moral theory — the fundamental premise upon which Epicurus built his moral theory is essentially [be`etsem] false. What is the fundamental premise and why is it false?

The fundamental premise in Epicurus' moral theory is that moral good consists in feeling good. This is, however, a mistake. It consists not in feeling good but in being good: a person is not moral in virtue of eating steak [oyf mit yoykh; lit., chicken with gravy] even if he gets to eat it his entire life, and has continuing pleasure, and suffers no harm, from eating it. To be moral he must be such as to be accepted as good from a standpoint other than that of feeling good.

Furthermore, quite often feeling good, or personal utility, may actually poison morality, and wherever the bacillus of the former shows itself, it kills the latter. Thus, for example, to save a drowning person is certainly a moral act; but, done for monetary gain, it loses its moral character, because the job of a life guard is not accepted by us as any more moral than that of the shoemaker or tailor.

This does not mean that every moral deed is rendered invalid [posl] if one takes pleasure [fargenign] in it personally. On the contrary, often the pleasure itself is a moral good. For example, the joy one feels in finding out that one's friend is out of trouble is good,

---

9 As already stated, Hobbes himself attempts to prove his theory of pity from the alleged fact that suffering that cannot happen to us ought to be of no concern to us, "... for calamity arriving from great wickedness, the best men have the least pity." But it is not difficult to find a simple reason why good men have no pity for troubles that come from wickedness, because we assume that such troubles ought to come, and involve no evil. The fact is, that good men wish from the beginning that the wicked should be punished for their sins, because they assume that such a punishment represents a moral good.

likewise the occasional pleasure one has in doing good deeds or from a spiritual achievement. But there is a difference between this kind of pleasure and the personal advantage which is the motive for good deeds in Epicurus' and Hobbes' moral theory. What is the difference?

The difference is that this particular pleasure follows from a good principle. Why do we have pleasure from good deeds? Because this is what we have wished for, and the good wish was fulfilled; the pleasure here serves only as an expression of the good wish. The same wish is expressed by the good deeds themselves and by this means the deeds and the pleasure from the deeds are literally [mamesh] the same thing. On the other hand, in Epicurus and Hobbes' egoist moral theory, the good deeds and the pleasure follow only from the wish to feel good — a wish which does not evoke in us the sympathy that a moral factor does.

The later materialists, therefore, had to take yet a different way. Here is what Buechner says of morality: "What we call moral feeling stems from a social instinct or habit, which every human (or animal) society develops and must of itself develop, if it is not to be lost due to its own incompetence."[10]

What does the term "social instinct" mean? It means that we are naturally inclined to sympathize with another's joy and suffering and to behave in accordance with the sympathetic feeling. This amounts to [iz shoyn] true altruism, which is exactly the opposite of Epicurus' and Hobbes' egoism and which was, in fact, taken over by Hobbes' opponent, Lord Shaftesbury. Yet the marriage [shidekh] between materialism and altruism is not very successful. Why?

Because according to materialism, consciousness is nothing more than property of certain bodies to reflect themselves and therefore each body should have a consciousness only of itself. This is in accordance with the theory of egoism, according to which everyone's feelings express the state and the requirements of his own body. Altruism requires, however, that one man's feelings should express the state and requirement's of another's body — just as a mother

---

10 Cf. the chapter concerning morality in *Force and Matter* op. cit.

suffers when the state of her child's body is in disorder — so whence will the materialism derive such feelings?

It will undoubtedly be said that these feelings do not reflect the state of another's body, but rather the consciousness which the sympathizer obtains by the manner in which his body is affected by the sufferer's body. This is certainly true. But it is also true that the feeling of sympathetic suffering does not express the meaningless effect which matter of one body has caused in the matter of another body, but rather it is related directly to the consciousness of another's suffering. When the cat risks her life to save her kittens from the eagle's claws, it is not because of the pain that the image has caused in her eyes, but rather because the consciousness of her child's danger evokes feelings in her, feelings which impel her to accept any pain, as long as she can save her offspring.

This is, naturally, difficult to understand in accordance with the materialist premise that thought is only the movement of matter. This premise is the more difficult when we take into account that these altruistic feelings themselves have the ability to move matter because the sympathizer acts in accordance with his feelings. But this leads us to the problems of the interaction between body and consciousness, which will be treated in the next chapter.

———◈———

Chapter Seventeen

The Relation Between our Bodies and our Minds

A.

Our cognitive behavior points to cooperation between two factors, our body and our mind. Take any cognition you will — it begins with bodily contact and ends with a presentation in the mind. Again, behavior begins usually with a thought and ends with bodily movement.

It appears also that these two factors work reciprocally, the body causes effects in the mind, and the mind causes effects in the body. I am deep in thought, when I suddenly hear someone call my name, and I turn around to see who called me. In this case there is, first, contact with my body (stimulation of my ears by a certain sort of air wave) which causes my mind to interrupt my thought and begin to construct an idea from what the brain took note of; finally, the mind again causes the body to turn around to the side from where the call came.

This is what is called "interaction" between body and mind, the body moves [makht arbetn] the mind and the mind moves the body. Does such an interaction, between body and mind, really go on, or is it only apparent [dukh zikh azoy]? There are differing views concerning this.

Until a couple of hundred years ago, nobody — philosophers, scientists, and the man on the street — doubted that their cognition and behavior were the result of an interaction. But recently this belief was shaken, and other ways were sought to account for cognition and behavior.

B.

What happened? How did the premise of interaction — which accords so well with everyone's inner experience and which explains our cognition and behavior so simply — suddenly fall into disfavor [gevorfn an umkhen]? For this there are a number of reasons:

(1) First, this premise was made to suffer from the general bias against old beliefs, a prejudice which dominated the intelligentsia of the Renaissance era. The fact that many things which had been taken for true turned out to be false, naturally led to beginning to doubt everything that had been believed till then and this general doubt did not bypass the premise of interaction. After all, nobody had ever seen this interaction with his own eyes [fleyshige oygn].

(2) Second, this premise had to suffer from the awesome [gevaltign] prestige that mechanics suddenly received. The discovery that mechanical laws govern unexpected regions of the universe, led to the belief that everything, including organic matter, is subject to these laws only. This is also easy to believe, since in that way the entire universe becomes for us an open book.

(3) This belief became even stronger in view of the discovery that the elements of organic matter are the same as those of inorganic matter; the difference between the two lies only in their proportion, i.e., in quantity — a difference that does not touch the laws involved with any quantity of matter. Also, organic matter is only a small part of the matter that we observe in the universe — so [iz] why should this small part not be subject to the same laws that rule everything [else]?

(4) By the way [agav], one of the most prominent interactionists, the French philosopher René Descartes, had already admitted that the greater part of organic matter is in this respect actually no different from inorganic matter; Descartes was in fact the first to set forth the theory that the behavior of animals other than man takes place mechanically. In the nineteenth century, in turn [vider], Darwin came and removed the barrier between men and other living things. That is, just as the behavior of the other animals, the behavior of men is only a result of mechanical laws.

(5) In the same century, physicists formulated the principle [klal] of conservation of energy, that energy is never increased nor diminished, but merely transformed from one substance to another, and this principle goes against the premise of interaction, because if mind is able to move the body, then motion, i.e., physical energy, comes from a nonphysical source and thus in the physical substance there is an increase in energy which was not there before.

(6) Aside from this, there is a logical difficulty with interaction — we cannot understand how things of such different natures as body and mind could have reciprocal effects. It would certainly not occur to anyone to think that his mere wish for warmth should have the power to set coals on fire, or cause them to creep into the stove [arayntsukrikhn in oyvele]; likewise, a wish should not be able to move a nerve or a muscle of the human body.

(7) But most of all, we consider [shtelt men zikh up oyf] the experimental work in the laboratories, and medical experiments, that show, that the functions formerly ascribed to the mind are actually [gor] done by the brain. It has been discovered that even when purely logical thoughts occur, the brain must be working, because the temperature of the brain rises then. It has further been discovered that when the brain is damaged, the power of thought is affected, and when the damage is repaired the power of thought returns to normal. That is, it is a mistake to ascribe the function of thought to the mind; and if so it is also a mistake to ascribe to the mind the function of causing the body to do what it does — a function which is also merely a thought.

C.

But if not the mind, then what causes the behavior of my body? Why did I turn around when someone called me?

The answer is [iz der terets], that that behavior is caused mechanically, through movements that occur continually in my body, or which are caused by outside stimulation [a shtoys fun droysn]. Thus, for example, the turning of my body in the direction from which the call comes is merely a result of irritating or moving the

nerves and muscles, irritations and movements which were initiated
by the stimulation of certain sound waves on my ear drum.

But do I not evidently feel that I turned around, because I wanted
to, and I in fact do not turn around when it is not worthwhile for me
to do so. How do we contend with this feeling?

It is said that the said feeling is merely an illusion; true, we find
that when motions occur in my body which turn it around, I have also
a desire to turn around; similarly, when movements to turn my body
are arrested by contrary motions, I then have a wish not to turn. I
therefore think that these wishes are the cause of my turning around
or not turning around, but actually this is not so; turning or not
turning would take place even if we had no such wishes.

But from where do we derive this very thing, that the movements
of my body are always accompanied by a wish which accords with
their result? — Is this itself not an unusual wonder, requiring
explanation? Well, for this there are various explanations:

One explanation is, that the movements themselves bring about
the very desire which accords with their result — the wish to turn
around is produced by the movement that occurs in the body at the
time of turning. The wish thus accompanies the movement, because
the former is caused by the latter.

This particular explanation does not break completely with the
interactionist premise of causality between body and mind, but
reverses the causality — instead of an interaction in which the wish is
the cause of turning around, it has now become its effect.
Furthermore, in some cases this explanation is entirely consistent
with interactionism — this is, when even for interactionism the mind
is taken to be an effect of bodily movement. So both agree that the
idea that somebody called me is only an effect of the motion in the
brain, itself caused by the stimulation of my eardrums by sound
waves.

The main difference between these two explanations lies thus in
this: that while in interaction the mind is sometimes a cause and
sometimes an effect of bodily motions, in the second explanation the
mind is never a cause and is always an effect. Mind is thus never a
cause even of mind, since each thought is an effect of bodily motions.

The mind therefore does nothing; it is nothing but consciousness, and therefore this theory is called "epiphenominalism."

Other explanations break entirely with the premise of interaction — neither the body causes effects in the mind, nor does the mind cause effects in the body. All effects in the body follow from bodily causes, and all ideas follow from ideas; these are two streams running in parallel, not meeting one another in any point. Those who assume this explanation are therefore called "parallelists."

But if both streams have no connection with one another, then whence the excellent agreement, after all, between ideas and bodily movements? Why is it always the case when my ears are stimulated by such and such air waves that I have the idea that someone is calling me, or when a movement to turn around occurs in my body I have the wish to do so? This is explained in various ways and therefore there are several varieties of parallelism.

One theory is that the bodily movement and the idea which simultaneously arises represent the same thing — the same existence is expressed both by space and by thought, and when in space there is the form of such a bodily movement, it has in the mind the form of such an idea. This is identity, or two-aspect, parallelism, which Spinoza adopted and whose standpoint has already partially been explained in this volume.

According to a second theory, mind and bodily movement are not the same thing, but the course of both are ab initio ordered in such a way that the same idea should occur always simultaneously with the same bodily movement. This is the theory of "pre-established harmony," which was adopted by Leibniz, Spinoza's contemporary.

A third theory seeks to explain this harmony between the two streams through phenomenalism — every internal idea is able to be manifested to the outer senses as a certain bodily form; my internal consciousness that someone is calling me is seen, or can be seen, by the eye, as such and such course of bodily motion. This is called "ideal parallelism," which is adopted by a certain group of Idealists, while epiphenomenalism is of course the theory of the materialists.

We will now see whether the theories of epiphenomenalism or parallelism better explain the abovementioned connection between body and mind.

D.

First concerning materialist epiphenomenalism, which itself is divided into two theories. According to one theory, mind is not something different from bodily motion: "Mind is a movement of body," says Buechner in the name of a prominent materialist [materialistishe godl]. According to a second theory, mind is not itself a bodily movement, but is an essential [ikkerdike] effect of bodily movement, an effect which cannot for its part cause anything.

Now [iz] the first theory had almost trickled out by the beginning of the twentieth century (only the behaviorists later tried, without success, to revive it). Everyone understood then that in order to identify mind with bodily movement, one must overlook the element of consciousness, which is the foundation of mind.[1]

The neo-materialists, therefore, assumed the second version of epiphenomenalism, that thought is an effect and not a cause of bodily movements. But this version of epiphenomenalism is associated with such great difficulties that all in all it is not much better than the ancient materialist version. These difficulties can briefly be set forth as follows:

(1) First it is entirely against our direct internal experience — we feel manifestly, that our mind is not simply [glat] an extraneous observer [zaytiger tsushoyer], but on the contrary the most important factor in our deeds: a general begins an invasion of the enemy after he has well planned it; sometimes a person will take his own life

---

1 Here it is not necessary to dwell upon this, because in this volume (Chapter 17, section G) the matter has been discussed already and there it was demonstrated that the feeling of a toothache, for example, is something more even of the consciousness of a movement. For a reader who is more interested in this question, it was worthwhile looking over the article concerning the "soul" in *An Introduction to Philosophy*, by F. Paulsen (tr. P. Thilly), as well as *Matter and Spirit*, by J. B. Pratt, to whom the author owes most of the material in this chapter.

because he cannot stand the feeling of pain. Is this all a delusion? Would the general write the same orders even if he had not any consciousness of what is going on and what he is doing? Or would the sick person take his own life even if he felt no pain?[2]

(2) Next, it is not plausible that mind should be entirely idle [yoyshevbotl]. This goes against even Darwin's theory of organic evolution, which materialists of course think the world of [haltn an oylemumloye]. According to that theory, the course of progress goes on thanks to the "survival of the fittest," i.e., whatever possesses a progressive trait is in a better position to exist, because this trait helps in the battle for existence. This very principle is not applicable to the progress of mind, if we should suppose that mind can do nothing and everything goes on without it, because it then does not help at all in the battle for existence.[3]

---

2 Certainly, the *possibility* that this all should be only a delusion cannot be excluded — just as we were deluded in the past into thinking that humans cannot live on the antipodes because it would mean that they would be standing feet up and head down, or as we are deluded even today that the moon is no bigger than a saucer. But such a possibility does not justify us in dismissing [upzogn] a veridical experience. "A doubt," say our Sages, "does not overrule a certainty" [Hebrew: ein safek motzi midei vadai]. This is, as a matter of fact, the foundation of Realism, namely that we must assume what our experience tells us, so long as it has not been proved that it is deceiving us. And the materialists are, indeed, Realists — they are even too good Realists, because they allow only what is experienced or could be experienced if our senses were a little sharper, while a nonmaterialist Realist allows also what we cannot experience with our senses, as long as there is a good ground for it. And if a mere *possibility* does not give us the right to dismiss an experience arriving through the external senses, we should certainly not because of it dismiss inner sense, which is received more directly and therefore more securely than the outer sense.

3 Perhaps one will try to dispute [dingn] this argument: it will be said that although mind does nothing itself, on the other hand, its progress is a bedfellow of the progress of the bodily organization, which fortuitously has the nature to be knowable. This would be fine, if we knew everything going on in our body. In fact, however, the bodily machinery is knowable only when something is not in order and must be repaired. So, for example, a healthy person would not know at all through his internal experience, that he has a heart, or blood circulation, or digestive system. He finds out about them only when something is out of order and must be looked after. And finding out is in fact through a command that he must

(3) This theory seems to have going against it as well the principle of conservation of energy, which requires that energy should never be lost, but it either continues to work as kinetic energy, or it is stored as potential energy — it must either do something or be able to do something. According to this theory, it emerges, that the energy that the body discharges while framing a thought (because while the body frames a thought it does something and doing something means discharging energy) is entirely lost, because the thought does nothing and can do nothing.

(4) This theory appears to go against the logic of causality, and here is why: if we say that the mind cannot cause a bodily movement, this is only because the cause can only produce that which it has in it (not ex nihilo); and since having within it means having as a part of that which one is, and since bodily movements are not a part of mind, they cannot be produced by it. But if so, bodily movements should not be able to cause mental events, because these are also not part of bodily movements.[4]

(5) Aside from all this, there is still a large doubt whether mechanics itself is altogether able to create a machine which would automatically produce a Babylonian Talmud; Rashi's commentaries

---

look after it, through a feeling that does not let him rest until everything is back in order. This is all very understandable when the looking after would help to remove the disorder, if the feeling of hunger, for example, would compel us to provide the necessary food. If, however, consciousness should be unable to do anything it also cannot help remove the disorder, so why does it happen to be [grod] connected with it?

4 This was actually Spinoza's chief argument against interactionism. This is what we read in Part I, Proposition III of the *Ethics*: "If two things have nothing in common with one another, one cannot be the cause of the other." This is built on the reasoning that the effect is only a conjoining of parts which already existed separately in the causes. This particular argument, however, falls away when we allow the idea of emergence, namely, that the effect represents something new. But on the other hand, epiphenomenalism can gain little from this because the question remains, why can the causality of bodily movement go to the mind and not from the mind to bodily movement? If bodily movement can give birth to mind as emergence it should equally be the case that mind can give birth to bodily movement as emergence, and, trivially, [a pshite shoyn] that thought should be able to give birth to thought.

on the Talmud or Bible; or Maimonides' *Code*, his *Commentary to the Mishnah*, or his *Guide to the Perplexed*; and other volumes [sforim], of which every sentence is a logical pearl. Meanwhile, nobody has succeeded in creating a pen [epes a pen] which should by itself write a simple note [aynfachn brill].[5] Epiphenomenalism is a remote, doubly doubtful theory [a vaytn sfek-sfeke] — maybe such a thing can never be fashioned, and even if it can, there is a doubt whether it exists.

The upshot [untershte shure] of all this is, therefore, that the relation between body and mind is inexplicable via epiphenomenalism, both in the ancient materialist version and also in the neo-materialist version. We will now see whether this relation is better explained by parallelism.

E.

First, concerning Spinoza's identity, or two-aspect, parallelism, which seeks to explain the relation between body and mind through taking the two as the same thing. This looks similar to the ancient materialist version of epiphenomenalism, and therefore it must also be rejected as meaningless — because how can we suppose that such

---

5 To prove that such a thing is possible one imagines a mouse in a trap, which continues running around, looking for a way out and after a considerable time of "trial and error" she can find almost every concealed exit. This should take place also in a human brain, when it looks for a way out of a problem; trying out various incorrect ways, which are blocked by "synapses," it finds in the end the open correct exit. It must however be noted immediately that the case of the mouse in the trap is also not so comprehensible according to the mechanical laws which we experience. When the mouse bumps into the wires that block the exit, she does not jump backwards immediately, which would happen with a ball, rather she bites, and pulls, and exhibits many other activities that can indirectly help her get out. It must also be supposed, that the mouse is conscious of everything she does and that her consciousness conforms to the facts, when she knows that she has approached the wall then she really has approached there and when she knows that she is running back then she really is running back, etc., because otherwise we cannot compare her case to that of what goes on in the human brain. Does a ball, then, have also consciousness when it runs up to the wall and when it bounces back?

and such bodily movement should be simultaneously the idea of that very movement? And how can we suppose at all, that body and mind "things which have nothing in common," should represent the very same thing?

It will be said that for Spinoza the body and the mind do not in fact represent the very same thing, because they are various expressions of the same thing. But what is that supposed to mean? Is it as different particulars of the same universal?[6] Or as the same thought is expressed in various words or languages? But if so they are in fact different things, which are only partly similar and such things are not connected in any automatic parallelism, i.e., if there is only one thing here, the other thing must not simultaneously be — the particulars of a universal must not all simultaneously exist, just as it might be imagined that one language is spoken and another is not.

Others try to be helpful with an analogy to the internal and external sides (concave and convex) of a curve — the same line appears different from one side than from the other side. What one forgets thereby, is that we are talking, once again, not about the same thing, but about different things — about the different areas that stand in relation to the points of the curve. The points of a curve stand in different directions of space, some stand nearer to the eastern side and some to the western side; those that stand nearer to the eastern

---

6 It really appears as though this is what Spinoza had in mind. His logic seems to go that way: since each existing thing must represent existence (existence must be detected [derhert vern] in every existing thing and it must therefore be the substance of everything), the result is that when there exists a thing there must be existence. And since existence is a universal which includes all the expressions of existence, it must further result that when there is existence then all the expressions of it also *are*, because if some expression should be missing the result would be that existence both is and is not.

The error in this logic is derived from misunderstanding the relation between the universal and the particular, a misunderstanding which has already been discussed in this volume: the universal does not include all its particulars, but, on the contrary, it is included in each one of its particulars. Accordingly, the outcome is, that when some things do exist and some things do not exist it would not mean that the same existence is and is not, but rather it means that one existence is and another one is not — i.e., that existences are only as numerous as there are things, and this does not represent a contradiction in existence.

side stand, perforce, further from the western side; likewise, those that stand closer to the western side stand, perforce, further from the eastern side; when you look from the eastern side, the former appear pushed in and the latter pushed out. In the same matter, conversely, when you look from the western side the latter appear pushed in and the former pushed out.

That there is no analogy between the two can be seen from the very fact, that while the two sides of the curve present an analytic unity — the concavity of one side is taken for the convexity of the other side — in our case there is entirely no unity allowed; there the concavity and the convexity cause one another reciprocally, but here "one thing cannot be the cause of the other." In other words, in that case it is nonsense to take the two for a non-unity, while in our case it is nonsense to take them for a unity.

F.

This is apparently what induced Leibniz to substitute, for identity parallelism, the parallelism of "pre-established harmony," which does not require the absurdity of taking different things to be the same. But this parallelism has other difficulties, which show themselves whenever we try to imagine the possibility of the "pre-established harmony" between mind and body.

These possibilities are four: (1) There is harmony both between body and mind and also in body itself as well as mind itself, i.e., not only do the same bodily movements take place simultaneously with the same ideas, but the bodily movements themselves follow one from another always in the same mechanical ordering, just as the ideas themselves continually follow one from another in the same intellectual ordering; (2) There is harmony only between body and mind, but not within bodies themselves or the mind itself; (3) There is harmony between body and mind, just as in the mind itself, but not in the bodies themselves; (4) There is harmony between body and mind, just as in the bodies themselves, but not in the mind itself.

It appears from Leibniz' words, actually, that he had pictured this harmony in accord with the first possibility; this is seen from several paragraphs in his *Monadology*. Thus, for example, he says there in paragraph 78: "The soul follows its own laws, the body its own laws." It appears also from his analogy of the harmony between the soul and the body to the harmony of two clocks which go each of them in his own way.[7] But one example from experience is enough to prove that this possibility is excluded:

Let us imagine that someone is engrossed in a mathematical problem, when suddenly a stone falls upon him. His previous thoughts and aspirations are immediately interrupted by a feeling of pain, which is altogether different and which also appears to come from another source, from a blow to the body. Leibniz would surely say, that this particular feeling does not come from the blow to the body but from the soul itself — how so? Calculating in advance that the body would in that moment receive such a blow, the Creator straightaway [glaykh] created the soul in such a way, that in the same moment it should receive a feeling of pain, in order that there should be harmony between it and the body. But on the other hand, he would have to add, that this feeling does not fit in to the previous courses of his thoughts or aspirations of the soul — because what relation is there between the pain of a wound and the solution of a mathematical problem?[8]

In the mind itself, therefore, there is no complete harmony. On the other hand, in the body itself it is plausible that there is complete harmony, for if we assume that some ideas or aspirations come to the surface [shvimn aroyf] in a definite time because it was so calculated in advance to agree with the movements of the body, we must then

---

7 Cf. *The Philosophical Writings of Leibniz, Selected and Translated by Mary Morris*, p. 115.

8 This presents a great difficulty for Leibniz' theory. Mainly, when in par. 22 of his *Monadology* we read explicitly: "Every present state of a simple substance is a natural consequence of its preceding state . . ." And since the soul is in fact for Leibniz a simple substance, according to him every state of the soul is a natural consequence of its preceding state. Here it cannot even help that we should explain bodies and thus bodily movements only as ideas, because the ideas of impulse and of pain, after all, have nothing to do with the solution of a mathematical problem and thus the result must be the states of the soul are not natural consequences of each other.

also assume that the movements of the body can be calculated in advance, i.e., that they go on according to a definite reckoning, a definite order. It is superfluous to say that this is also confirmed by experience, which shows us evidently that the movements of bodies follow certain mechanical laws.

This is therefore the only possibility in which the "pre-established harmony" can be accepted — a corporeal world in which the states follow one another in a definite order and a mental world in which the states are merely arranged so that they should harmonize with or reflect the states of the corporeal world. This smells very strongly of epiphenomenalism in its second version and thus has, therefore, several of the difficulties of that particular epiphenomenalism.

First, it is difficult to understand the whole affair [gantse uvde] of the mind. Even if we should not assume Leibniz' premise, that everything in our world is ordered in the best possible way, we cannot deny the fact, that every organ of living creatures is useful, or at least was once useful, for their survival — so why should the mind, the "entelechy," or the organ par excellence, be taken for a useless reflection of what goes on in the body? What good is [oyf velkhe gute yor] the necessity of pains, the aggravations, and the worries which can accomplish nothing for us, since without them everything would go on exactly the same way?

It is also difficult to understand why the mind is so selective, why some things it reflects and some things not. Of course it is possible to say that our mind is limited, that it was established to think only those thoughts which reflect what is closely connected with our body. But is, then, the effect upon the eye of a house a half mile away more closely connected with our body than the blood circulation, which goes on in our entire body?

It is also difficult to understand from whence our ideas of interaction are derived, why we make the mistake of thinking that body and mind influence each other reciprocally. And even if we should assume, for lack of something better [zoln mir shoyn afile onnemen], that this mistake is natural, that when two things occur in parallel our mind from its nature is disposed to think a causal connection between them, it remains difficult to understand from whence is derived the definite order in this causal connection, why do we always think in some definite cases that the bodily state causes the ideas and in other definite cases we think the opposite, that the ideas cause the bodily state.

G.

It remains, then, merely to consider ideal parallelism, which is a couple of hundred years younger than its first two brothers, and is by now, therefore, worked out in the light of modern science. Nevertheless, it is not difficult to find the same family defects — we need only look how it interprets concrete happenings.

Let us take the following event: I stand and look in a show window, when suddenly I feel a hand on my shoulder; I turn around and spot [derzey] my brother. If someone were to make an inspection [onkukn], during that time [beshas mayse], with the most powerful [grestn] microscope, combined with a fluoroscope, he would not see what was in my consciousness, but something entirely different: he would not see in me the feeling of a hand on my shoulder, the urge [vuntsh] to turn around to see whose hand that is, the image of my brother and the feelings that that image evoke in me — but instead, he would see only a surge of bodily movement, extending from the shoulder to the brain and back to certain muscles, which contract and expand and cause, by this means, the turning of the body, etc.

Usually, we assume that the difference between these two sorts of cognition is an objective one. What I cognize in myself is essentially something different from what the outside observer [zaytiger tsushoyer] can see in me; it seems to us that the two sorts of cognition represent two sequences of events, which are united in one scene, of which I see one part and the outside observer sees another part. The idealist parallelisms assume, however, that these two sorts of cognition represent the same events — my feeling of a hand on my shoulder, or my urge to turn around, are cognized externally, by the sense of vision, as a such and such bodily movement.

This means, however, that mind is a movement of matter — a theory which has already been mentioned in the name of a prominent materialist [materialistishn godl] and which the idealist parallelisms all reject as absurd — so how is the same theory whitewashed [gekashert] as idealist parallelism? In other words, in what does the difference between epiphenomenalism in its first version and idealist parallelism consist, a difference that makes the former theory absurd and the latter not?

The main difference between these two theories consists in this, that while in epiphenomenalism the physical world is taken for the primary [ikker] existence and psychological states only as secondary [a tofl], here, conversely, we take psychological states as the primary existence and the physical world as secondary; according to epiphenomenalism existence began with matter and motion, only with time some combinations of matter or some movements began to manifest themselves as as states of consciousness, while in this theory it's the opposite: "The psychological domain represents reality just as it is through itself and for itself; on the other hand, the physical side is on the level only of an external appearance."[9] And this very difference is supposed to [zol] account for [derklern] why epiphenomenalism must be rejected as absurd, while the analogous theory of idealist parallelism is not absurd — how is this?

If matter or movement should become consciousness, that would mean that a thing has become something different from what it was, i.e., that it has produced from itself which was not there before, ex nihilo. Conversely, if consciousness should be manifested also as matter, it would not be different from what it is, because the manifestation of body is also consciousness — consciousness of such and such form. This is the explanation of Paulsen's argument: "Thoughts cannot be conceived as products of matter, while matter can be conceived as a product of thought."[10]

This argument is not bad and from the standpoint of logic, therefore, the idealist parallelist would allow himself easily to swallow it. Troubles begin, however, when we get to experience. Let us take the example of my feeling of a hand on my shoulder. According to this particular theory, it should follow that the observed

9 Cf. p. 92 in Thilly's translation of Paulsen's *An Introduction to Philosophy*.
10 Paulsen, p. 111, op. cit.

fact of this is only a manifestation of my feeling — but if so, from whence is derived the sudden feeling of a hand on my shoulder?

The idealist parallelists labor [matern zikh] to explain this through "panpsychism" — what is that [vos heist]? Every body is in essence a consciousness, which manifests itself only for our external senses as a body. The hand and the shoulder are, therefore, essentially also consciousnesses, and when my brother's hand touches my shoulder, what is actually happening is that one consciousness touches another — a consciousness connected with my brother touches a consciousness connected with me — and from this contact between consciousnesses can very well ensue the feeling of a hand on my shoulder.

Now this explains quite well why I delude myself to think that my feeling followed from a physical contact, because I can cognize the external consciousness from which it actually follows, only as a physical manifestation. This, further, can explain also why my brother deludes himself to think that the physical touch of his hand caused the feeling in me, since the consciousness that goes on internally in his organs is even for him so obscure [tunkl], that he is in a position to cognize it only with his external senses, but in that way it is impossible to understand the way how one consciousness seeks to come in contact with the other one — a way, which is entirely unsuited to the nature of consciousness.

Let us consider an example: I see my brother from afar and I would like to speak with him. Now what does my consciousness do in order to realize that wish? It walks? It moves in space? Is not the whole story [gantse mayse] of movement and of space merely an appearance [ershaynung] before the outer senses — an appearance which is only the "equivalent" of an internal consciousness — so what became of the internal consciousness? Why do we feel, internally as well, that the contact must be made through an approach in space by a movement?

It will perhaps be said that all this is derived from the fact that the higher consciousness does not make contact itself, but delegates this to its servants [meshorsim], the consciousnesses which are connected with it and which it is in a position to cognize only with its external senses and thus only as bodies, as a hand, feet, mouth, etc. And because the acts of its servants are also cognized by consciousness only with its outer senses, it is in a position only to cognize how the made contact is manifested physically. But if the movement in space is merely an appearance and in fact a direct contact between consciousnesses takes place, why then must it take so much time till this contact is made? Why must we go for days in order to come into personal contact with people?

Even here there is a partial reply, which we find in Kant's *Transcendental Idealism*, namely, just as space and movement, so is time only an appearance as well. But when we take up Kant's road we must accompany him until the idea of an unknown "noumenon," i.e., that not only space and time, but also consciousness and will are merely appearances, because consciousness and will cannot, in fact, be pictured through time's form of the past, present, and future — when I am now conscious of something, that something must already have existed a moment earlier and when I wish something, I must wish it before the future. But so far the idealist parallelists cannot go, because their entire objective is to detach the truth from appearance, i.e., to attain for us that which is rid of appearance.

Aside from this, there are here many more things in our experience, which look quite strange [modne] in light of idealist parallelism: here, a stone fell upon someone and killed him. The stone is according to this theory a completely obscure consciousness; while a person represents, on the contrary, a high level of consciousness. Does it not, however, appear strange, that the weaker consciousness should be able to push a stronger consciousness out of existence? Do not our internal experiences teach us the reverse, that the stronger impression thrusts aside the weaker impression, or that the stronger will suppresses always the weaker one?

We could find many such anomalies [modnekaytn] — but why go to look for rotting trees, when the whole forest is burning? Our entire experience is markedly opposed to this sort of parallelism: our experience tells us explicitly that there exist, as a matter of fact [be'etzem] not only wills and consciousnesses, but also space, bodies, and movements; just as it tells us explicitly that between bodies and consciousnesses or wills there are relations of reciprocal causality.[11]

It is said that our experience is not reliable [farleslikh] — and here is the proof [vehoraye], we have also false experiences, such as dreams, illusions, etc. One forgets, however, that the fact that we know that some experiences are false, points to, surprisingly [gor], the opposite, the reliability of our experience — it shows, that we possess also the ability to sift out [oyszipn] falsehood from our experience, from what is only appearance.

On the other hand, if we should not believe our experience, we should assume that all the bodies around us are only appearances, false images — then why should we think that behind these images there are consciousnesses? The only answer to this is "analogy" — just as I am a consciousness and I appear before my senses as a body, it is reasonable that all things that appear before my senses as bodies are consciousnesses. But if I support myself only by this analogy, I would have to suppose, that all bodies are nothing different from my consciousness, because I know only that that which appears before my senses as bodies is my own consciousness.

This denial of experience must, therefore, lead to solipsism — to the premise that only I myself exist and all other existents are merely appearances in my consciousness. Nobody would like to dwell, however, on solipsism, because with that theory one can't go to market — a solipsist cannot pretend that his theory is such that other people must also assume it as true, because according to his theory, nobody else exists to suppose it to be true.[12]

---

11 There is even an hypothesis [svore] that the whole idea of causality stems from this internal experience, because in that experience we cognize it explicitly — I feel explicitly that my hand moved because I wanted it to. By contrast, in the other cases of causality we see only that one event succeeds another.

12 The other arguments that Professor Pratt cites against idealist parallelism will be omitted here for the reason that they can be strongly disputed [men ken sizkh oyf zey shtark dingn].

H.

So we see, that there are difficulties not only for interactionism but also for all the other theories having to do with the relation between body and mind. We see, as well, that interactionism has an important edge [mayle] over the other theories, in that while the other theories are against our direct experience, interaction actually does agree with it. But this is not all. When one investigates fundamentally the difficulties of interaction, it actually appears that they are derived from prejudice and false logic. How so?

Seven reasons why interaction has been rejected have been cited above. The first two reasons are not arguments: the first reason represents only a conviction [aynredenish] that everything must be different from what we take it for; the second reason represents only a preference for mechanics — but convictions and preferences are essentially nothing more than prejudices.

The third reason is based upon a parallelist premise, that the same elements must remain, in all combinations, with the same qualities. This is, however, denied by the postulate of "emergence," which holds that elements, when found in a combination, display different qualities from those they display outside the combination, or in other combinations. We cannot, therefore, infer the sole dominion of mechanics by an analogy with the elements. This is especially when the issue is the analogy between inorganic and organic matter, where we cannot even say that the elements are the same, because organic matter adds the unknown element of life.[13]

Even less is Decartes' postulate of the "animal-machine" taken seriously [rekhn men zikh mit] today, the postulate which is the basic premise of the fourth reason. Today no one has any doubt that an animal is something more than a mechanical machine; that just as a human, it possesses feelings through which it is impelled [getribn] to do, or not to do, specific things; that when a dog, for example, is

---

13 In this volume, in the eleventh section of Chapter 12, it was demonstrated that the logic of "majority rules" has also to do with similarity and what is not similar is not subject to that logic.

wounded or hungry he suffers pain and that suffering compels him to do something to free himself from it. Darwin's bringing the human closer to the other animals does, therefore, nothing for the pretension of the sole dominion of mechanics, because that pretension is refuted with respect to the other living creatures just as with respect to humans.

What remain, therefore, are merely the last three reasons against interactionism — reasons which look serious and over which more than one philosopher has wrinkled his brow. But even here, "The devil is not so black [text has shreklikh, a misquotation from De Foe] as he is painted"; when we go deeper into these reasons we find in them too, the weeds of prejudice, sown by habit: our habit of seeing bodies put into motion by physical contact (pushing or pulling) creates in us an association between the two, so that whenever we imagine something put into motion we imagine also that it happened by physical contact. We think, therefore, that by nature [beteva] we cannot imagine anything else and nothing else can be depicted. But this is not correct — did we not as children imagine that a stone can be moved by saying "abracadabra" [algavish efen zikh]?[14] And do we then not see with our own eyes how the earth attracts to itself a falling stone even when the space between them is empty, so that the earth cannot touch the stone even indirectly?

This is one false prejudice. Another one is this, that we think that when something has caused a movement in one body, it must also cause a movement in another body of the same weight. This prejudice is much stronger than the first one, because aside from habit, it is supported by faulty logic — from the same cause the same effect must ensue. One thereby forgets, however, that here it is really a matter of different effects, because my body is not the same as another body; it has other relations; it is in a certain manner connected to my consciousness, while another body is not.[15]

---

14 It is superfluous to state that that which we cannot imagine, children cannot either — children too cannot imagine a thing that does not occupy space.

15 Concerning a physical cause of movement, a like distinction is not made. Why? Because by induction it has been found that physical movement is not connected with such a distinction — it is connected with extension, with inertia, and in general

A third prejudice is, that we believe that every cause of motion must add motion and that therefore when the consciousness causes a movement in the body it must add movement and thus increase the stock of physical energy. This prejudice is derived as well both from habit and also from faulty logic; it appears to us, that since being a cause of movement means moving, it must perforce also mean an activity of movement, as when one moves a ball he performs while doing so an activity of movement. It is however not hard to prove that a consciousness moves the body in a completely different way, a way which does not require an activity of movement. How so?

Because if the consciousness should move the body in the same way as someone moves a ball, it would have to know what it moves, just as he who moves the ball knows what he is doing. And since the movement of a limb [kerperlikher eyver] begins not from the limb itself, but is a part of an entire complex of movements of muscles and nerves which extend to the brain, then to know what it moves, consciousness would have to have knowledge of this complex. This does not mean that it would have to know all the nerves and muscles that enter into this complex, because since our body is set up like a machine, all the nerves and muscles may be set in motion by moving only one of them. But on the other hand, it would in fact have to know that nerve which starts up the complex of movements and this means that it would have to know all the motor nerves, found in the brain. Does our consciousness know these nerves?

---

that which is ordinarily in all bodies. This is, however, not the case with consciousness as a cause of movement. This is also not the case for a chemical or electric cause of motion: the same element can cause a movement in one element and not in another one, even a lighter one; oxygen reacts with carbon but not with helium. Certainly if we look we can find some kind of order, a lawfulness of positivity and negativity and reciprocal complementarity. But can we then not find a lawfulness also in the interaction that takes place only between consciousness and body, which are in some way connected in one personality? And is there not an order in that a person's consciousness can move only his own body and not another's, where there can well be another consciousness which should move it in another direction? Besides, my consciousness in another's body is not a consciousness at all, and therefore causality between the two by means of consciousness is not applicable.

Then in what way does consciousness move the body? Reason
yields that if we do not know this from somewhere else, we must
assume what consciousness itself tells us concerning it. Namely, that
it moves the body by orders. Meaning what? Through a command of
consciousness to do a certain deed the motor nerve is aroused, which
sets in motion the entire complex of nerves and muscles, which use
their own potential energy, which is needed for the movements to
carry out the order. In this way there is no accretion of energy, rather
potential energy becomes kinetic energy. In the same way,
apparently, it is arranged that when the senses set us up for
consciousness [shteln uns tsu bavustzayn] then the kinetic energy
becomes potential energy.

How can all this be done by an order or an arrangement? This
question, however [shoyn], has nothing to do with the argument from
conservation of energy, but with logical argument, which is supported
by the premise that a physical thing can effect, or be effected by, only
a physical contact. This particular argument is set forth here as the
sixth reason interactionism is rejected, and it is refuted by what has
here been proved, that the premise upon which it is supported is
nothing but a false prejudice, that in fact this premise is denied every
moment that we see that things fall to the earth or that positive and
negative elements seek to unite.[16]

Similarly the last argument against interactionism is no more than
a prejudice or conviction. We have persuaded ourselves that
according to interactionism, the body need not do anything while the
mind thinks — but from where do we know exactly how interaction
should work? From where do we know that the mind, while it thinks,
does not need to use the brain, let us say, in the manner that a typist
uses a typewriter or one who calculates uses an adding machine?

Of course, these particular analogies have little value, because
they are like conjectures that a blind person can make for himself

---

16 Gravity does not need a postulate of an unknown physical ether to bind all
things; and such a postulate can here also help very little, because every intervening
substance [mamoshes intsvishn] would represent a break [hafsoke] more than a
connection — in fact, a thing falls faster to the earth when in between there is less
substance.

concerning the nature of colors. But of equally little value are all the accounts of the ways and conditions in which body and consciousness can or cannot work together — accounts from which the last arguments against interactionism follow. After all, we do not possess a comprehensive science even concerning the nature of bodies and obviously not concerning the nature of consciousness — so how could we be in any position to calculate in advance everything that they can do or not do?

I.

I would like here to mention an important distinction between interactionism and the other theories concerning the relation of body and consciousness, a distinction, which brings us back to the problem of determinism and indeterminism, which occupied an important place in this volume, as freedom of the will occupies such an important place in our religion. But before we elucidate the distinction, it is necessary to make the following remark.

I believe that it is superfluous to prove the fact that the problem of determinism and indeterminism touches only our will, i.e., even indeterminists concede that our body is subject to certain mechanical laws (if only because according to interactionism the will is also is included as a mechanical factor). Even if we should agree with those who say that the behavior of individual electrons is random, that for no reason [on a far vos] they can begin to carry on [arumshtifn] and jump from one orbit to another, it must nevertheless be admitted, that this randomness, does not go so far as to subvert the lawfulness [aropfirn fun gezetslikhe derekh hayosher] of larger bodies with which we humans come into contact [hobn tsu ton] in experience. This has to be assumed, if only because otherwise physical science would be impossible.

From this it follows necessarily that those who hold that our consciousness, and thus also our will, cannot cause anything, and everything that we do comes from our bodies, must, perforce, reject in advance any possibility of indeterminism. Those who assume epiphenominalism, either in the first version or in the second, must from the beginning [shoyn mimele] also assume determinism.

The same goes for parallelism in all its shades: if the two chains of causes and effects, that of consciousness and that of body, proceed in parallel so that neither of them intercepts the other at any point, then the corporeal chain goes on only corporeally, i.e., only according to the mechanical laws and only deterministically; and if the chain of causes and effects in consciousness continually goes on parallel to the corporeal chain, so that to each effect in the second corresponds an effect in the first, then perforce the effects in the first chain must indeed be just as determined as in the second.

It thus emerges, that interactionism is the only theory that allows the possibility of free will. And since our religion espouses freedom of the will, in our religion interactionism must be presupposed.

J.

Interaction includes two activities: one through which a bodily movement creates consciousness and a second activity through which consciousness creates a bodily movement. These two activities are dissimilar both concerning their relative importance and also concerning the complexity of their accomplishments — the first represents a much greater accomplishment and is much more complicated than the second.

First, concerning the importance of their accomplishment: the second is only an activity, a bodily movement, or, as has been interpreted in this volume, an order to the body to move in such and such a way. On the other hand, the first represents the creation of a new being, a creation ex nihilo.

Then concerning complexity: the second activity is simply action, an action involving only movement. On the other hand, the first represents a cognition of a great deal of different objects — objects of different senses and objects which are received differently through each sense; objects of body and consciousness, of the intellect and feeling, of good and evil, of reality and illusion, etc.

This is not all. The object of the first activity is even very often contradictory: the same thing evokes in one the opposite feeling in another — that which one takes for good, another takes for evil, what for one is real, for another is an illusion. Even the same person can sometimes have the opposite opinion at a time from what he had in another time.

The first activity of interactionism requires, therefore, a separate analysis and a separate inquiry — the object of the activity must be analyzed and the basis of its reliability, and how far it is in fact reliable — what is real and what illusory — must be investigated. But this must await another work.

———•❧•———

Index of Topics and Names

Page

Index of Biblical and Rabbinic Citations